The Development of American Federalism

The Development of American Federalism

William H. Riker
Wilson Professor of Political Science
University of Rochester

Kluwer Academic Publishers
Boston   Dordrecht   Lancaster

Distributors

for North America: Kluwer Academic Publishers, 101 Philip Drive,
Assinippi Park, Norwell, MA 02061, USA

for the UK and Ireland: Kluwer Academic Publishers, MTP Press Limited,
Falcon House, Queen Square, Lancaster LA1 1RN, UK

for all other countries: Kluwer Academic Publishers Group, Distribution
Center, Post Office Box 322, 3300 AH Dordrecht, The Netherlands

Library of Congress Cataloging-in-Publication Data

Riker, William H.
   The development of American federalism.

   Bibliography: p.
   Includes index.
   1. Federal government — United States — History.
   I. Title.
   JK311.R55   1987   321.02'0973   87-2942
   ISBN 0-89838-225-4

Contents

Preface

The chapters of this book have diverse origins. They were written over the period 1954–1984. Several (i.e., three, four, seven, and ten) were originally published in scholarly journals. Several (i.e., one, eight, nine, and eleven) are excerpts from my previous books: *Soldiers of the States* and *Federalism: Origin, Operation and Significance.* And several (i.e., two, five, and six) were written for conferences and are now published here for the first time.

Despite the fact that this history suggests they are quite unrelated, these chapters do indeed center on one theme: the continuity of American federalism. In order to emphasize that theme, I have written an introduction and an initial commentary for each chapter. These commentaries, taken together, with the introduction, constitute the exposition of the theme.

Some of these chapters (four, six, and ten) were written with my students, Ronald Schaps, John Lemco, and William Bast. They did much of the research and analysis so the credit for these chapters belongs to them as much as to me.

Chapter five is based quite closely on William Paul Alexander's dissertation for the Ph.D. degree at the University of Rochester, 1973. Unfortunately Dr. Alexander died before he could condense his dissertation for publication as a paper. But, following his plans, I have revised it into chapter five. Since the time series in that chapter are essential for the analysis of the development of American federalism, I am glad to be able to present this important contribution to the audience for which Dr. Alexander intended it.

I take the opportunity of this preface to thank a number of other people who have helped me understand American federalism: Anthony Birch, William T. Bluhm, Daniel Elazar, Richard F. Fenno, Ronald May, Dale Neumann, Vincent Ostrom, Peter Regenstrief, and Aaron Wildavsky.

Introduction

I planned this book in 1954 as a set of papers on the federal features of each part of American government. In the course of writing *Democracy in the United States* (1953, 1964), which included a description of the national government, I had discovered that almost no commentaries then existed on these specifically federal features. Of course, the role of the Supreme Court as the arbiter of federalism and indeed the actual arbitration itself had been exhaustively studied, although almost always in terms of the narrow and practical interests of Constitutional lawyers rather than for scientific interpretation of the whole Constitution. That one institutional feature aside, the federal aspects of Congress, the Presidency, administration, and political parties had been only casually described. So my research program was to describe these features systematically. (Part III of this book is the product of that program as initially conceived, with chapters on Congress, the Presidency, administration (of the militia), and political parties.)

For guidance in this research program, I assumed as an axiom that institutions are self-perpetuating. That is, I assumed that institutions, once consciously formed, continually influence—with participants often unaware—the formation of the tastes of the next generation so that its members in turn clarify and render consistent the essential features of the institution as initially constructed.

This assumption does not preclude conscious revolutionary rejection of existing institutions. Monarchies are indeed destroyed. But destruction, I assume, is always conscious and always a matter of great moment. Otherwise people follow the old habits and institutions are, of course, no more that habits writ large.

Nor does this assumption preclude adjustment to changing circumstances. All institutions are "preserved" in that way, i.e., by being slightly changed. Of course, in order to preserve, one must understand the thing preserved. And given such understanding, people clarify their institutions, identifying and emphasizing their essential features. Thus, the assumption that institutions are self-perpetuating necessarily involves also the assumption that they are progressively adjusted and clarified.

Given that assumption of stabilizing adjustments, a recurrent problem is to explain why institutions sometimes undergo radical changes, changes that seem revolutionary but occur without any revolution. In the case of the study of American federalism, this problem has seemed particularly acute. The conventional interpretation was (and is) that an initially peripheralized federation (as of, say, 1789) has gradually become a highly centralized one. It is paradoxical, therefore, that the supposed historical experience of dramatic change is inconsistent with the theoretical assumption of clarification and refinement. This putative inconsistency has been extensively documented, relative both to the allocation of functions between federal and state levels, and to the actual expenditures of time and money in administrative activity.

My study of the militia (in part III) of course adds to this documentation. But it does so with a difference, because I found that military centralization occurred at a time (1830–1850) when, according to the historians of the Supreme Court, the system was peripheralizing in reaction against judicial centralization under John Marshall and that peripheralization occurred at a time (1880–1900) when, according to those same historians, states were being systematically restricted by the Supreme Court as part of the creation of "dual federalism" to prevent both state and federal regulation of industry.

The discovery of this unexpected absence of synchronization led me to reconsider the thesis of progressive centralization of an initially peripheralized federalism. One possibility, which saves the assumption that institutions are self-clarifying, self-stabilizing, and self-perpetuating, is that the system never was peripheralized. If it was centralized from the beginning, there is no inconsistency and no paradox. The centralization observed has always been there. Another related reconciliation is that the observed revolutionary change is a trivial feature of the system, while the deep political properties of the system are constant. If the political structure of the government is more influential on outcomes than the administrative structure and if the political structure remains constant while the administrative structure changes, then the administrative change is not of itself very important.

Thus the supposed inconsistency may be resolved by a reinterpretation of the conventional history. There has indeed been intense centralization of effort and expenditures. But the essential federal structure, as seen in political control, has retained just about the same position on the scale of centralization that it has had since 1788. The change from the Articles to the Constitution was the main step in centralization, and a more or less steady state has continued since then.

This reinterpretation, if it is correct, strengthens the assumption that the institutions of federalism, as they exist at any one time, guide the learning and development of tastes and preferences in later time periods so that the federal institutions have been self-adjusting and self-perpetuating. Two prominent features of our history support this interpretation: we might have destroyed our federation in two ways—by breaking it up or by becoming fully unitary. At the time of the Civil War, which was a conscious proposal to break up, we chose decisively to keep what we had. At the other extreme, there has been no serious movement to centralize completely, though a few radical splinter groups have suggested it. The conscious and unconscious rejection of both these possibilities indicate how deeply the habits of centralized federalism have formed American tastes.

The chapters in this book provide the evidence for this reinterpretation. The first chapter, however, has simply an introductory purpose. It provides some definitions, explains the motivation for federal constitutions, compares them with other kinds of governments, and shows why federation is such an attractive political structure in this century. (I have reprinted it also because it includes the initial statement of one of the very few well-attested sociological laws about institutions, namely the law of federal origins.) The subsequent chapters all relate closely to the resolution of the supposed inconsistency. The chapter on the origins of American federalism shows that the framers of the Constitution wanted a unitary government but invented centralized federalism as a practical political compromise. The following chapter about putative Dutch influence on American federalism is a footnote to the discussion of the invention. It shows that the one avenue for the transmission of earlier federal ideas was effectively closed.

In part II the first two chapters deal with the measurement of federalism. In the chapter on disharmony a statistical measure is explained and justified, and in the chapter on measurement this statistic is applied to American federalism to show that, while administration has been centralized, political structure has not. The third chapter, on federal stability, offers two general reasons for the fact that American federalism has neither collapsed (like, say, the West Indian federation) nor become unitary (like, say, the United Kingdom).

In part III some institutional reasons for the stability of American federalism are examined. The chapter on the Senate shows that despite the facade of indirect election, the Senate was from the beginning a centralized institution. The excerpts from *Soldiers of the States* explain the military centralization (probably inherent in the Constitution, but not realized until after the War of 1812), while the chapter on the Presidency, on the other hand, shows why centralization could be carried no further than it has. The except from *Federalism* on administrative centralization summarizes the detail on that subject. And the last selection on party organization explains why the structure of political parties, though admitting much administrative centralization, nevertheless prevents political centralization.

These chapters are thus held together by their relation to my thesis that American federalism has remained remarkably constant for 200 years. They are directed to 1) defining federalism as a constitutional form, not as mere administrative centralization (a consistent misinterpretation by economists: Musgrave, 1965; Oates, 1972); 2) demonstrating its initial centralization in the United States; 3) measuring its development; 4) showing its stability in the face of administrative adjustments.

A brief introduction to each section and even briefer headnotes to each chapter carry the general argument along.

A Note on Ideology

This collection of chapters spans more than 30 years. It would be strange indeed if, during that entire time, I had maintained exactly the same ideological stance. And, as will doubtless be apparent to one who reads all the chapters, I have not.

In the half-century after the first world war the world was flooded with statist confidence in the beneficence of powerful government, e.g., communism, fascism, welfare statism, peronism, etc., which in the United States took the form of, first, the New Deal, and, later, the "great society." In the last two decades, however, disillusionment with big government has set in, with a revival of nineteenth century liberal values, or at least with a recognition that government is as likely to be a force for evil as for good. My own ideological migrations have been much in the spirit of the age: from New Dealer in the fifties to liberal, anti-statist in the eighties.

These ideologies have quite different implications for federalism: The statism of the New Deal implies that the national government should be unfettered. Since federalism restrains the national government by setting the scene for conflicts between the states and the nation, the appropriate stance for a New Dealer is to seek to eliminate federalism. On the other hand, the liberal goal of protecting rights from governmental attack justifies restraints like federalism and separation of powers that occasion intergovernmental and interbranch deadlocks.

Given my ideological shift, I have also changed my evaluation of federalism. Initially I regarded it as an impediment—minor, perhaps— but still an impediment to good government. Now I regard it as a desirable, though still minor, restraint on the leviathan. (Of course, however, I have always regarded it as a necessary condition of nationhood in 1787 and hence a feature that must, as a practical matter, be accepted with the Constitution as a whole.)

The variation in my ideological judgment has been reinforced by a fundamental change—during the 1960s—in the political significance of federalism. Prior to that time, the moral meaning of federalism was ambiguous. It was liberal as a restraint on statism. But it was profoundly illiberal because the main local value it protected was, initially, slavery, and, later, legal disabilities for blacks. Thus liberals might oppose federalism on racial grounds (like the Radical Republicans from the 1850s to the 1880s) or favor it on politico-economic grounds (like the Supreme Court that, partially in the name of federalism, struck down the most extreme statism of the New Deal). Conversely, statists might oppose federalism on politico-economic grounds (like the original New Dealers who formed national cartels) or favor it on racial grounds (like the Southerners who composed a good third of the New Deal coalition).

The civil rights reforms of the 1960s removed this ambiguity by eliminating the protection for local repression. With the racial dimension of judgment thus removed, it became possible, for the first time in American history, to value federalism unambiguously as a deterrent to statism, a deterrent that liberals could readily support and that statists might believe restrictive and unpleasant.

This political clarification, of course, helped me to reverse my ideological judgment. But since the chapters were written over a long period they reflect differing ideological stances. This does not disturb me nor does it, in my opinion, impede republication. As the reader can see, my description of federalism and of its historical variations remains pretty much the same, despite shifts in ideology. So the description itself is consistent, a practical refutation, I believe, of the claim by opponents of social science that moral premises preclude useful generalization.

I THE ORIGINS OF FEDERAL GOVERNMENTS

The chapters in this part concern the origins of federal governments. The first selection begins at the beginning. That is, it offers a well-attested law about the origin of federations. The second selection describes the invention of centralized federalism at Philadelphia in 1787. The third considers the influence of ideas about the Dutch federation on the framers of the American Constitution.

1 THE ORIGIN OF FEDERAL GOVERNMENT

William H. Riker

Commentary. Suppose one wishes to consolidate some existing political units. How might this be done? The answer is presented here as the law of federal origins. One possible method of consolidation is, at minimum, an alliance, in which all the units retain full autonomy except their (only loosely binding) obligations to their allies. The converse possibility, at a maximum, is empire, in which one unit conquers and rules the others. In between are various kinds of federations in which the units create a superior and general government to coordinate their actions, but retain some freedom from control by that superior.

The bargain to create such a federal government is described in the first section. The necessary conditions under which the bargain is made are set forth in the second section, namely that politicians, both those who offer and those who accept the bargain, seek to meet an external military or diplomatic threat or to expand militarily or diplomatically without the distraction of conquering their potential partners.

From William H. Riker, *Federalism: Origin, Operation, Significance* (Boston: Little, Brown and Co., 1964), pp. 1–16.

3

Some questions have subsequently been raised by critics about the persuasiveness of the evidence that these conditions are necessary. The necessity is easy to see in federations arising in war or revolution (e.g., the United States, Switzerland), in fear of conquest (Canada), in anticipation of conquest (Yugoslavia), or in anticipation of aggression (Australia). But Dikshit (1971), for example, argued that while these conditions described the formation of federations in an earlier era, in this century they have been formed for different reasons. He offered West Germany and India as examples. They satisfy the conditions perfectly, however: the West German federation, which inherited the federal form from imperial Germany (where it was clearly a device for military expansion) and even from the Holy Roman Empire (where it clearly served the same purpose), readopted federalism after Hitler to provide a mode of welcoming East Germany, were it ever to be detached from the Soviet empire. Similarly India in 1947–1948 followed the suggestion of the Government of India Act of 1935, not because of intellectual agreement on the merits of this kind of decentralization but because of straightforward military concerns about Pakistan and the consequent desire to incorporate both the princely states with their military resources and possibly portions of Pakistan itself into the Indian polity. (Certainly, Dikshit's suggestion that India lacked military incentives is not borne out by its subsequent history of several wars and military conquests.)

A better criticism of my military-diplomatic conditions was offered by Birch (1966), who compared them with conditions offered by several previous writers. K.C. Wheare (1946) had required an amalgam of something like my military conditions, plus economic associations and ideological sympathy. Deutsch (1957) required economic and ideological association, plus shared communications and shared elites, but did not require any military or diplomatic condition. Birch preferred the military-diplomatic conditions because they established "the importance of certain kinds of political considerations in the formation of federations" and because he thought "this may be counted as a real, if limited, gain in a period in which it seems fashionable to assume that economic and social factors are pre-eminent" (1966, p. 33).

Nevertheless Birch feared that the military-diplomatic condition was unnecessary in certain cases, so he tested it out on three then recent federations: a proposed east African federation, Nigeria, and Malaysia. Since there seemed to be neither military threat nor expansionist ambition in east Africa, the fact that the proposed federation never materialized is negative support for the condition. In the other two cases, federations were in fact formed, though the presence of either military threat or expansionist ambition seemed questionable. I had seen a military-diplomatic threat against Nigeria from the pan-Africanism of Ghana. A few years later, however, this threat seemed negligible as Ghana reduced itself to insignificance with a dictatorial government and a statist economy. Still, even, the initial pan-African threat was probably not very strong, and this fact raises some questions about the validity of the condition. In the case of Malaysia, I had seen a threat from Indonesia, which was not, however, directed at the Malay or Singapore components so much as at Sarawak and Sabah. Birch found, however, that in both cases federation significantly reduced the danger of empire building by one member (in Nigeria) or the danger of internal revolutionary action (in Malaysia). Hence he proposed to revise the condition to allow for internal as well as external military threats.

I am inclined to accept this emendation provisionally with respect to Nigeria, though it is still not clear that the Nigerian federation can survive. It has had one huge civil war and most of the time since the war it has been a nonfederal military dictatorship. This suggests that the union can survive only by military force, not by a federal bargain.

Subsequent events in Malaysia confirm the original form of the condition. The Indonesian threat related primarily to the states in Borneo, and these remain in the federation. Where the threat was simply internal, namely Singapore, the federation dissolved.

So the status of the condition with two decades of new evidence is strong. Only Nigeria offers a possible counter-instance and Birch's emendation clearly covers it.

It is important to understand the force of this law of federal origins. If framers overlook these necessary conditions their federations are likely to fail. Thus, British colonial officers, having observed the success of the federal form in earlier British colonies like the United States and Canada, assumed, probably under the influence of writers like Wheare, that Britain could by its directive create new federations in Africa, the West Indies, etc. Since, however, they did not understand the necessary conditions, they were only adventitiously successful. The case of Malaysia is instructive. The truly threatened areas in Borneo remain while the unthreatened Singapore has left.

Today one hears often of other possibilities for federation: in western Europe and in the entire world. West European federation is conceivable, provided the threat of Soviet domination is sufficiently strong (as it may become when the United States withdraws). World federation is, however, hard to imagine because there is no coherent military threat to all prospective members.

A Theory of Federalism

This is an Age of Federalism. In 1964, well over half the land mass of the world was ruled by governments that with some justification, however slight, described themselves as federalisms. Thus,

in North America: Canada, Mexico, and the United States
in South America: Argentina, Brazil, and Venezuela
in Europe: Austria, the Soviet Union, Switzerland, West Germany, and Yugoslavia
in South Asia: Australia, India, Malaysia, and Pakistan
in Africa: Congo, Ethiopia, and Nigeria

are all in one way or another federalisms. Furthermore, most of these governments are creations of the nineteeth and twentieth centuries. The Swiss federation is of medieval origin; the United States was formed in the late eighteenth century; and the other federalisms in the Western Hemisphere were formed in the nineteenth century. Except for Germany, Australia, Switzerland, and Austria (which dates from 1901), the federalisms of the Eastern Hemisphere are products of the worldwide political reorganizations following the two world wars. Truly, the twentieth century is an Age of Federalism, which is a constitutional bargain only rarely and sporadically struck prior to the nineteenth century.

The Popularity of Federal Constitutions

The recent popularity of federal constitutions is not surprising because federalism is one way to solve the problem of enlarging governments—a problem that is one of the most pressing political concerns in the modern world. Like so many other modern problems, this one is a consequence of rapid technological change. Each advance in the technology of transportation makes it possible to rule a larger geographic area from one center, to fill a treasury more abundantly, to maintain a larger bureaucracy and police, and, most important of all, to assemble a larger army. There seem to be enough ambitious politicians in the world at any one time to guarantee that at least one government will use the new technology of transport to enlarge its area of control. And, once one government enlarges itself, then its neighbors and competitors feel compelled to do likewise in order, supposedly, to forestall anticipated aggression. Hence it is that technological change and a sense of competition together guarantee that governments will expand to the full extent that technology permits.

At the dawn of written history, most governmental units were tiny, consisting typically of an urban place and a few square miles of farms and villages. But with technological advance, imperial dominions became possible. Some of these in the ancient Near East and central and south Asia were based on the domestication of the horse; others like the Egyptian and Chinese were based on the exploitation of a river system as a channel of transport. The Roman empire is especially interesting for it was first created by control of the Mediterranean (*mare nostrum*) as a channel of tranportation and was expanded by the invention of the Roman roads to control western Europe. Even so, the ancient empires were small by modern standards, and at its height Rome probably ruled less land and fewer people than are now ruled from any one of these cities: Washington, Ottawa, Brazilia, Moscow, New Delhi, Peking, and Canberra. A necessary condition for these numerous large governments of today is of course innovation in transportation. First came the navigational discoveries (compass, triangular sail, sextant, trigonometry, etc.) that permitted the so-called expansion of Europe and, second, the innovations in land transportation (the steam railroad, the automotive engine, road building and earth moving, the airplane, etc.).

The initial form of most of the great modern governments was empire. That is, large territories were accumulated by conquest when the technologically sophisticated Europeans subdued the relatively primitive inhabitants of America, Asia, and Africa. Thus were created the Spanish, Portuguese, Dutch, British, French, German, Russian, and Belgian empires. Of modern empires, only the Austrian, Turkish, and Chinese involved the conquest of territory inhabited by people as technologically sophisticated as the conqueror, and even in these cases the conqueror had some kind of technological superiority in transportation and military equipment.

But empire, which was the characteristic form of European domination of the world in the eighteenth and nineteenth centuries, has not been popular or successful in the twentieth. I think there are at least two reasons for the contemporary failure of imperialism. One is that the imperial powers exhausted themselves in conflict with each other so that they were no longer strong enough to control their dependencies. This is a process that started as early as the several American revolutions against England, Spain, and Portugal, all three of which were weakened or diverted by intra-European warfare at the time the revolutions occurred. Today this process is ending as Africans gain freedom from the European empires debilitated by two world wars. A special case, but still a part of this process, is the dismemberment of a defeated empire after an inter-imperial war, as when the German and Turkish empires were divided up by the winners in 1919 or when the United States took over the remnants of the Spanish empire in 1898. The other reason for the failure of imperialism is that the dependencies learned enough modern technology from their masters to challenge imperial control. (Those dependencies largely inhabited by descendants of European emigrants were, of course, the quickest to learn and the first to challenge, as in North and South America; but by the twentieth century even most of the indigenous peoples had learned enough to rebel.) For these two reasons, therefore, the imperial form of territorial expansion has gradually been discarded—and as the discarding goes on, the very act of discarding itself contributes to further discarding, as exemplified by the recent and continuing dismemberment of the Dutch, Belgian, and Portuguese empires, all of which have been ludicrous anachronisms in the twentieth century and all of which are now collapsing almost in sympathetic imitation of the collapse of the British and French empires.

The collapse of imperialism forces a constitutional alternative on all successful rebels: Since they necessarily rebel within the subdivisions established by the imperial power for its own convenience in governing, one alternative is to establish the freed subdivisions as independent political units. But the subdivisions, coordinated as they have been by the colonial office in the center, are not usually large enough to take advantage of the technological conditions that made the empire possible in the first place. Hence, if the newly independent subdivisions stand alone as political entities, they are highly vulnerable to yet a new imperialism. This is what happened, for example, to the Balkan rebels against the Austrian and Turkish empires. Freed from one imperial master as a result of nineteenth century revolutions and World War I, and yet too small to support large armies, they fell victim in World War II to Hitler's abortive Third Reich and then to Stalin's Communist hegemony. The whole of Africa and the Near East is now Balkanized in a similar way and it is not fanciful to suggest that something of a similar future awaits these new nations. The other alternative for successful rebels is to join several former imperial subdivisions together. But if they join the subdivisions in one centralized political unit, then the rebels have merely exchanged one imperial master for a lesser one. Thereby much of the justification for rebellion is lost. The subdivisions can, however, be joined in some kind of federation, which preserves at least the semblance of political self-control for the former subdivisions and at the same time allows them (by means of the government of the federation) to make use of the technological advantages in the size of treasuries and armies and thus to compete successfully with their neighbors.

In this sense federalism is the main alternative to empire as a technique of aggregating large areas under one government. Although it probably does not so clearly assure large treasuries and armies, it does assure them to some degree—and it avoids the offensiveness of imperial control. It is this combination of attributes, I believe, that accounts for the twentieth century popularity of the federal kind of constitutional bargain and explains why today all the governments of large territories (except China) have federal constitutions at least in name.

Kinds of Federal Constitutions

Only in the modern world, however, has federalism been an effective alternative to empire. Although the notion of federalism has existed from ancient times, ancient and medieval federalisms (with one exception) succumbed rather quickly to imperial onslaught. By contrast, modern federalism has been notably successful, at least in the Western Hemisphere. Much of the reason for this difference in performance stems from the invention in 1787 of a new kind of federalism, so that in the modern world *centralized* federalism has generally replaced the *peripheralized* federalism characteristic of earlier eras.

The essential institutions of federalism are, of course, a government of the federation and a set of governments of the member units, in which both kinds of governments rule over the same territory and people and each kind has the authority to make some decisions independently of the other. But this notion admits of a great many actual constitutional arrangements, some of which may operate effectively and others may not. The numerous possible federal constitutions may be arranged in a continuum according to the degree of independence one kind of the pair of governments has from the other kind. The range of possibilities in this relationship is between the following minimum and maximum:

> *minimum:* the ruler(s) of the federation can make decisions in only one narrowly restricted category of action without obtaining the approval of the rulers of the constituent units. (The minimum is *one* category of action, not zero, because if the ruler(s) of the federation rule nothing, neither a federation nor even a government can be said to exist.) Some ancient federations were federations in this minimal sense because their rulers were authorized to make decisions independently only about military tactics and then only during the course of a battle.
> *maximum:* the ruler(s) of the federation can make decisions without consulting the rulers of the member governments in all but one narrowly restricted

category of action. (The maximum number of categories is *all but one*, not simply all, because, if the rulers of the federation rule everything, the government is an empire in the sense that the rulers of the constituent governments have *no* political self-control.) The Soviet Union may be an example of a federation at the maximum. Although the government of this federation is, by its written constitution, one of delegated powers somewhat like that of the United States, still the guarantee of independence to constituent units seems only nominal, except, perhaps, in the area of providing for the cultural life of linguistic and ethnic minorities around whom the union republics are constructed. If, in fact, the union republics are fully able to decide about cultural life without consultation with the government of the federation, then the Soviet Union is a totally centralized federalism. If, however, the union republics cannot freely decide even in this area, then the Soviet Union is an empire, not particularly different from the Tsarist empire it succeeds.

Of course, relatively few federalisms lie at either extreme. Those which lie in between are spaced according to the number and importance of the areas of action in which the ruler(s) of the federation decide(s) independently of the rulers of the subordinate governments. Those which are closer to the maximum than to the minimum are described as *centralized*, whereas those closer to the minimum than to the maximum are *peripheralized*.

Although this distinction between kinds of federalisms seems fairly precise, the precision is somewhat spurious. There is no mechanical means of toting up the numbers and importance of areas of action in which either kind of government is independent of the other. Both the notion of number of categories and the notion of importance are evaluative and hence relative to the cultures from which each specific federalism springs. Nevertheless, there is one rough standard by which it is possible to assign any particular federalism to one category or the other. If a federalism is centralized, then the ruler(s) of the federation have and are understood to have greater influence over what happens in the society as a whole than do all the rulers of the subordinate governments. And, having this influence, they tend to acquire more. Thus, an identifying feature of centralized federalism is the tendency, as time passes, for the rulers of the federation to overawe the rulers of the constituent governments. Conversely, if a federalism is initially peripheralized, the rulers of the subordinate governments have, in sum, greater influence over the affairs of the whole society than do the ruler(s) of the federation. Having the initial advantage, the rulers of the subordinate governments tend to acquire more; and thus an identifying feature of peripheralized federalism is the tendency, eventually, for the rulers of the constituent governments to overawe the ruler(s) of the federation. Using these standards, observation of the historical development of particular federalisms enables the observer to assign them to either the centralized or the peripheralized category.

Once these standards for categorization have been enunciated, the significance of the distinction between centralized and peripheralized becomes apparent. Peripheralized federalisms—with their tendency to minimize the role of rulers of the federation, with their tendency to permit the rulers of constituent units to aggrandize themselves at the expense of the federal officials, and with their tendency to allow even those decisions originally intended for the rulers of the federation to revert to the rulers of the subordinate governments—can hardly be expected to provide effective government. They fall gradually apart until they are easy prey for their enemies. Centralized federalisms, on the other hand, become more like unitary or imperial governments in time and thus render the whole federation able to function more effectively in a hostile world. It is this difference between gradual disintegration and gradual solidification that explains the contrast between the failure and relative rarity of ancient and medieval peripheralized federalisms and the success and popularity of modern centralized ones.

Ancient and Medieval Peripheralized Federalisms

The first appearance of what can be called federal governments occurred in ancient Greece after the Peloponnesian War. The circumstances that inspired the invention were exclusively military, either the threat of Sparta, the threat of Macedon, or the threat of Rome, all three of which were imperial powers that promised to and in fact did absorb the miniscule city-states that tried to defend themselves with a federal combination. Since the exclusive purpose of these federations was military, the constituent cities delegated to the federal rulers only military authority, retaining for themselves decisions on diplomatic matters such as whether or not to make war, whether or not to conclude treaties, and other affairs highly relevant to military decisions. As a consequence, the military function was ill-performed; the poor performance was used by the rulers of constituent units as a justification for further restrictions on the authority of the federal military officials; and such restriction led in turn to even worse military performance. First Macedon, then Rome, triumphed. And the notion of federalism was not heard of again until the Middle Ages.

It reappeared when circumstances essentially similar to those of the Greek city-states were replicated. In northern Italy and southern Germany medieval cities formed military federations to resist the encroachments of nascent nation states, all of which were essentially imperial in nature. These Italian and Suabian federalisms went through exactly the same cycle as the Greek federalisms had 1,500 years earlier and for exactly the same reasons. Only one of them survived into the modern world: the Swiss confederation—and it survived not because of its constitutional form but because of its unique geographic advantages for defensive military operations.

In the sixteenth century the Dutch federation was formed as an incident in the struggle for the independence of the low-country bourgeoisie from the feudal imperialism of the Spanish crown. This federation survived for over 200 years (until formally demolished by Napoleon), although it was for all practical purposes a simple monarchy after 1672. . . .

Modern Centralized Federalisms

Although the Dutch federalism was only extralegally centralized, the American federalism after 1787 was legally and constitutionally centralized. The innovation involved in this new government is the crucial event in the history of federalism. . . . It is sufficient to say now that the first American federalism (established informally in 1776 and formally in 1781) was modelled on the ancient federalism and on the supposed structure of the Dutch republic. So long as the Revolutionary War was in progress and all the really important federal decisions rested in the hands of the military commander, General Washington, the peripheralized feature of the government under the Articles of Confederation did not impede effective action by the central government. As soon as the war was over, however, this peripheralized federalism began, characteristically, to fall apart. The reform of 1787 transformed the federation into a centralized one, which survived and prospered. Because it prospered, other constitution-makers copied it. These adaptions also prospered and were copied, until now, as I previously noted, over half the world is ruled by federal governments. . . .

The Origin and Purposes of Federalism

In the previous section I interpreted federalism as a bargain between prospective national leaders and officials of constituent governments for the purpose of aggregating territory, the better to lay taxes and raise armies. This bargain can be defined quite precisely so that, when presented with an instance of a constitution, one can say whether or not it belongs to the class of federalisms. The rule for identification is: a constitution is federal if 1) two levels of government rule the same land and people, 2) each level has at least one area of action in which it is autonomous, and 3) there is some guarantee (even though merely a statement in the constitution) of the autonomy of each government in its own sphere. Since such constitutions have appeared frequently in the last century and three-quarters, the class of federal bargains is large enough to admit of some generalizations involving it. Because the class is both precisely defined and relatively large, one can rise above the undisciplined uniqueness characteristic of historical commentary, even though each instance of a federal bargain is of course imbedded in a unique historical context.

Conditions of the Federal Bargain

As bargains, the acts of making federal constitutions should display the main feature of bargains generally, which is that all parties are willing to make them. Assuming that they do display this feature, one may ask what it is that predisposes the parties to favor this kind of bargain. From the theory set forth in the previous chapter, I infer the existence of at least two circumstances encouraging a willingness to strike the bargain of federalism:

1. The politicians who offer the bargain desire to expand their territorial control, usually either to meet an external military or diplomatic threat or to prepare for military or diplomatic aggression and aggrandizement. But, though they desire to expand, they are not able to do so by conquest, because of either military incapacity or ideological distaste. Hence, if they are to satisfy the desire to expand, they must offer concessions to the rulers of constituent units, which is the essence of the federal bargain. The predisposition for those who offer the bargain is, then, that federalism is the only feasible means to accomplish a desired expansion without the use of force.

2. The politicians who accept the bargain, giving up some independence for the sake of union, are willing to do so because of some external military-diplomatic threat or opportunity. Either they desire protection from an external threat or they desire to participate in the potential aggression of the federation. And furthermore the desire for either protection or participation outweighs any desire they may have for independence. The predisposition is the cognizance of the pressing need for the military strength or diplomatic maneuverability that comes with a larger and presumably stronger government. (It is not, of course, necessary

that their assessment of the military-diplomatic circumstances be objectively correct.)

For convenience of abbreviation I shall refer to these two predispositions as 1) the expansion condition and 2) the military condition.

The hypothesis of this chapter is that these two predispositions are *always* present in the federal bargain and that each one is a necessary condition for the creation of a federalism. I am tempted, on the basis of my immersion in this subject, to assert that these two conditions are together sufficient. But, since I cannot possibly collect enough information to prove sufficiency, I am constrained to assert only the more modest hypothesis of necessity.

In order to prove this hypothesis, I have examined *all* the instances of the creation of a federalism since 1786, giving most detailed attention to the invention of centralized federalism in the United States. (More exactly, I have examined all the instances I have been able to discover. It is quite possible, however, that I have overlooked some obscure instances.) For those federalisms that have survived, I am able to show that the two conditions existed at the origin; and, for those that failed, I am able to show that either the conditions never existed or they existed only momentarily. Though such evidence does not constitute absolute proof of the hypothesis, it comes as close to a proof as a nonexperimental science can offer.

Before this proof is undertaken, a word about the significance of this hypothesis. To those whose first acquaintance with the literature on federalism is this chapter, the hypothesis may seem obvious and trivial. But it is not; and to show why it is not I shall briefly examine two widely asserted fallacies about the origin of federalism.

One is the ideological fallacy, which is the assertion that federal forms are adopted as a device to guarantee freedom. Numerous writers on federalism, so many that it would be invidious to pick out an example, have committed this ideological fallacy. It is true, of course, that federalism does involve a guarantee of provincial autonomy and it is easy to see how some writers have confused this guarantee with the notion of a free society. Indeed, in certain circumstances, for example by encouraging provinces to have different policies or even simply to be inefficient, federalism may provide interstices in the social order in which personal liberties can thrive. And I suppose it is the observation of this fact that leads one to the ideological fallacy.

The worst error involved in this fallacy is the simple association of 1) federalism and 2) freedom or a nondictatorial regime. Only the most casual observation of, for example, the Soviet Union or Mexico demonstrates, however, that even though all the forms of federalism are fairly scrupulously maintained, it is possible to convert the government into a dictatorship. In the two examples mentioned, the conversion has been accomplished by a strict one-party system, which suggests that the crucial feature of freedom is not a particular constitutional form, but rather a system of more than one party. But in other countries, e.g., Brazil, Argentina, imperial Germany, even federalism and a multiparty system have been unable to prevent dictatorships, so probably some even more subtle condition is necessary to maintain free government. What it is I cannot say, but I am certain that there is no simple causal relationship between federalism and freedom.

Even though it is objectively false that federalism preserves freedom, it is still possible that uninformed constitution-writers might believe they were providing for freedom simply by making the federal bargain. And if they did, then the ideological fallacy would be no fallacy at all. But there is almost no evidence that they have so believed, or at least no evidence that such a belief was a primary motivation. Theoretically, it is unlikely that writers of federal constitutions are so motivated. As men engaged in expanding a government, they are much more likely to be preoccupied with practical expedients for the moment than with provisions for the distant and not clearly foreseen future. As centralizers, they are much more likely to be concerned with centralization itself than with fears that centralization may go too far. Entirely apart from these theoretical considerations, however, there simply is almost no evidence that they have been motivated in the way the ideological fallacy asserts. Most so-called evidence for this proposition is essentially anachronistic in nature, e.g., citations from *The Federalist* papers to indicate the motives of the framers six months previously, conveniently overlooking that the authors of *The Federalist* papers throughout the Convention were in favor of unitary government and had almost nothing to do with the invention of centralized federalism. If one examines the debates of authors of federal constitutions and the political circumstances surrounding them, . . . it is abundantly clear that practical considerations of expansion rather than ideological considerations of safe-guards for freedom animated framers of federalisms. Only in the instances of Latin American federalisms can even moderately convincing cases be made for the latter motivation and under close examination even these instances collapse.

Alongside the rather crude ideological fallacy is the subtler and initially more impressive reductionist fallacy, which is the assertion that federalism is a response to certain social conditions that create some sense of a common interest. On the basis of a theory of this sort, British colonial administrators have encouraged a number of federalisms, some successful, some not. It is the fact of some failures that is interesting—for they indicate the inadequacy of the theory. Perhaps the most exhaustive statement of this kind of theory is contained in the work of Deutsch and his collaborators (Deutsch, 1957, p. 38) who produced a list of nine "essential conditions for an amalgamated security-community" of which class the class of federalisms is a subclass:

> (1) mutual compatibility of main values; (2) a distinctive way of life; (3) expectations of stronger economic ties or gains; (4) marked increase in political and administrative capabilities of at least some participating units; (5) superior economic growth on the part of at least some participating units; (6) unbroken links of social communication, both geographically between territories and sociologically between different social strata; (7) a broadening of the political elite; (8) mobility of persons at least among the politically relevant strata; and (9) a multiplicity of ranges of communications and transactions.

There are many defects in such a list. It is apparent that these conditions are not sufficient to bring about amalgamation for, if they were, federalisms like the Central American Federation would never have broken up or a pan-Arabic movement would reunite the Arabic parts of the former Turkish empire. Nor are all these conditions necessary, for a great many successful amalgamations have violated some or even all of them, e.g., the Swiss confederation seems to have violated conditions 1) and 2) during most of its history and nineteenth century colonial empires violated almost all conditions. If these conditions are neither jointly necessary nor sufficient, it is hard to imagine in what sense they are "essential."

The trouble with the Deutsch list is that it attempts to reduce the explanation of the political phenomenon of joining together to an explanation of the social and economic condition of the population. In bypassing the political, in bypassing the act of bargaining itself, it leaves out the crucial condition of the predisposition to make the bargain. What this list amounts to is a set of frequently observed conditions in which politicians can develop a predisposition to unite in some way or another. But it omits any mention of the political conditions in which, given some of these and other social and economic conditions, the actual predisposition to bargain occurs. The theory I have set forth, on the other hand, is confined to the political level entirely. It assumes some sense of common interest, of course, and then asserts the invariant conditions of forming one kind of larger political association, namely, federalism. (Incidentally, by confining the theory to a specific kind of amalgamation, the theory has a political focus that Deutsch and his collaborators failed to achieve.)

2 THE INVENTION OF CENTRALIZED FEDERALISM

William H. Riker

Commentary. Federations, more than any other kind of government, benefit from written constitutions. In traditional governments, where the lines of authority may stretch back farther than human memory, people can discuss disputes about their political institutions by citing precedents, as, for example, the British "cite" their "unwritten constitution." Since federations, on the other hand, originate in particular bargains struck at a particular time for a particular purpose, written constitutions are useful, even necessary, records of the terms of the bargains. Indeed, to write and adopt a constitution is to agree on the bargain itself.

Since constitution-writing is thus planning an institution, it is easy to think of constitutions as social inventions comparable to mechanical inventions. But this is somewhat anachronistic. It may be that framers of constitutions are simply intent on solving an immediate problem with a unique set of rules. They may well not be aware that their product will, like a true invention, have diverse applications and immense long-run consequences. So to talk about their activity as "inventing" may be pretentious and misleading,

This paper was presented at Indiana University, May 1985, on the occasion of the inauguration of Vincent Ostrom as Bentley Professor of Political Science.

17

especially if they see themselves simply as political manipulators trying to win on some particular set of issues.

Nevertheless, from our contemporary point of view, the framers at Philadelphia produced an invention of great value in many parts of the world; so I am willing to risk an anachronism in order to talk about how they invented centralized federalism. (In its original form this material was presented as an illustration of a theory about how institutions may flourish because they accomplish an unanticipated social purpose. I have stripped away this theory because it is irrelevant here. Some hints of it remain, and I leave them in place to remind us of the dangers of anachronism.)

Federalism is a constitutional form for gathering several governments together to take actions, mostly military, that would be impossible for the governments separately (Riker, 1964). It is midway on the scale between alliance and empire. Alliance permits joint action, while the allied governments retain full authority. In an empire (or unitary or consolidated government), the imperial government can take any action because it has absorbed all authority from the local governments. Federation is in between in the sense that the central government has full authority in certain spheres, e.g., military or foreign affairs, while the constituent governments (which are the allies of alliances and the local governments of empires) retain full authority in other spheres, e.g., criminal law.

The advantage of alliance is that it preserves the member governments. Its defect is that, since every decision requires both discussion and unanimity, the allies are often paralyzed. The advantage of empire is that direction and decision are centralized into one set of officials unlikely to stymie each other; but the defect is that local interests are sacrificed to imperial interests. Federalism is a nice compromise because it allows the pursuit of imperial goals without sacrificing interests of localities.

One would expect, therefore, that federation would be a frequently established constitution, especially since a federal compact avoids the effort of imperial conquest and the subsequent bitterness of the conquered. In fact, however, for the 2,500 years of recorded history prior to 1787, federation was a constitutional rarity: a few instances in ancient Greece and the Near East, a few medieval leagues (of which Switzerland, as later revised on the American model, is the only survivor), the Holy Roman Empire (if indeed it could be called a government at all), the Dutch Republic (1570–1800, although it was a de facto monarchy after 1672), and the United States from 1776 to 1788. Since 1787, however, federations have proliferated to include: most of the large units of the former British,

Spanish, and Portugese empires (though some of these abandoned the federal form because it was not militarily necessary); the Soviet Union (briefly, although it still retains some federal constitutional mythology); Germany; Austria; Yugoslavia; and many short-lived federations in Africa and Asia (parts of the former Turkish, Dutch, and French empires).

What makes the difference before and after 1787? Doubtless the invention at Philadelphia is necessary. Before 1787 federations were invariably peripheralized, that is, fairly close to the alliance end of the scale. Those federations were able, usually, to wage the war that brought the members together initially, but after the first success members squabbled and fought, sometimes breaking up, other times centralizing completely. Naturally, founders of nations rejected the federal form as inefficient compared with the imperial (or national) model.

After 1787, however, federations on the American model were sufficiently centralized that the government of the federation could perpetuate itself even after the situation that occasioned it had completely changed. Framers of many constitutions saw that federations were capable of surviving and therefore were at least as efficient as empires. So when federation seemed appropriate, e.g., when a group of more or less equal and independent states could, by combining, achieve some military or diplomatic objective, then framers were willing, indeed eager, to adopt the federal form. On this basis, then, the centralized federalism of 1787 became a model copied worldwide.

It may of course be that the high frequency of federalism among new constitutions of the last two centuries was as much a function of the decomposition of empires as it was of the improvement of federalism. That is, it may be that there are more federal governments simply because there are more governments. Still, the federal form has been popular for a reason. Typically provinces in empires are not an efficient size for independent governments. So, as empire ends, it is desirable to combine provinces in some way: either by conquest or by federation. That the choice in the last two centuries has so often been federation is testimony to the fact that the change in federalism has rendered it more usable.

American Federalism Before 1787

How was this new kind of federalism invented? Initially, of course, American federalism was peripheralized in the way that were all previous federal governments. But something happened in 1787 to change the terms of the federal relation. Let me outline the history of the event.

Prior to 1774 the colonies in British North America were imperially coordinated into one "Atlantic" unit by the government in London. The Continental Congress of 1774, which was based on nongovernmental committees, began to usurp the London authority. The colonial committees gradually transformed themselves into independent state governments, with all the functions of the predecessor colonial government and most of the relevant functions of the government in London. Thus an area governed by several local governments inside an empire came to be governed by usurping committees and, ultimately, by a confederation of usurping committees. In the constitutional debates prior to the Civil War, Whigs and Republicans often denied, in an effort to bolster the case against states rights, that the states were ever independent. They asserted, on the contrary, that the Congress had, by the Declaration, directly seized authority from London. It is true that the Declaration temporally preceded all new state constitutions; but the committees were de facto governments well before the Declaration was adopted. Hence, Congress took over, not from London but from the committees (Adams, 1980). For example, Washington, the continental commander, took over troops of Massachusetts and Connecticut. In this sense the new national government of 1776 was a federation of new quasi-governments.

It was a highly peripheralized federation, as one would expect from its local origins. Indeed, it was about as peripheralized as its contemporary Swiss confederacy and a great deal more peripheralized than the Dutch republic (Riker, 1957). When the Congress finally formalized itself with a constitution, the Articles of Confederation (written in 1777 and fully ratified in 1781), the central government was granted very limited powers (over some military and foreign affairs, currency, Indian trade, post office, and territorial disputes between the states), while the states reserved everything else to themselves. Functionally, therefore, the central government declined in significance when the peace deprived it of its most important activity. Furthermore, form followed function. The delegates to Congress were local rather than national officials because they were appointed annually by state legislatures and (in an unnecessary provision) were subject to recall. Each state had one vote in Congress, just like the allies of an alliance, and could absolutely veto amendments to the Articles both in Congress and in state legislatures. An extraordinary majority (9/13 or about 69%) was required for decisions on foreign affairs, the military commander, and appropriations and borrowing, which meant that collegia of five states could veto. Only minor matters could be dealt with by majority rule. Consequently, the real decision on important matters was pushed back from Congress to the state legislatures.

The Background of the Philadelphia Convention

After the peace treaty in 1783, the work of Congress lost significance. So nationalists agitated for constitutional reform. Those who feared a reopened war with Britain or a confrontation with Spain, those who abhorred the fiscal irresponsibility of state governments, and those who yearned for commercial expansion attempted to amend the Articles, first (by the impost) for national tariffs, then (by the Annapolis Convention) for national commercial regulation, and finally (by the Philadelphia Convention) for a general strengthening of the central government. In the autumn of 1786 the pivotal actors in bringing about the Philadelphia Convention were Virginians because their legislature, responding to the proposal at the Annapolis Convention, called for attendance at Philadelphia even before Congress could officially summon a Convention.

Since Virginians thus forced the hand of a reluctant Congress, they felt obliged to offer something for discussion or at least to open debate at the Philadelphia Convention. James Madison felt the obligation so strongly that he wrote out the elements of a plan for reform (as we know from his letters to Jefferson, Randolph, and Washington (Rutland, 1975, vol. IX, pp. 317, 369, 382). Furthermore, the Virginians were so eager for reform that they assembled in Philadelphia exactly on time while delegates from most other states were one or two or three weeks late. Then, while waiting for stragglers, they perfected the Virginia plan. Governor Edmund Randolph, the titular head of the Virginia delegation, offered the plan as the first substantive business of the Convention, and it became the basis, first, of the discussion, and, ultimately, of the Constitution.

Of course, the plan was significantly revised because the Convention considered it four times: first, as originally submitted, in the Committee of the whole, where, as amended, it was reported to the Convention; second as amended in that report, in Convention, where it was referred, as further amended, to a Committee on Detail; third, as revised in the Committee on Detail, in Convention again, where, as further amended, it was referred to the Committee on Style; and fourth, as revised by the Committee on Style, in Convention again, where, as further amended, it was finally adopted. Nevertheless, throughout that extensive procedure, the fundamental form of the Virginia plan remained clearly recognizable: a government of three parts (legislature, executive, judiciary) somewhat independent of each other and each endowed with national authority; a two-house legislature subject to a conditional veto by an executive; and a judiciary with jurisdiction over a wide range of questions. Indeed, the only significant changes in all those revisions were the methods of selecting the executive, the upper house, and the judiciary, and the elimination of the national veto over state laws. By contrast, the one alternative plan seriously offered, the New Jersey plan, provided for something extremely close to the Articles, essentially the Articles augmented with some additional functions for Congress. The New Jersey plan was, however, decisively rejected, so that the Convention necessarily did no more than elaborate on the Virginia plan. The Virginia plan provided for a national government, clearly superior to the states. It proposed that Congress be empowered "to enjoy the Legislative Rights vested in Congress" by the Articles, "to legislate in all cases to which the several States are incompetent, or in which the harmony of the United States may be interrupted by the exercise of individual Legislation," and, perhaps most significantly, to negative all laws passed by the several States," contravening in the opinion of the National Legislature the articles of Union." Such a broad grant of authority would of course reduce the supposedly sovereign states to mere provinces. But, just to make certain, perhaps, that this effect actually resulted, the central government was to be entirely separate from the states electorally: the lower branch of the legislature, while apportioned by states, was to be popularly elected (rather than by state legislatures); the upper branch was to be elected by the lower; and the two branches together were to select the executive and judiciary. Thus the state governments were to be *completely* excluded from the creation of the national government. Furthermore, this independent national government with full authority to govern was to supervise the states, not only with a veto on state laws but with full responsibility to guarantee republican government in the states.

Clearly, there was nothing federal about the Virginia plan. During the ratification debates the following winter, Antifederalists often proposed to be horrified by the "consolidated government" provided in the Constitution. Think how much more horrified they would have been had the Virginia plan not been modified.

James Madison's Goals in the Virginia Plan

It was no accident that the Virginia plan was centralizing. This is what the Virginians presented after they had discussed for two weeks and presumably agreed to it, although George Mason, who refused to sign the Constitution out of truly parochial economic interests, may have regretted his easy initial acquiescence. We know from Madison's writings and Washington's letters, even Mason's letters in May 1787 (Farrand, 1964, vol. III, pp. 22–24) that the plan was what they wanted. We know also that

Madison was the author of the Virginia plan. So it is possible to specify quite precisely the goals of the Virginians and thus to show that the plan was not intended to be federal. This, then, is what I shall do in the next two sections by, first, analyzing Madison's state of mind in the spring of 1787 and by, second, showing on textual grounds that he was in fact the author of the Virginia plan.

That Madison's goal was to centralize government and to subordinate the states is easily demonstrated by an analysis of the practical and philosophical criticism he wrote about American government in the spring of 1787, just at the time he was formulating the details of the Virginia plan. His criticism is set forth in a paper entitled, "Vices of the Political System of the United States" (Rutland, 1975, vol. IX, pp. 345–358), which was apparently intended as an aid to his own education and thinking. (It was a companion piece to his notes on Ancient and Modern Confederacies— prepared in the spring of 1786—in which the analysis of each confederation contained a section entitled "Vices of the Constitution" (Rutland, 1975, vol. IX, p. 346). The 12 vices of the political system of the United States were:

1. *Failure of the states to comply with Constitutional requisitions*: Madison's remarks under this rubric (e.g., that the failure "results from the number and independent authority of the States," is "uniformly exemplified in every similar Confederacy," and is "permanently inherent...[and]...fatal to...the present system") completely convey his hostility to federalism both in general and to the American in particular.
2. *Encroachment by the states on the federal authority*: The not-very-serious examples cited by Madison (i.e., Georgia's wars and treaties with the Indians, unlicensed compacts between Virginia and Maryland and between Pennsylvania and New Jersey, and Massachusetts troops raised to put down Shays) indicate that he wished to subordinate states even when they "encroached" in easily justifiable ways.
3. *Violations of the law of nations and of treaties*: Madison here referred to the failure of states to enforce or abide by the peace treaty. Presumably he, like Jay and Washington, feared that these failures might reopen the war. In any event, his cure for this defect was to subordinate the states so fully to Congress that they would be unable to violate treaties.
4. *Trespasses of the states on the rights of each other*: Under this rubric Madison included not only state grants of monopolies to their own

citizens, excluding citizens of other states, but also (indeed especially) paper money and legal tender laws that infringed on contracts between local citizens and citizens of other states. To oppose these traditional police powers of states, few of which actually violated the Articles, indicates that Madison intended to deprive the states of much of their domestic authority.

5. *Want of concert in matters where common interest requires it*: Madison referred here to commercial regulation, patents, etc., which "may at present be defeated by the perverseness of particular States." This also may be interpreted as an attack on the customary domestic authority of states.

6. *Want of guaranty to the states of their Constitution and laws against internal violence*: Madison may here have referred to Shays' rebellion, but mainly he was criticizing the potential unrepresentativeness of state governments, which he thought could only be cured by an increase in central authority (presumably to permit it to displace unrepresentative state governments in the way the central governments of India and Argentina have often displaced unrepresentative state governments).

7. *Want of sanction to the laws, and of coercion in the government of the Confederacy*: Madison noted that the federal government lacked the power to coerce any one and that the Articles were, under the guise of a constitution," nothing more than a treaty of amity...between so many independent and Soverign States." Why, he asked, was coercion omitted? Because, he answered, the framers of the Articles overoptimistically expected interstate cooperation which, however, dissolved in the postwar self-interest of the states.

8. *Want of ratification by the people of the Articles of Confederacy*: Madison believed that this feature permitted states to ignore the Articles and was, therefore, further evidence that the Articles were merely an alliance.

9. *Multiplicity of the laws in the several states.* Madison, like a contemporary libertarian, regarded the multiplicity of laws as a "nuisance."

10. *Mutability of the laws of the states*: The instability of the laws was, he said, "vicious" and "a snare."

11. *Injustice of the laws of the states*: Madison's commentary under this rubric is almost as long as the commentary on the previous ten. Today this passage is remembered mainly as the first version of his argument (in the Tenth *Federalist*) for an "extended republic." As a commentary on his state of mind in the spring of 1787, however, the main value of this passage is his emphasis on the possibility

that, in a small jurisdiction, demagogues would retain office with bribes (like paper money) that selfish citizens would accept. By inference, therefore, the remedy for injustice is to transfer authority to the largest and highest level of government.

12. *Impotence of the laws of the states*: Madison broke off at this point and did not explain this vice.

Summarizing, the vices fall into two categories: 1) the excessive authority of the states, which weakens the center (numbers 1, 2, 3, 7, and 8), and 2) the bad government by the states, which results from their excessive authority (numbers 4, 5, 6, 9, 10, 11, and 12). In either case the cure was, so Madison thought, to subordinate the states.

But lurking underneath these vices of structure is a vice of personnel about which, in my opinion, Madison felt even more deeply. He thought that the third vice, violations of treaties, resulted, inter alia, from the "sphere of life from which most . . . members [of Legislatures] are taken." And he thought that the eleventh vice, injustice of laws, resulted, in part, from an "honest but unenlightened representative" being duped by a "favorite leader, veiling his selfishness under the professions of public good, and varnishing his sophistical arguments with the glowing colors of popular eloquence." Clearly he thought most state legislators were simple men, myopic (e.g., unable to recognize the dangers of paper money), and easily manipulated by demagogues. By contrast, as he wrote to Washington (Rutland, 1975, vol. IX, p. 384, 16 April 1787), the Congressmen were more farsighted and responsible: "There has not been any moment since the peace at which the representatives of the union would have given an assent to paper money or any other measure of a kindred nature." Thus the deeper danger of state governments was their small size because to staff them it was necessary to select from too low a social and educational level. This would not be a serious defect, so Madison implied, if state governments did nothing of importance and had no control over the national government. Hence followed his deep rationale for the Virginia plan. Important affairs could be handled at the national level by the best men (doubtless men like himself who understood paper money) if the states were thoroughly subordinated to the center and the election of national officials separated entirely from electors in the state government.

Madison's Authorship of the Virginia Plan

The testimony of the "Vices. . . ," which Madison finished in April 1787, two to six weeks before he arrived in Philadelphia, indicates that he despised the peripheralized federalism of the Articles. It is to be expected,

Table 2–1. History of the principal features of the resolutions of the Virginia Plan

Resolution no.		Included in Madison's letters to		
		Jefferson 19 March 1787	*Randolph* 8 April 1787	*Washington* 16 April 1787
1	Correction and enlargement of Articles	x	x	x
2	Proportional representation of states	x	x	x
3	Two-branch legislature	—	x	x
4	First branch	—	x	x
	POPULARLY ELECTED	—	x[a]	x[a]
	term	—	x	x
5	age, stipends, ineligibility, *recall*	—	—	—
	Second branch	—	x	x
	ELECTED BY FIRST	—	—	—
	term	—	x	x
	age, stipends, ineligibility	—	—	—
6	Legislative authority	x	x	x
	as vested in Congress	—	x	x
	when states incompetent or harmony interrupted	—	—	—
	negative on unconstitutional state legislation	x[b]	x[b]	x[b]
	military power	—	x	x
7	Executive (separated powers)	x	x	x
	chosen by national method	—	x	x
	specifically, the national legislature authority	—	undecided	undecided

	Item			
8	Council	—	x	x
	executive officers	—		x
	national judiciary	—		—
	conditional veto	—		—
9	Judiciary	—	x	x
	supreme and inferior tribunals	—		x
	chosen by national method	—		x
	specifically the national legislature	—		—
	admiralty jurisdiction	—	x	x
	interstate and foreign jurisdiction	—	x	x
	taxes, impeachment	—		—
	national peace and harmony	—	x[c]	x[c]
10	Admission of new states, nonunanimous	—		—
11	Guarantee of republican government	—	x	x
12	Continuance of Congress until adoption	—		—
13	Amendment of new Articles by states only	—		—
14	Binding state officers by articles	—		x[d]
15	Ratification by state conventions	x	x	x

Note. Items in upper case: resolution more nationalistic than Madison; in italic: resolution less nationalistic than Madison.

[a] Madison offered the alternative of election by state legislatures.
[b] Madison emphasized "all" state legislation.
[c] Madison inferentially stated.
[d] Madison mentioned only state judges.

therefore, that he would seek to eliminate the federal structure. Of course, if centralized federalism had been invented, he might simply have wished to replace peripherialized with centralized federalism. But, in fact, centralized federalism had not been invented, so, in the absence of any other alternative, he was compelled to eliminate federalism entirely. This is what he tried to do with the Virginia plan.

That Madison conceived the Virginia plan is entirely certain. During March and April of 1787, he wrote three surviving outlines of proposed constitutional provisions. Writing from New York, where he was serving in Congress and where he doubtless discussed the subject with New Yorkers like Alexander Hamilton and with Congressmen like Rufus King of Massachusetts, Madison described provisions to Jefferson (in France) 19 March 1787, to Randolph (in Virginia) 8 April 1787, and to Washington (in Virginia) 16 April 1787. Surveying these letters in temporal sequence, one can see how Madison's proposals were fleshed out until they were almost exactly the Virginia plan. See table 2–1, where the left column lists the provisions of the plan and the three right columns list the provisions in Madison's letters. It is apparent from direct examination of the table that the letters anticipate almost all of the provisions of the plan.

Nevertheless, the best evidence that Madison himself developed the Virginia plan is not the textual history as set forth in table 2–1, but rather the internal coherence of plan itself. Almost every feature of the plan is aimed at Madison's goal, as inferred from the "Vices...," namely that national decisions and national officials be independent of and superior to state governments, state decisions, and state officials. The Virginia delegates who went over the plan in the two weeks prior to the Convention did not significantly depart from the tenor of Madison's proposals. Their retention of his tone indicates that he dominated in these preliminary discussions—as would be expected because he was the only one who was fully prepared—and that the other Virginians in effect ratified his intent to jettison the federal system.

It is true that the other Virginians weakened Madison's plan. In three distinct instances they allowed for a feature of federalism. First, they provided that members of the lower house of the legislature be subject to recall. This was strikingly out of harmony with the whole plan and indeed with other revisions the Virginians made. Madison had allowed in his letters to Randolph and Washington for the selection of the lower house either by popular vote or by state legislatures. The delegation deleted state legislatures, thereby, in the spirit of Madison's plan, excluding state government from the generation of the national government. Recall, however, brought state government back into the process because in that era one could imagine recall only by state legislatures. How can one explain the delegates decision to simultaneously promote and demote state legislatures? The explanation is, I believe, that, like Madison, the Virginians wanted to exclude state legislators from influence but also they wanted the plan to pass. I suspect they believed that recall was a right deeply cherished (especially in New England) but seldom exercised—I can discover no instance of recall from Congress 1776 to 1788, probably because, with short terms, it was unnecessary. Hence the addition of recall was an inexpensive (because unused) bait for New England votes, a trivial weakening compared with the strengthening by deletion of election by state legislatures.

The second weakening toward federalism of Madison's proposals was the change of the national negative on state laws from Madison's formulation "in all cases whatsoever" to cases "contravening in the opinion of the National Legislature the articles of Union." This must have pained Madison greatly for, as I will show in a later section, he profoundly desired this provision. For him it was a substitute for imperial centralization and he identified it with the "Kingly prerogative," doubtless the main weapon to subdue intransigent states. Again, I think, the other Virginians regarded their change as a matter of sophisticated persuasion. Like most other delegates, they did not believe this provision was important and they therefore modified it for the sake of not alienating those who might believe the mere assertion of the right to be in itself offensive.

A third weakening, namely, the exclusion of the national legislature from the process of amendment, seems a similar kind of conciliation, a bid for votes with a rarely used provision.

Aside from weakening with these three only slightly federalistic provisions, the Virginians strengthened with several highly nationalistic ones. As already noted, they deleted state legislatures as prospective electors for the lower house. They further excluded the states by providing the lower house elect the upper and both together choose the executive and judiciary. (By contrast, Madison had simply proposed that the executive and judiciary be national, without specifying the method of selection.) Finally, they provided that the national government (not states) admit new states, with less than unanimity (so no veto), and they required all state officers (not just judges) to swear to support the national constitution. Of course they amended Madison in a number of other ways that were neutral with respect to centralization. But insofar as they affected the federal relation, they offered a highly nationalistic plan which was an extention, doubtless with Madison's enthusiastic participation, of his own proposal to dispense with federalism.

The Virginia Plan on the Floor of the Convention

But, of course, the Virginians were not able to eliminate federalism. On the floor of the Convention the delegates reversed the Virginians on: 1) the representation of states, 2) the election of the upper house, 3) the national veto on state laws, and 4) the election of the executive; and they added one especially important federalistic provision: 5) the residence of legislators.

What came out of the Covention was, therefore, a centralized national government modified with provisions to preserve the states, which is exactly the content of centralized federalism as admired and copied worldwide.

It is not to be supposed, however, that anyone planned this result. Rather, each of the modifications was undertaken in sequential isolation in the sense that earlier modifications were not typically reconciled with later ones. Furthermore, the motives for specific modifications sometimes involved federalism and sometimes involved quite unrelated considerations. The sum of the modifications is thus a jumble. In subsequent sections I review their history—not to tell well-known stories again, but to demonstrate the temporally isolated and ideologically uncoordinated nature of the event.

The Representation of States

As is well known, the main dispute in the Convention concerned federalism, specifically, whether states were to be represented equally or according to population or wealth. Proportional representation was a crucial feature of the Virginia plan, and the delegates from Virginia and Pennsylvania met before the Convention to coordinate strategies to obtain it (Farrand, 1964, vol. I, pp. 10–11). But smaller states (especially Delaware, New Jersey, and New York) were similarly determined to retain the equality of the Articles, and devised the New Jersey plan as an alternative. This issue occupied the framers much of the time from 30 May to 16 July, and the disputes became so bitter that the Convention almost broke up. Many of the leaders on both sides viewed the issues on representation as a choice between national (i.e., unitary) or federal government, and in table 2–2 I have collected some direct verbal expressions of the parallelism between the two dichotomies. The settlement on representation (i.e., proportional in the lower house, equal in the upper) is the main feature of our centralized federalism and the median between peripheralized federalism and unitary governments. But the compromise for this settlement was not motivated by an intention to improve

Table 2–2. The choice on representation as a choice between nationalism and federalism

---

I. By Proponents of Equality:
    Paterson (New Jersey): "If we argue...that a federal compact... exists,... we...find an equal soverignity to be the basis of it....This is the basis of all *treaties*" (Farrand, 1964, vol. I, p. 250, 16 June 1787, emphasis added).
    L. Martin (Maryland): "...contended that an equal soverinty in each state was essential to the federal idea....(H)e read...passages in Locke and Vatell and also Rutherford: That the States being equal cannot... confederate so as to give up on equality of votes without giving up their liberty" (Farrand, 1964, vol. I, pp. 437–438, 27 June 1787).
    Ellsworth (Connecticut): "No instance of a Confederacy has exisited in which an equality of voices has not been exercised by the members of it" (Farrand, 1964, vol, I, p. 484, 30 June 1787).

II. By Proponents of Proportionality:
    Randolph (Virginia): "The true question [i.e., between the New Jersey and Virginia plans] is whether we shall adhere to the federal plan or introduce the national plan" (Farrand, 1964, vol. I, p. 255, 16 June 1787).
    King (Massachusetts): "...he considered the proposed Government as substantially and formally, a General and National Government over the people of America. There will never be a case in which it will act as a federal Government on the States and not on the individual Citizens" (Farrand, 1964, vol. II, p. 6, 14 July 1787).

---

federalism. Rather it was a practical expedient to save the Union (and the Convention) from dissolution.

Proportional representation had won on the preliminary bouts, and delegates from small states reacted intensely. Gunning Bedford (Del.) even threatened that the small states would "find some foreign ally [sci: Great Britain] of more honor and good faith, who will take them by the hand and do them justice" (Farrand, 1964, vol. I, p. 492, 30 June 1787). The crucial vote on representation (Farrand, 1964, vol. II, p. 15, 16 July 1787) was the closest possible, 5–4, with Massachusetts divided and unable to vote. If the two changelings from Massachusetts had voted as they had previously, the vote would have been a tie and the compromise would have failed. So the two from Massachusetts (Elbridge Gerry and Caleb Strong) were the pivotal voters in the sense that their shift changed the outcome. We have a pretty good idea of their motivation and it had little to do with federalism. They were simply trying to save the Union. Gerry, who was chairman of the committee that recommended the compromise, justified it half-heartedly:

> Tho he had assented to the Report in the Committee, he had very material objections to it. We were however in a peculiar situation. We were neither the same Nation nor different Nations. We ought not therefore to pursue the one or the other of these ideas too closely. [Query: Are the two ideas federalism and nationalism?] If no compromise should take place what will be the consequences. A secession he foresaw would take place;...two different plans will be proposed, and the result no man could foresee. If we do not come to an agreement among ourselves some foreign sword will probably do the work for us (Farrand, 1964, vol. I, p. 532, 5 July 1787).

Strong, who otherwise spoke seldom, explained his intention thus:

> The Convention had been such divided in opinion. In order to avoid the consequences of it, an accommodation had been proposed. A committee had been appointed; and though some of the members of it were averse to an equality of votes, a Report had been made in favor of it. It is agreed on all hands that Congress are nearly at an end. If no Accommodation takes place, the Union itself must soon be dissolved. It has been suggested that if we can not come to any general agreement the principal States may form & recommend a scheme of Government. It is probable that the large States themselves will under such circumstances embrace and ratify it. He thought the small States had made a considerable concession...and that they might naturally expect some concession on the other side. From this view of the matter he was compelled to give his vote for the Report taken all together (Farrand, 1964, vol. II, p. 7, 14 July 1787).

Clearly Gerry and Strong were uneasy about deserting the large states and they justified it out of fear of secession. Perhaps Gerry also had some dim vision of centralized federalism ("neither the same Nation nor different Nations") but mainly he feared a "foreign sword."

It is thus apparent that constitutional theory had little to do with the compromise on representation. Rather it was based simply on the small states' insistence on positioning themselves well for further negotiations and on the pivotal voters' fear of secession. In that provision, therefore, centralized federalism is an unanticipated consequence of practical judgments on other matters.

The Election of the Upper House

The second peripheralizing revision of the Virginia plan, i.e., the method of election of the upper house, was, however, a conscious modification of the nationalism of the plan because of a constitutional theory about federalism. John Dickinson (Del.) explained his motion for state legislatures to elect the upper house with a federalistic rationale:

The preservation of the States in a certain degree of agency is indispensible. It will produce that collision between different authorities which should be wished for in order to check each other. To attempt to abolish the States altogether, would degrade the Councils of our Country, would be impractical, would be ruinous (Farrand, 1964, vol. I, p. 153, 7 June 1787).

Thus, the initial rationale for the revision appears to be federalistic. In a diversionary footnote Madison implied that Dickinson's intent was to preserve small states, not the federal system. Nevertheless, Dickinson's supporters—Sherman (Ct.), C. Pinckney (S.C.), Mason (Va.)—echoed his federalism. And the opposition to Dickinson was nationalistic, not large state, in tone:

Wilson (Pa.):   "If this amendment passes—we shall not have a national Govt...." (Farrand, 1964, vol. I, 158, 7 June 1787). So he proposed popular election.

Madison (Va.): We are about to form a national Govt. and therefore must abandon Ideas founded alone in the plan of confedn (Farrand, 1964, vol. I, p. 158, 7 June 1787).

Read (Del.):   proposed "that the Senate should be appointed by the Executive Magistrate out of a proper number of persons to be nominated by the individual legislature" (Farrand, 1964, vol. I, p. 151, 7 June 1787).

The debate on Senatorial elections had small state delegates and large state delegates on each side, so the issue was not a matter of positioning small states. Rather it was as Dickinson said, a matter of perserving some of the peripheralized federalism of the Articles. Furthermore, the preservationists won, unanimously indeed. Madison and Wilson could not even carry their own delegations. In general, the framers were nationalists, but they were not prepared, even the Virginians were not prepared, to abandon federalism completely.

On the other hand, the preservationists were not truly anti-national. Dickinson, as will be discussed, favored the national veto of state laws. In general, the framers did not think deeply about what they were doing for federalism. Soon after the decision on Senatorial elections, the framers decided, without debate and unanimously, to delete recall of members of the lower house (Farrand 1964, vol, I, p. 217, 12 June 1787). Recall had been added to Madison's plan by the Virginia delegation and it was not consonant with popular election. So the deletion of recall cleared up an inconsistency in the Virginia plan as it had been introduced. On the other hand, having revised the plan to make the upper house with its long terms, responsible to state legislatures, it would have been appropriate to provide for the recall of Senators. But the framers overlooked this possibility. In the absence of recall, Senators soon learned that they could ignore their direct constituents (Riker, 1956). Consequently, Senatorial elections without recall did little to preserve federalism. By the twentieth century, the agitation for the seventeeth Amendment (direct election of Senators) was not regarded as a threat to the federal system.

The National Veto on State Laws

The third peripheralizing revision of the Virginia plan, namely, the deletion of the national legislative veto of state laws, was supported and opposed on grounds of constitutional theory, but ultimately the decision was made on opportunistic grounds. Madison had consistently regarded the veto as the substitute in the new American circumstances for the "Kingly prerogative," the thing that made the Empire work and would, in the new form, so he hoped, make the American empire work. Hardly anyone else was as entranced as Madison with the veto—only Charles Pinckney (S.C.) and James Wilson (Pa.). Furthermore, there were close substitutes. So it is not surprising that the provision was deleted.

The Virginians were apparently unwilling to allow as wide a veto as Madison's ("all cases whatsoever"). They limited it to laws "contravening...the Articles of Union." In that form it was not initially objectionable. Two days after the Virginia plan was introduced, the veto passed without debate or dissent, even with an addition for laws "contravening any treaties" (Farrand, 1964, vol. I, p. 54, 31 May 1787). That easy victory inspired Charles Pinckney (S.C.) to propose a veto on "laws which they [national legislators] judge to be improper," which is almost Madison's original veto. Pinckney's motion was not well received: Only Madison (Va.), Wilson (Pa.), and Dickinson (Del.) supported it, while Williamson (N.C.), Gerry (Ms.), Sherman (Ct.), Bedford (Del.), and Butler (S.C.) opposed. The motion lost 3 to 7 with Delaware divided (Farrand, 1964, vol. I, p. 170, 8 June 1787).

The three supporters were Massachusetts, Pennsylvania, and Virginia, which suggests a large state-small state conflict with Dickinson a personal aberration. And it is true that the intense opposition which developed later was led by John Lansing (N.Y.) and Luther Martin (Md.), both small-state delegates and both later active opponents of ratification of the Constitution. Lansing was indeed intense: "The States will never feel a sufficient confidence in a general Government to give it a negative on their laws" (Farrand, 1964, vol. I, p. 250, 16 June 1787); "If this influence [i.e., legislative veto] is to be attained, the States must be entirely abolished"

(Farrand, 1964, vol. I, p. 337, 20 June 1787). And Lansing's intensity impressed others. When the veto came up the second time, it got short shrift. After brief debate, it was defeated, 3 to 7, with Pennsylvania now in the negative.

More interesting, perhaps, than the failure is the reason adduced for opposition by, especially, Gouverneur Morris (Pa.): He "opposed this power as likely to be terrible to the States, and not necessary if sufficient Legislative authority should be given to the Genl Government" (Farrand, 1964, vol. II, p. 27, 17 July 1787), and again he "was more and more opposed to the negative. The proposal would disgust all the States. A law that ought to be negatived will be set aside in the judiciary department and if that security should fail; may be repelled by a National law" (Farrand, 1964, vol. II, p. 28, 17 July 1787). Morris' comments were made just after the small-state success on 16 July on equal representation in the Senate. Morris had been the most determined opponent of equal representation, and on the morning of 17 July he reopened that question, only to discover he had no support whatever. Doubtless somewhat chagrined, he may well have finally recognized the depth of feeling on the small state side and may well have come to believe that it ought to be placated. Nevertheless, his opposition to the national veto does not involve a concession to federalism. He himself listed, in the sentences just quoted, three close substitutes for a veto: 1) large national legislative authority, 2) judicial review and supervision of state laws, and 3) national legislation to repeal unconstitutional state laws. In addition there were two other substitutes suggested and adopted: 4) specific prohibitions on state laws, as in Article I, section 10 (e.g., prohibitions on paper money, as urged by Gerry as a specific substitute for the legislative veto (Farrand, 1964, vol. I, p. 165, 8 June 1787), and 5) the supremacy clause, which certainly establishes judicial review of state laws and which was adopted immediately after the legislative veto was rejected—adopted moreover by unanimity, without debate, and on the motion of L. Martin (Md.), the most extreme advocate of peripheralized federalism at the Convention. One suspects that Morris and Martin had an agreement. Whether they did or not, we know for certain that Martin regarded the supremacy clause as a moderate substitute for the legislative veto (Farrand, 1964, vol. III, p. 286, 19 March 1788). Since the supremacy clause was indeed a perfectly adequate substitute, as John Marshall subsequently demonstrated, it is not surprising that the Convention again and finally rejected a motion for a legislative veto. Softened by requiring a two-thirds majority the motion was nevertheless defeated, 5 to 6, mainly on the ground that it was now unnecessary.

The legislative veto was especially dear to Madison. In reporting to

Jefferson on the work of the Convention, Madison devoted more attention by far to the deletion of the veto than any other subject (Rutland, 1975, vol. X, pp. 206–219, especially pp. 209–214, 24 October 1787). He was clearly pessimistic about whether a Constitution without it would survive: "If the supremacy of the British Parliament is not necessary as has been contended, for the harmony of that Empire; it is evident I think that without the royal negative or some equivalent control, the unity of the system would be destroyed. The want of some such provision seems to have been mortal to the ancient Confederacies, and to be the disease of the modern" (Rutland, 1975, vol. X, p. 210). Despite Madison's pessimism, however, the deletion of the veto did not in fact moderate the nationalism of his plan. As Luther Martin subsequently observed, the coupling of the supremacy clause with an elaborate system of federal courts provided almost the same degree of national control (Farrand, 1964, vol. III, p. 287, 19 March 1788). This fact is what Marshall, and subsequent judges, exploited to provide almost systematic review of state laws.

The conclusion is, therefore, that, in deleting the veto over state laws, the framers did not really reject Madisonian nationalism, although for rhetorical reasons they toned down the projection of it in the Constitution.

The Election of the Executive

The fourth peripheralizing revision of the Virginia plan involved the election of the executive. While the Virginia plan provided for election by the national legislature, the Convention substituted an electoral college in which the states might play a significant part. Yet the motive for the revision was the constitutional theory of the separation of powers. Federalism was only incidentally and opportunistically involved. Consequently, it can, in this case also, easily be said that the framers were not intentionally modifying the Virginia nationalism.

The opposition to the Virginian method of election grew out of the political experience of the Pennsylvania constitutional theorists, especially James Wilson and Gouverneur Morris. One main dividing line in Pennsylvanian politics was the attitude toward the unicameral legislature. This constitutional feature was, in the popular mind, identified with radical and myopic populism and the radical party consequently called themselves Constitutionalists. The conservative party, called Republicans, believed that their cause would be best advanced by a constitution with a separately elected executive and upper and lower houses. James Wilson, as the main spokesman in the Convention for this political theory, urged popular election of the executive and the other house. He got nowhere with his proposal for popular election of the Senate (Farrand 1964, vol. I, p. 52, 31 May 1787), for popular election from large districts (Farrand, 1964, vol. I, p. 154, 7 June 1787), and for election by popularly chosen electors (Farrand, 1964, vol. I, p. 406, 25 June 1787). But his proposals for the Executive did better, especially when taken over and sponsored by G. Morris (Farrand, 1964, vol. I, p. 79, 2 June 1787, by electors popularly chosen in districts; vol. II, p. 24, 17 July 1787, by citizens; vol. II, p. 399, 24 August 1787, by the people; vol. II, p. 399, 24 August 1787, by popularly chosen electors; vol. II, p. 399, 24 August 1787, by electors; and finally vol. II, p. 525, 6 September 1787, by electors chosen as the state legislature might direct).

As is apparent from this list of motions the matter was bitterly contested, and the Convention wavered a long time. The proponents of election by the national legislature were, of course, motivated by both nationalism and elitism. They feared that popular election would be uninformed (G. Mason [Va.]: "It would be as unnatural to refer the choice of a Chief Magistrate to the people, as it would, to refer a trial of colours to a blindman" Farrand, 1964, vol. II, p. 32, 17 July 1787), or that election by state officials would be too peripheralizing (Edmund Randolph [Va.]: "A Natl. Executive thus chosen [i.e., by state executives] will not be likely to defend with becoming vigilance and firmness the national rights agst State encroachments" (Farrand, 1964, vol. I, p. 176, 9 June 1787). The opponents of election by the national legislature were eager to separate powers in the national government in the interests of a Montesquieu-ian notion of liberty. G. Morris remarked: "Of all possible modes of appointment that by the Legislature is the worst. If the Legislature is to appoint, and to impeach or to influence the impeachment, the Executive will be the mere creation of it" (Farrand, 1964, vol. II, p. 103, 24 July 1787). As the controversy progressed Madison himself was persuaded to change sides and he then rationalized, with characteristic eloquence, the alternative methods of election:

> If it be essential to the preservation of liberty that the Legisl:Execut: & Judiciary powers be separate, it is essential to a maintenance of the separation, that they should be independent of each other. The Executive could not be independent of the Legislature, if dependent on the pleasure of that branch for appointment ... (Farrand, 1964, vol. II, p. 34, 17 July 1787).

The matter was fought over repeatedly. The Convention initially adopted election by the national legislature (Farrand, 1964, vol. I, p. 79, 2 June 1787), then reversed itself to election by electors (Farrand, 1964, vol.

II, p. 51, 19 July 1787), then reversed again for election by the national legislature (Farrand, 1964, vol. II, p. 98, 24 July 1787, comfirmed vol. II, p. 118, 26 July 1787), then tied on election by electors (Farrand, 1964, vol. II, p. 339, 24 August 1787), and finally, having sent the matter to a committee in which the electoral college was invented, adopted the electoral college (Farrand, 1964, vol. II, p. 520, 6 September 1787).

As this history of wavering suggests, each new revision was accompanied by some new coalition. Support for popular election by itself was not large, mainly Pennsylvania and Virginia (after Madison was converted). But since electors implied some extra weight for small states, they (i.e., Connecticut, New Jersey, Delaware, and Maryland) joined the separationist side on some votes. This small-state bloc solidified against election by the national legislature when, on a large state motion, the Committee required a joint ballot of the two houses, which would give extra weight to the large state representatives in the lower house and certainly eliminate the equality of states in the upper house. As a result of this maneuver two small states (New Jersey and Delaware) became consistent allies of Pennsylvania and Virginia in support of electors.

At the same time the consistent supporters of legislative election (Massachusetts, North Carolina, South Carolina) were joined by the distant states (New Hampshire and Georgia). The distant states were not concerned with constitutional theory but the prospect of an electoral college meeting somewhere in the middle states appalled them with its travel costs.

The ultimate resolution consisted of election in an electoral college, which would decide by an absolute majority, or, in the absence of an absolute majority in the college, of election by an absolute majority in the House of Representatives where each state delegation would have one vote. Futhermore, the electors were to be chosen as directed by the state legislatures and were to meet only in their respective states, forwarding their votes to the Senate.

This elaborate institution satisifed each member of the ultimately victorious coalition. The separationists (i.e., Pennsylvania and Virginia) probably expected that, as actually happened, electors would eventually be chosen by popular election. Some delegates thought that the college, meeting in separate states, would never agree on a majority candidate so that the electors, however chosen, would not be decisive, but G. Morris, for example, accurately predicted that, since each elector was to have two votes and since a majority of electors was decisive, an "eminent and generally known" character would receive the necessary one-fourth of the votes (Farrand, 1964, vol. II, p. 512, 5 September 1787). Thus the separationists obtained something close to their ideal of popular election. Since the small states were slightly overrepresented in the electoral college (based on the number of representatives and Senators from each state) and were equally represented in an election in the House, they obtained something of their ideal of equality. As for the distant states, they were satisfied by the provision that the electors for each state were to meet in that state without trips to some distant national capital.

This remarkable compromise resulted in the adoption of the electoral college by a vote of 9 to 2 with only North and South Carolina dissenting. Clearly, this compromise was opportunistic. It had very little to do with the theory of federalism, even though in the end it modified the nationalism of the Virginia plan. Indeed, if it had anything to do with constitutional theory, it was with a theory about the separation of powers and was neutral with respect to the dispute on federalism (Riker, 1984).

The Residence of the Legislators

The fifth peripheralizing revision of the Virginia plan was an addition, the requirement that legislators be inhabitants of the state from which elected. The effect of this apparently innocuous provision is that national executives or political leaders cannot place their supporters in legislative seats but must rather find their supporters among those who already have legislative seats. If executives can place their supporters, then political parties are likely to be leader-centered and national in tone. If, however, executives must select their supporters from those already elected, then political parties are likely to be decentralized and localized in tone.

Given the great significance of this provision for the subsequent development of federalism, it might be expected to derive from constitutional theory about federalism. In fact it came up almost by accident and certainly was not derived from constitutional theory. It first appears in the Convention in the paper of the Committee on Style in a rough draft in Randolph's handwriting with emendations in Rutledge's. There it is listed along with personnel qualifications. That is, its form is: "previous residence for one year" and it is coupled with a property qualification. There are two crossed out marginal notations: "qu: if a certain term of residence and a certain quantity of landed property ought not to be made by the convention further qualifications" and "These qualifications are not justified by the resolutions" (Farrand, 1964, vol. II, pp. 139–140). When it was originated, Randolph, probably, thought of this feature as a customary age and property qualification.

On the floor, however, it was recognized that nationalism was involved. Those with a bent toward perpheralization—(Mason (Va.), Dickinson (Del.), Mercer (Md.), even Ellsworth (Ct.)—emphasized the need for "local knowledge," and G. Mason specifically discussed the British practice of nonresidency, without, however, recognizing the ministerial role in filling rotten boroughs: "If residence be not required, Rich men of neighbouring States, may employ with success the means of corruption in some particular district and thereby get into the public Councils after having failed in their own State. This is the practice in the boroughs of England" (Farrand, 1964, vol. II, p. 218, 8 August 1787). On the other hand, nationalists (e.g., G. Morris [Pa.], Wilson [Pa.], Read [Dl.]) recognized the localism inherent in the provision. G. Morris observed that the residency requirement "is improper, as in the 1st. branch, *The People at Large*, not the *State* are represented" [Madison's emphasis] (Farrand, 1964, vol. II, p. 217, 8 August 1787). And Read [Dl.], who was the most nationalist of small-state delegates and who persistently proposed the abolition of the states, remarked "we were now forming a *Natil.* [Madison's emphasis] Govt and such a regulation would correspond little with the idea that we are one people" (Farrand, 1964, vol. II, p. 217, 8 August 1787).

Despite the verbal recognition on the floor of the relation of residency requirements with the constitutional issue between nationalism and federalism, the bulk of the actual debate, as well as the voting, concerned a choice of words ("resident" or "inhabitant") and a choice of time (one, three, or seven years of previous or current residence). The framers did not pursue at length the deeper significance of the subject. Habituation was incorporated to guarantee "local knowledge" just as a minimum age was incorporated to guarantee some maturity of judgment. Federalism thus came in by the back door.

How Centralized Federalism Was Invented

Had the Virginia plan not been modified, the framers would surely have produced a national government, something they would have called "consolidated" and we "unitary." What they actually produced was, however, centralized federalism, something far closer to the imperial end of the scale between alliance and empire than had been the federalism of the Articles. This new federalism was centralized because it was founded on the fully national plan, but it was federal because in some ways it provided for the survival of state governments. Even though we have greatly centralized administration in the last two centuries, the states themselves remain politically significant. And even though a civil war demonstrated the dominance of the center and the impossibility of secession, still the states remain the basis of political parties which are barely more centralized than they were one and two centuries ago.

Those modifications that preserved the states are, I believe, the ones I have analyzed. It is apparent, however, that the intent of the framers in so modifying was not to preserve federalism—though they were happy enough to use the name rhetorically when they sought ratification. Rather, it was exactly the federalism of the Articles that they sought to transcend. It is true that two of the modifications were inspired and justified by federalist theory: the election of Senators and the deletion of the national veto. But these were the least important, federally, of the several modifications. At a later time the provision on Senatorial elections, which the framers had constructed casually and loosely, seemed so insignificant that states casually abandoned it. And the deletion of the veto—itself intended to be highly nationalist—was accepted because there were close nationalist substitutes already in place. The really important modifications, on the other hand, were not undertaken primarily for federalist reasons. While they were recognized at the time to involve some federalist concerns, the main intent behind them was to solve practical problems in an opportunistic way. Thus equal representation was, for the two pivotal voters, a practical concession to the minority's threat of secession. Thus, also, the method of electing the President resolved the conflict between nationalism and the ideal of the separation of powers. It reintroduced federalist features only incidentally and off-handedly. And thus, finally, residency, which even the framers thought of as mostly a trivial matter of personnel qualifications, turned out in an unanticipated way to strengthen the states almost more than any other provision.

So federalism was preserved, but not on purpose. Although this reinvented federalism turned out to be highly successful, it is hardly possible to attribute its success to the prescience of the framers. They were mostly intent on centralizing at the expense of federalism, not on preserving federalism at the expense of centralization.

3 DUTCH AND AMERICAN FEDERALISM

William H. Riker

Commentary. *When this essay was originally published in isolation from other work on federalism, it served only as a caution against the too ready attribution of causal influence in the history of ideas. From the distance of the twentieth century it is all too easy to see some connection between the sixteenth and seventeenth century experience in the low countries and the eighteenth century experience in America. But centuries, easily tele- scoped in history books, are long in the life of men. Let the reader ask how much he or she knows about his or her great-grandparents' thoughts in 1887. After such reflection, it is easy to see that the Dutch experience of two centuries previous could not have influenced American decisions simply because American decision-makers knew only a few mistaken "facts" about Dutch government. Nor could these erroneous ideas have had any independent influence because the framers used them, not as information about Dutch experience but as a metaphor for their own experience with the Articles of Confederation.*

When reprinted in the context of the study of federalism, this demonstra- tion of the irrelevance of Dutch experience for American constitution-framing takes on a new significance. If the framers learned little or nothing from the

Reprinted from the *Journal of the History of Ideas*, 1957, vol. 18, pp. 495–521.

Dutch, whose constitution was, for them, the most obvious example of an important federal government, then the federalism they provided for must be entirely their own work. So it is. And that is why I reprint this rather technical essay here. The framers did indeed invent something new in 1787, and the independence of their invention from the influence of other constitutions reveals the full extent of their accomplishment.

Since the United Netherlands was by far the most successful of modern federal republics prior to 1787, one might reasonably suppose that the framers of the United States Constitution drew heavily on Dutch experience. And indeed, when the records of the Constitutional Convention and the state ratifying conventions are superficially examined, it appears that our heritage from the Netherlands is considerable. The records show that members of the conventions referred to the government of the United Provinces more frequently than to any other modern European government, except that of Great Britain. In all, Dutch institutions are mentioned 37 times, and 10 of these references are substantial discussions of history and authorities.[1] John Marshall remarked, as he began his highly rhetorical interpretation of the Dutch constitution in the Virginia ratifying convention (Eliott, 1856, vol. III, p. 25): "We may derive from Holland lessons very beneficial to ourselves," and the tone of most of the rest of the 37 references is quite similar. It might seem justifiable, therefore, to conclude that Dutch institutions of the seventeenth and eighteenth centuries have a significant historical relevance to our own (Wheare, 1953, p. 43).

But the pitfalls in the study of the history of ideas are many, and some of them are in the path here. Despite the framers' fairly extensive discussions, despite their own obvious confidence in their knowledge, despite, even, their citation of authorities, close examination of their speeches reveals that they had only a cursory knowledge of Dutch history and that they knew even less about the operation of Dutch institutions. Nearly all the framers who spoke on the subject seemed certain of one statement about the Netherlands; and in this they were mistaken. Nearly all seemed to believe that the decisions of the general government required unanimity of the seven provinces—an even more stringent requirement than in the Continental Congress. But, misled by inaccurate commentaries, they did not know what this requirement meant or how it worked in practice or what significance it had in Dutch politics. And, of course, they did not know that unless they allowed for significant exceptions they were wrong. Because, however, of the superficial similarity of this supposed rule of

Dutch legislatures to the provisions about legislative decision in the Articles of Confederation, they concentrated on this constitutional rule—torn out of its political and historical context—and quite erroneously interpreted it in the light of their own recent experience. As a consequence, their discussions of Dutch institutions, far from constituting an attempt to learn from Dutch history, are simply a device for praise or calumny of the Articles of Confederation, from the history of which the framers had learned much. As a member approved or disapproved of the Articles, so he eulogized the Netherlands as "a free and happy republic" or condemned it as an example of "the characteristic imbecility of federal governments."

Tempting though it may be, therefore, to conclude from the records that our federalism owes something to the example of this earlier one, such a conclusion is nevertheless false. Constitutional experience is not readily transmitted from one culture to another; and, as suggested by the detailed examination of the supposed transmission of ideas from the Netherlands to America, an examination to which the rest of this essay is devoted, statements about the influence of one constitution on another are difficult to substantiate.

I

One of the reasons Dutch experience could exert little influence on the United States is the paucity of information about the Netherlands available to members of the Philadelphia convention. John Adams, then the only American ambassador to The Hague ever actually in residence and hence one of the few Americans qualified to speak on Dutch politics, was in Europe in 1787. Only one of the delegates at Philadelphia, Pierce Butler of South Carolina, purported to discuss Dutch affairs on the basis of a traveler's knowledge. Yet his one contribution was so clearly without foundation in the customary interpretation of Dutch politics that the following day Dr. Franklin, in one of the few speeches he personally delivered, reviewed Dutch history in some detail in order to point out Butler's errors (items 1 and 2, note 1). Butler had asserted that the direction of Dutch military affairs was so divided that the States-General had recently been forced to employ a French commander. Franklin demonstrated on the contrary that the employment of a French officer was merely an incident in the perpetual conflict between republicans and the House of Nassau and that the danger to the republic was not the division of military command but rather the concentration of it in the hands of a stadtholder. Franklin's 300-word epitome of Dutch history from 1570 to 1787 is, with one exception, reasonably accurate in fact, consistent in interpretation, and obviously based on knowledge obtained at the French court in the previous decade. His prestige and the content of his speech were sufficient to crush Butler's pretentions to authority. So far as the record shows and quite understandably, Butler did not mention his travels again.

Since the members of the convention lacked personal knowledge of Dutch politics, they were forced to rely on published accounts. Here language was a barrier. So far as I can discover from an extensive reading of biographies and papers, all of the framers were ignorant of Dutch and thus lacked access to any comprehensive account of Dutch history or to the several collections of state papers. Consequently they could know only what was written about the Dutch constitution in English and, for the best educated, in French, though it is not certain that they used any French sources. Numerous Latin works on the Netherlands were available of course; but by the latter part of the 18th century Latin had ceased to be the language of history writing and diplomacy. Few of the framers read Latin with facility, and even one as well educated as Madison would ask Jefferson to get titles in French rather than Latin. It may be safely assumed, I believe, that none of the framers ploughed through any of the detailed Latin chronicles of affairs in the Netherlands.

Materials on the subject in English or French were, however, difficult to come by. At least one of the framers, James Madison, who is not undeservedly called "the father of the Constitution," had for some years sought to study Dutch government. In March 1784, he wrote to Jefferson, who was then at Annapolis, asking him to buy books: "You know tolerably well," he added, "the objects of my curiosity. I will only particularize my wish of whatever may throw light on the general Constitution and droit public of the several confederacies which have existed. I observe in Boinaud's [sic] catalogue several pieces on the Duch [sic], the German, and the Helvetic. The operation of our own must render all such lights of consequence."[2] Jefferson delayed the purchases until he went to the better and cheaper bookstores of France, where, during the winter of 1784–1785, he selected a library of 192 volumes. He shipped it 1 September 1785, and Madison received it 24 February 1786, nearly two years after the original request (Boyd, 1951, vol. VIII, pp. 460–464). But not one volume in the 192 dealt more than cursorily with the Netherlands. Clearly, it was not easy for an isolated Virginia planter to study the "droit public of the several confederacies." Madison did subsequently acquire a copy of De Witt (?), *Political Maxims*—he read from it at the Virginia convention—and this acquisition ought to be regarded, I think, as part of the everyday heroism of the scholarly politician.

Madison's difficulty in getting books was partly occasioned by the fact that there were few titles to get. The catalogue of Jefferson's library, as he sold it to Congress in 1815, lists only two works in English published prior to 1787 on Dutch history and public law, and these are in fact about the only ones that were readily available.[3] Indeed, every scrap of specialized or detailed knowledge about the Netherlands used in the several conventions can be readily traced to one of the following short list of sources:

1. Sir William Temple, *Observations upon the United Provinces of the Netherlands*. (London, 1672. The third edition of 1676, which has minor additions, seems to be the one customarily found in the United States. It was reprinted in 1932, from the third edition, by the Cambridge University Press with an introduction by G. N. Clark. I shall quote from this reprint.) Sir William, who was subsequently Swift's patron, served as ambassador to the United Provinces in 1668. On the occasion of the Anglo-Dutch war of 1672, he used the leisure of his political retirement to write this delightful and discursive little essay on Dutch geography, history, trade, manners, religion, and government. On this last subject he is fairly well informed and well organized. His work displays sympathy with republican forms and, considering that his country and his subject were at war, a surprisingly friendly attitude toward the Netherlands. The *Observations* was probably readily available to the framers, since it is listed in several almost contemporary library catalogues, especially the catalogue of the Library Company of Philadelphia.[4]

2. John De Witt, *Political Maxims of the State of Holland: Comprehending a General View of the Civil Government of that Republic, and the Principles on which it is Founded: the Nature, Rise, and Progress of the Commerce of its Subjects, and of their True Interests with Respect of all their Neighbors*, translated by John Campbell with a memoir of Cornelius and John De Witt. (London, 1743. There was a second edition in 1746; but since most copies in the United States seem to have been the first edition, I have used it for citations.) This work is a translation of *Aanwysing der Heilsame Politike Gronden en Maximen Van de Repulike Van Holland* (1669), which is in turn a revision and enlargement of Pieter De La Court, *Interest Van Holland* (1662). John De Witt was Grand Pensioner of Holland, 1652–1672, and the chief politician of the United Netherlands of this era. Intensely republican, he and his brother Cornelius were in 1672 lynched by a mob instigated by the party of William III. The De Witt volume is an analysis, still impressive today, of the commercial and political policy appropriate for Holland, as distinct from the United

Netherlands. Its main dogmas are: 1) that Holland ought to beware of monarchy, that is, of a stadtholder of the House of Nassau, 2) that Holland ought to avoid foreign alliances except in time of war even, apparently, too close alliances with the other provinces, and 3) that Holland ought to follow a policy of free trade, free seas, free religion, and peace. Unlike Sir William Temple, De Witt (?) did not describe the government of either Holland or the United Provinces, since he assumed that knowledge on the part of his readers. As a tract on public policy, this book is less informative than the more carefully organized and more introductory treatment in the traveler's essay. It was, however, readily available. The Library Company of Philadelphia almost certainly had a copy in 1787. The Boston library of the American Academy of Arts and Sciences had a copy in 1802 and, very probably, in 1787. Both Jefferson and John Quincy Adams had copies, although the dates they acquired them are unknown.

3. Philip Dormer Stanhope, Fourth Earl of Chesterfield, "Some Account of the Government of the Republic of the Seven United Provinces." This is item 433 of *Letters Written by the Right Honorable Philip Dormer Stanhope, Earl of Chesterfield, to his Son*, ed. by Mrs. Eugenia Stanhope (London, 1774, and often required thereafter). The most recent critical edition, from which I shall quote, is one edited by Bonamy Dobrée (London, 1932, 6 vols.), in which the "Account" appears in II, 605–612. Mr. Dobrée dates the essay from Chesterfield's second embassy to the Hague (1745), although he believes that Chesterfield added the notes in 1761. In any event, this characteristically lucid and succinct essay was intended to instruct his son and hence is a useful text for others who want instruction. Roughly two-thirds of the "Account" consists of a condemnation of the supposed requirement of unanimity of legislative decision in the States General. This essay is without question the most influential source of information the framers had, possibly because it was the most readily available. According to Evans, *American Bibliography*, the *Letters* were printed in full in New York in 1775, in Boston in 1779, in Providence in 1779, in Philadelphia in 1786, and, in abbreviated form, in several other places.

4. Benjamin Franklin, "Speech to the Philadelphia Convention" (item 2, note 1). So far as I can discover, this epitome of Dutch history does not depend on any written source but is simply a distillation of what Franklin knew about the Netherlands, which, though little, was considerably more than what any one else at the convention knew. Since his speech was not printed, it probably had little influence beyond the convention; but we do have the assurance of Madison's notes that the speech was actually delivered.

5. An oral tradition, the existence of which can be clearly discerned, consisting chiefly of the belief that legislative decision in the States General was by unanimity of provinces. In the debates in the Continental Congress in the summer of 1776 on the provisions of the Articles of Confederation, Dutch institutions were several times mentioned in connection with the draft article: "In determining questions each colony shall have one vote." According to John Adams' notes, Roger Sherman of Connecticut cited the practice of "the States of Holland" in support of the draft (Ford, 1906, vol. VI, p. 1081). So also did Stephen Hopkins of Rhode Island (p. 1105). According to Jefferson's notes of the same debate, James Wilson of Pennsylvania argued against the draft thus: "the greatest imperfection in the constitution of the Belgic confederacy is their voting by provinces. The interest of the whole is constantly sacrificed to that of the small states" (p. 1106).

Dr. Benjamin Rush of Philadelphia discussed the Dutch forms in more detail than anyone else, saying that the "decay of the liberties of the Dutch republic proceeded from...: 1. the perfect unanimity requisite on all occasions. 2. their obligation to consult their constituents. 3. their voting by provinces. This last destroyed the equality of representation:...." (p. 1105). According to John Adams' notes, Dr. Rush cited the Abbé Raynal as his authority, doubtless referring to his *Histoire du Stadhoudérat Depuis Son Origine Jusqu'à Présent* (Paris, 1747, although I quote from the fourth edition, The Hague, 1748). At the time Raynal wrote, the English had just succeeded in installing William IV, son-in-law of George II of England, as stadtholder, much to the discomfiture of the French, who supported the republic. Raynal, as a civil servant of the French monarchy, attacked monarchy (in its low country form) and defended republican institutions (for the Dutch). While one would not thus expect severe criticism of the republic from him, he did say that "*si les deux tiers pouvoient conclurre [sic] pour tout le corps, le Gouvernement en seroit plus sur et plus fort*"(p. 83). We can be certain that several members of the convention of 1787 received this tradition about the weakness of legislative decision in the Netherlands. Roger Sherman and James Wilson, both of whom discussed Dutch government in these terms in 1776 and both of whom doubtless heard Dr. Rush's speech, were present at the Constitutional Convention of 1787, where Wilson again discussed Dutch government in detail. Benjamin Franklin and Elbridge Gerry were present in Philadelphia in both 1776 and 1787. Since Franklin participated actively in the debate with Sherman, Hopkins, Wilson, and Rush, one can be certain that he carried this tradition in his person. Furthermore, Jefferson gave his notes on this debate in 1776 to Madison, and they remain in

Madison's papers to this day. Hence it can be assumed that Madison read at least once the abstract of Dr. Rush's severe condemnation of Dutch voting procedure.

In addition to these five sources, perhaps 50 or so other works had been published in English or French, and might therefore have influenced the framers. The most important of these works are listed and described in the Appendix. Some of them doubtless contributed to the tradition that assigned the requirement of unanimity to Dutch legislatures; but since, so far as I can discover, none of the detailed references in the conventions derive from them, I have consigned them to a concluding note.

In addition to knowledge gained from books, the framers of course possessed the common and often inaccurate information of educated men of their time and place, i.e., such statements as: that the United Provinces were a republic, that they had successfully revolted against Spain some two hundred years previously, that they had prospered in trade and fisheries, that their present circumstances in the war with England were exceedingly perilous, and that, as Montesquieu blandly told them in a sentence (*The Spirit of the Laws,*, Book IX, chapter 3), all the provinces had an equal voice in the States General.

II

The 37 discussions of the Netherlands in the several conventions may be divided into two categories, those that depend simply on the stock of common statements of the sort mentioned in the previous paragraph and those that depend on some specialized knowledge. All but one of the 13 discussions in the second category depend on the five sources listed above; and the one that does not, Pierce Butler's already mentioned speech, depends on a traveler's observation rather than a written source. In most of the instances, the source is apparent, not merely by reason of similarity of content, but by reason of verbal parallels and direct quotations.

Turning to a demonstration of the framers' dependence on these few sources, James Wilson's speech of 16 June 1787 (item 3, note 1, above) is one of the earliest discussions of the Netherlands in the convention and, I believe, one of the most influential. It is reported in the notes of Madison, Robert Yates, Rufus King, and William Paterson. All four of these auditors agree that he emphasized that the affirmative vote of all provinces was necessary to legislative decision. Paterson's notes on the Netherlands passage of the speech consists of only nine words and Madison's notes are somewhat confused, but Yates and King make it clear that Wilson told or read the following story from Lord Chesterfield:

...When I was soliciting the accession of the Republic to the treaty of Vienna, in 1731, which the Pensionary, Count Sinzendorf, and I, had made secretly at the Hague, all the towns in Holland came readily into it, except the little town of Briel [i.e., Brill]; whose deputies frankly declared, that they would not give their consent, till *Major-Such-a-one*, a very honest gentleman of their town, was promoted to the rank of Lieutenant Colonel, and that, as soon as that was done, they would agree, for they approved of the treaty. This was accordingly done in two or three days, and then they agreed. This is a strong instance of the absurdity of the unanimity required, and of the use that is often made of it (vol. II, pp. 605–607, ed. Dobrée).

This story was used again by John Lansing in the New York convention (item 7, note 1); but he gave it both a new source and a new application. Lansing says "an important measure was delayed by the dissent of a single town until one of its citizens was accommodated with a commission." Obviously this is Chesterfield's story, but Lansing attributed it to Sir William Temple, who nowhere mentioned such an event. (Indeed, Temple, in reciting the details of his embassy, remarked on pages 71–72 that such bribes were unnecessary.) While Wilson used the story to condemn the Articles insofar as they required unanimity in decision, Lansing, an Anti-federalist, used it to show that the Articles were superior to the constitutions of other confederacies, such as the Dutch, whose experience was therefore, so he argued, irrelevant to a judgment of the Articles.

In a speech on June 28, Madison commented (item 4, note 1): "Holland contains about 1/2 the people, supplies about 1/2 the money, and by her influence, silently and indirectly governs the whole Republic." The simple statistical fact, which is several times repeated in the conventions, could well have come from Temple, De Witt, Chesterfield, or indeed from several of the writers cited in the Appendix, all of whom mention that Holland paid 58 guilders out of every 100 assessed by the States-General. The inference about Holland's influence doubtless came, however, from Chesterfield. Temple did not notice and of course De Witt would not admit the overweening influence of the province of Holland; but Chesterfield observed: "It is very natural to suppose, and it is very true in fact, that Holland...should have great weight and influence in the other six provinces" (II, p. 607). In connection with his story of the Major from Brill, Chesterfield explicity asserts that Holland had a controlling influence in the other provinces.

Gouverneur Morris, echoed by Butler (Farrand, 1964, vol. II, pp. 31, 202) asserted that in Holland "their Senates have engrossed all power." This too is clearly reminiscent of Chesterfield, who wrote in the second paragraph of his essay. "It is very true, that the sovereign power is lodged in the States-General; but who are those States General? Not those who are commonly called so; but the Senate, Council, or *Vrootschaps* [i.e., vroedschaps] call it what you will, of every town, in every province that sends deputies to the Provincial States of the said Province." This comment about the town councils occurs in connection with assertions that the people have lost all right to vote and that the councils perpetuate themselves by co-option. Hence the phrase, "engrossed all power," is a fair summary of Chesterfield's observation.

Chesterfield is also the source, I believe, for a paragraph in Oliver Ellsworth's speech to the Connecticut convention (item 6, note 1). Ellsworth emphasized the rôle of the stadtholder who was, he said, necessary "in order to set their unwieldy machine of government in motion." "Without such an influence," he concluded, "their machine of government would no more move, than a ship without wind, or a clock without weights." Considering that Chesterfield assigned the same rôle to the stadtholder—even to the point of using the metaphor of clock machinery: "...a Stadtholder was originally the chief spring upon which their government turned" (vol. II, p. 609)—considering that he alone of the five sources discussed the stadtholder's duties in detail, considering that he ascribed to William the Silent a Machiavellian intent to render a stadtholder necessary to break deadlocks that resulted from the unanimity requirement, and considering finally that both he and Ellsworth empha-sized Holland's hostility to the office (though, of course, De Witt does that also), it seems likely that Ellsworth relied on Chesterfield, at least indirectly. It should be noted, however, that the Abbé Raynal hints at something like this when he says (pp. 84–85): "*On crut devoir terminer tous ces arrangemens* [i.e., of the Union of Utrecht] *per intéresser personellement le Prince d'Orange à la conservation de l'edifice, qu'il avoit lui même construit; il fut élu Stadhouder.*" But since this remark is brief and buried, it seems unlikely that it could have inspired Ellsworth, even if he had had access to the *Histoire du Stathoudérat*.

De Witt's (?) *Political Maxims* is the source of two major analyses of Dutch government in the ratifying conventions, one by Rufus King (item 5, note 1) and one by James Madison (item 8, note 1). Citing John De Witt, "a celebrated political writer, formerly pensioner of Holland," King noted 1) that provinces of the United Netherlands were free to comply or not as they chose with requisitions of money by the States-General, 2) that Holland paid 58 parts in 100 of the war with Spain, 3) that two provinces paid not a single guilder, 4) that Holland collected requisitions from other provinces by force, 5) that the Prince of Orange doubled the requisitions, collecting only from Holland, so that Holland paid all the expenses of the war. Items 2 through 5 in this list appear in exactly this order on page 257 of *Political Maxims*. It seems likely that King had the volume before him as he prepared his speech. Although Madison's speech is not quoted verbatim, but merely summarized, it is apparent that he quoted from the same passage. The reporter cited items 2 through 4 on the foregoing list in that order, even naming, as in *Political Maxims*, the recalcitrant provinces, Gelderland and Overissel.

The same material, much abbreviated serves Chancellor Livingston in the New York convention (Eliott, 1856, vol. II p. 214) for a one sentence condemnation of the Dutch confederation which, he said, "permitted the burden of the war to be borne, in great measure, by the province of Holland; which was, at one time, compelled to attempt to force a neighboring province, by arms, to compliance with their federal engagements." The *Political Maxims*, or a verbal tradition based on it, must have been the source for Livingston's comment because any of the more extensive sources of the story (e.g., Lothian, pp. 80–82) would have made it clear that not Holland, but the States General, sent a force to compel payment.

Later on in the Virginia convention, William Grayson undertook to explain party politics in the Netherlands (Eliott, 1856, vol. III, 290) or rather to state the names and chief principles of the two opposing parties. Since these names and principles are similarly set forth (on page xxxiv) in the "Memoir of Cornelius and John De Witt" which serves as an introduction to *Political Maxims*, it can, I think, be safely assumed that this volume is also the source of Grayson's information.

Sir William Temple, although mistakenly cited by Lansing in the New York convention, is clearly enough the source of two discussions of the Netherlands in the Virginia convention. Governor Randolph (item 9, note 1) observed: "Consult all writers—from Sir William Temple to those of modern times—they will inform you that the government of Holland is an aristocracy." And so Temple does (p. 58), though he used the stronger and perhaps more accurate word, "oligarchy." One of the "writers of modern times"—possibly the only one—is certainly Chesterfield, who makes the same observation in a footnote to the first sentence of his essay. When Edmund Pendleton and Madison echoed Randolph (Eliott, 1856, vol. III, pp. 310, 617), they emphasized that the people had no right to vote. Since Chesterfield in the second sentence of his essay observed that the unfranchised people "have nothing to do but to pay and grumble," it seems likely also that Chesterfield is also the source that impressed these latter two.

Randolph, as a proponent of the Constitution, wished to condemn the government of the Netherlands, which he identified with the government of the Articles. George Mason, on the other hand, as an adherent of the

Articles, used Temple's *Observations* to demonstrate the felicity of the Dutch people (item 10, note 1). The reporter simply summarizes and does not cite the source of Mason's quotations: but it seems to me fairly certain that Mason quoted selected paragraphs from the fourth chapter of Temple's work.

So it appears that, for all the members besides Franklin (and perhaps Butler) every bit of detailed information about the Dutch in the several conventions probably came from Chesterfield, De Witt, or Temple, or perhaps indirectly from Raynal. It is possible that some of the brief references could have derived from some of the works listed in the Appendix. But since all the extensive references derive clearly from these three books, which were also the three most readily available, it is reasonable to suppose that these and the oral tradition were the framers' only sources.

III

The foregoing analysis has demonstrated the paucity of information about the Netherlands available to the framers of the Constitution. Lacking, except in the case of the aged Franklin, a deep personal experience with European politics, they were forced to rely on the written word. Lacking a knowledge of Dutch, they were forced to rely on books in English or French. This meant a library of at most 50 or so volumes, of which only three or four were easily available and regarded as authoritative. Of these, one was the observation of an ambassador who had spent only a short time in the Netherlands; the second was a tract that grew out of party politics in Holland (the implications and innuendoes of which must certainly have been obscure to the framers); the third was an inaccurate pamphlet written as a political duty by a French civil servant who had never been in the Netherlands; and the fourth was a seven-page essay which, although written for a schoolboy aged 12, is the most judicious and informative of the four. The first pair of these works was based on experience as of 1668; the second pair as of the mid-1740s. A library of three and a fraction volumes, the two most recent of which were 40 years out of date, the others 120 years, could hardly be expected to provide sympathetic or detailed understanding of Dutch government from 1579 to 1787.

In short, the framers had little to learn from. Further, they learned little from what they had. Considering how remote Dutch affairs were from their own, a complete mastery of those works is about all that one might reasonably expect from an American politician of the 1780s. But it is abundantly clear that the framers had not mastered even these sparse materials.

Even the best of them were quite vague about Dutch affairs. Pierce Butler's misinterpretation of his observation has already been mentioned. Butler, though a man of judgment, had no scholarly pretensions. Madison, however, did pretend to a knowledge of Dutch history. Yet when he took notes on Franklin's speech, he both improved and confused the detail. Franklin's written speech reads in part:

> On his [i.e., William the Silent's] Death, They [i.e., the provinces] resum'd and divided those Powers [i.e., of the Stadtholder] among the States and Cities. . . . In the last century the then Prince of Orange found means to inflame the Populace against their Magistrates, excite a general Insurrection in which an excellent Minister, *Dewit*, was murdered, all the old Magistrates displac'd, and the Stadtholder re-invested with all the former Powers.

Madison's notes on the last sentence are:

> Still, however there was a party for the Prince of Orange, which descended to his son who excited insurrection, spilt a great deal of blood, murdered the de Witts, and got the powers revested in the Stadtholder.

Of course, Franklin may not have delivered his speech as written; but since he felt his infirmities of age sufficiently to write out all his speeches, it is very likely that he read this speech word for word. Assuming that his spoken words tally with his written ones, Madison's deviations are of considerable interest. Franklin referred presumably to the murder of only John De Witt. Madison uses the plural, thereby including Cornelius—an action that indicates some special knowledge. On the other hand, Madison mixed up the genealogy of the House of Nassau. Franklin referred to the "then Prince of Orange," thereby carefully dodging the genealogical problem. It was a wise choice of words, for the descent of the House of Nassau was somewhat involved: from William the Silent (d. 1584) to his son Maurice (d. 1625), from Maurice to his brother Frederick Henry (d. 1647), from Frederick Henry to his son William II (d. 1650), and from William II to his posthumous son William III, who was chosen stadtholder in 1672 and King of England in 1689. Madison, apparently unaware of these genealogical facts, transformed William III, the "instigator" of the murder of the De Witts, into a son of William the Silent, whereas he was in fact the great-grandson. A slip of the pen, perhaps, but not a slip likely to be made by one conversant with the course of Dutch history.

Franklin clearly knew enough about Dutch chronology and the descent of the House of Nassau to avoid Madison's error. But Franklin too seems hazy on detail. For example, he asserted that on the death of William the Silent the Stadtholder's powers were divided among the "states and cities" and from that event he jumped to the accession of William III. It is certainly true that Prince Maurice did not immediately attain his father's position; but Franklin overlooked entirely the rôles of both Maurice and Frederick Henry, both of whom were, like their father, stadtholders of five provinces. Franklin intended, of course, only a brief history, but one has the impression that he ignored William's sons because he was unaware of them.

One would not expect American politicians of the 1780s to know much Dutch history of the previous two centuries, any more than one would expect American politicians today to know much about the history of, for example, Austria from the 1750s to the 1830s. But while this lack of knowledge of Dutch politics is quite pardonable and not at all surprising, it does substantially preclude the use of Dutch experience in the several conventions. Further, the lack of knowledge suggests the possibility that the framers' quotations from authorities may be misleading. Such is indeed the fact, for not one of the substantial quotations was judiciously abstracted from its source.

Madison and Rufus King in their respective conventions quoted extensively from De Witt. Both of them used the quotations to prove that the Dutch confederacy, like the government under their own Articles, was ineffective and unfair. It could not compel the payment of taxes, so they said. Yet the very passage they quoted relates that Holland [sic] sent troops to collect (presumably with success) from the recalcitrant state of Groningen. The Union of Utrecht was, they also said, unfair in that Holland had to pay more than its share of the cost of the Spanish war. (Parenthetically it should be noted that Madison and King were doubtless impressed by the parallel with their own states: Virginia and Massachusetts paid requisitions when the smaller states did not and thus bore more than their share of the cost of the central government.) They blamed this unfair taxation of Holland, just as they blamed their own unfair taxation, on the requirement of unanimity in legislative decision. Quite probably this unanimity (or rather extraordinary majority) was one of the chief factors in the excessive taxation of Massachusetts and Virginia; but, according to the very sources they quoted from, it was not so important a factor in the Netherlands. The author of *Political Maxims*, much as he complained of the injustice, did not blame the requirement of unanimity. Instead he blamed Prince Frederick Henry who, he asserted, packed the States General with his own men. And further: he complained not that Holland was balked in action by its failure to persuade the States to unanimity, but rather that Holland was out-voted by the Prince's men, "even in such matters wherein plurality of votes should have no place" (p. 259). Clearly, this Hollander did not think that the constitutional provision was a problem. He was angered, not by its existence, but by its desuetude.

James Wilson and John Lansing both refer to Chesterfield's story of the Major from Brill; but both also misapply it. Although the one wished to identify, the other to distinguish, the Continental Congress and the States-General, still both accepted Chesterfield's story as a sample of the normal course of public business in the Dutch Republic. Wilson concluded therefrom that, as a general rule, the requirement of unanimity leads to corruption. Lansing, who was certain no such corruption occurred in Congress, concluded that the operation of the two legislatures was quite different. The conclusions of both men were invalid, however, because the promotion of the Major was not a normal procedure, as Chesterfield himself specifically pointed out:

> The unanimity, which is constitutionally requisite for every act of each town, and each province, separately, and then for every act of the seven collectively, is something so absurd, and so impracticable in government, that one is astonished that even the form of it has been tolerated so long; for the substance is not strictly observed. And five provinces will often conclude, though two dissent, provided that Holland and Zealand are two of the five; as fourteen or fifteen of the principal towns of Holland will conclude an affair, notwithstanding the opposition of four or five of the lesser (vol. II, p. 607).

Furthermore, Chesterfield called the story of the major from Brill "a strong instance," that is, an exceptional instance, and then added:

> However, should one, or even two of the lesser provinces, who contribute little, and often pay less, to the public charge, obstinately and frivolously, or perhaps corruptly, persist in opposing a measure which Holland and the other more considerable provinces thought necessary, and had agreed to, they would send a deputation to those opposing provinces, to reason with, and persuade them to concur; but, if this would not do, they would as they have done in many instances, conclude without them. The same thing is done in the provincial States of the respective provinces; where if one or two of the least considerable towns pertinaciously oppose a necessary measure, they conclude without them. But as this is absolutely unconstitutional, it is avoided as much as possible, and a complete unanimity procured, if it can be, by such little concessions as that which I have mentioned to the Briel Major (vol. II, p. 607, note).

There can be no doubt that in the matter of unanimity the framers misapplied their sources. They also ignored the direct statement of Sir William Temple on this point, when he described the duties of the President of the States-General:

> [He] Makes the Greffier [i.e., the Secretary] read all Papers; Puts the Question; Calls the Voices of the Provinces; and forms the Conclusion. Or, if he refuses *to*

conclude according to the plurality, he is obliged to resign his Place to the President of the ensuing week, who concludes for him.

This is the course in all Affairs before them, except in cases of Peace and War, of Foreign Alliances, of Raising, or Coining, of Monies, or the Priviledges of each Province or Member of the Union. In all which, All the Provinces must concur, Plurality being not at all weighed or observed. . . .And in other important matters, *though decided by Plurality*, they frequently consult with the Council of State (Temple, 1672, p. 70, emphasis added).

On the whole, Sir William thought the system worked well. Speaking of the fact that, by persuasion, a committee of the States-General had obtained the agreement of all provinces to the treaty he had negotiated, he said:

Nor have they ever used, at any other time, any greater means to agree and unite the several Members of their Union, in the Resolutions necessary, upon the most pressing occasions, than for the agreeing-Provinces to name some of their ablest persons to go and confer with the dissenting, and represent those Reasons and Interests by which they have been induced to their Opinions (p. 72).

Clearly, the framers' major sources indicate that the Dutch were not nearly so disturbed by the requirement of unanimity as the framers supposed them to be. And two of them clearly state also that the rule was not as general as the framers supposed, for as Temple pointed out, the circumstances in which unanimity was required were few. Temple was quoting fairly accurately the provision of voting in the ninth article of the Union of Utrecht of 1579 and is, therefore, accurate in his statement of constitutional provisions. He too failed to understand, however, that the requirement of unanimity in the States General and the Provincial States was much mitigated by other institutions. In the States General, it is true, matters of war, peace, treaties, and taxes could not be concluded without unanimity and even then could not be concluded finally until approved by the provincial states in which each town had a veto power. And it is also true that in all other matters in the States General, the province of Holland, which had over half the people and wealth and which contributed over half of the taxes, army and navy, still had only one-seventh of the vote. But there were other national institutions besides the States General. The Council of State, which in the absence of a stadtholder was the executive head with authority to direct the army, negotiate treaties, prepare the agenda of the States, appoint judges, and govern the dependencies in Flanders and overseas, concluded by a plurality of members. Furthermore, one-fourth instead of one-seventh of its members were chosen by Holland. Even more significant a deviation from unanimity and provincial equality is found in the five boards of admiralty. These boards, located in Rotterdam, Amsterdam, and Hoorn in Holland, in Middleburg in Zealand, and in Harlingen in Friesland, were without doubt the most important administrative bodies in the Netherlands. Since the Navy was the most important part of the national defense system, since more of the funds of the generality went for it than for any other purpose, and since colonial expansion and foreign trade and hence the prosperity of the Netherlands depended on the protection of the navy, the admiralty was in the seventeenth and eighteenth centuries the very heart of the government. And here the notion of unanimity and provincial equality was ignored. Holland dominated three of the boards, especially the one in Amsterdam, which received one-third of the national naval funds while the others received only one-sixth each; and in all five taken together, Holland had 42% of the voting power.[5] In the East India company, a state within a state and in effect the Dutch colonial office, Holland was even more dominant, for Hollanders held 80% of the capital and had 76% of the voting power in the board of directors. Indeed, the merchants of Amsterdam, who probably held half the capital, held nearly half the directorships and were clearly in a position to dominate the affairs of the society. In short, in commercial and naval affairs, in a high degree, and in administrative affairs to a somewhat lesser degree, the principle of provincial equality was ignored and wealth and population served as the basis of representation. In an age when legislation was popularly regarded as less important than it is now, and when administration was the essential political activity, the disregard of the principle of unanimity in administration explains why Dutchmen at least were less upset than foreigners by the requirement of provincial unanimity in some of the business of the States General. Certainly, taking the Dutch government as a whole, the unanimity rule was not as serious a disability as foreign publicists suggested. It was indeed a far less stringent restriction on governmental activity than the provisions of the Articles of Confederation.

Leaving aside the failure of the framers to quote justly from their sources—a failure doubtless occasioned by their pardonable ignorance of Dutch affairs—the framers displayed radical misunderstanding of the Netherlands generally. They did not comprehend the depth of civic loyalty, which was far deeper than their own state patriotism and which was the social justification of the consititutional requirement of unanimity in some decisions. They did not comprehend the role of the House of Nassau, which often had had more of the loyalty of the common people than the patriciate of the town councils. They did not comprehend that unanimity on some legislative decisions by seven provinces that would fit into the state of New York four times was quite different from the unanimity of 13 large states sprawled out over 1,000 miles of coast. They did not even comprehend current events in the Netherlands. Contemporary history was neither much studied nor well reported in 1787 and hence they knew almost nothing about eighteenth century Dutch politics. If they knew about the strengthening of the stadtholderate in 1747–48, an event that minimized the problem of unanimity, or about the revolutionary movement of the 1780s, they gave no hint of their knowledge in their speeches.

Instead they read Dutch problems (what they knew of them) in the light of their own. Since they were worried about the provision of the Articles that required unanimity for amendment and an extraordinary majority for ordinary business, they assumed that Dutch politicians were worried about similar problems. But the Dutch had more pressing things to worry about than this (perhaps unwise) constitutional provision which they had long since learned how to manipulate and evade.

IV

The analysis has so far demonstrated that the framers of the Constitution had only inaccurate and inadequate information about the Netherlands. It follows that the actual Dutch political forms had little influence on our own.

But, if that is so, what then is the significance of the 37 references to Dutch institutions that crop up throughout the several convention reports? With the exception of Franklin's epitome of Dutch history and Mason's quotations from (presumably) Temple's *Observations*, all the extended and detailed references to the Dutch constitution, as well as many of the briefer ones, deal with its provision for unanimity in some legislative decisions. As I have already pointed out, the provision they deal with is an idealized one, torn out of its political context and only by illegitimate descent related to the one the Dutch people knew. But that idealized provision is still of no little importance. It provided an Awful Example.

Supporters of the Constitution and of a strong central government used the mythical provision of the Dutch constitution as an indication of the future of our confederacy. The Articles of Confederation contained superficially similar provisions: They required unanimous consent of the states for amendment (Art. XIII); they required nine-thirteenths of the states to declare war, ratify treaties, coin money, tax, borrow, construct navies, recruit soldiers and sailors, and appoint army and navy commanders (Art. IX); they required an absolute majority of seven-thirteenths, regardless of how many states were represented in Congress at the time of voting, on all other matters (Art. IX). The supporters of a strong central government in effect asserted that the miseries of the Dutch were the result of a corresponding provision. By analogy between Dutch institutions and ours, they prophecied similar miseries for the American confederacy, with its similar provisions, if a strong central government were not adopted. "Happy that country", said John Marshall (Eliott, 1856, vol. III, p. 225), "which can avail itself of the misfortunes of others." By observing what Madison called "the characteristic imbecility of federal governments" as displayed in this mythical constitution of a mythical Netherlands, we might, he urged, avoid the unhappy state of that besieged republic.

Regardless of its validity—which was dubious—this was an influential argument. At least it was sufficiently impressive to inspire opponents of the Constitution to answer it. In the New York convention, John Lansing (item 7, note 1) sought to distinguish the United Provinces from the United States:

> The United Dutch provinces have been instanced as possessing a government parallel to the existing confederation; but I believe it will be discovered that they were never so organized, as a general government, on principles so well calculated to promote the attainment of national objects as that of the United States.

In the Virginia convention, where the Dutch example was referred to more frequently and where the opponents of the Constitution were more articulate than elsewhere, there are several examples of a similar attempt to refute the argument drawn from the mythical Dutch constitution. Patrick Henry, the leading opponent of ratification in Virginia, remarked sarcastically of Madison's use of the Dutch example (Eliott, 1854, vol. III, pp. 160–161):

> Notwithstanding two of their provinces have paid nothing, yet I hope the example of Holland will tell us that we can live happily without changing our present despised government.

And James Monroe, the most learned of the Virginia opponents of the Constitution, argued at length that, because of the many differences of situation between the United States on the one hand and the Swiss and Dutch on the other, the experience of the latter two was irrelevant to the former (Eliott, 1856, vol. III, p. 211).

It does not seem likely that the Awful Example persuaded many people to support ratification. It was only one of the many subsidiary propositions in the argument for a strong central government. Yet, as in all such great controversies, each subsidiary proposition, however subordinate, contributed to the whole. The very fact that the opponents of the Constitution so vigorously disputed the relevance of the Dutch example indicates that it was a telling argument.

This Awful Example was not entirely of the framers' own construction, although it doubtless had more meaning to them than to those who had constructed it originally. As has already been indicated, the framers obtained it from several Anglo-French histories and commentaries on public law. And further, it was a part of a still wider European juristic tradition, a tradition that was based almost entirely on a two-century-old misreading of the ninth article of the Union of Utrecht. This article provided that no treaty of peace, no declaration of war, and no tax might be enacted or levied without the unanimous consent of the provinces, that all other matters would be decided by a plurality of votes of the provinces, and that, in the event of a disagreement on subjects requiring unanimity, the issue should be put to the stadtholders, who might in turn select an arbitrator. Hasty readers, mistakenly believing that war, treaties, and taxes are the only important subjects of legislation, had long before 1787 construed this to mean "unanimity of the provinces on all subjects." Those who so construed knew little more than this one detail about the Dutch republic. They did not know the structure of the council of state nor the boards of admiralty nor the customs by which Dutch politicians operated under the ninth article. Since most of the European knowledge of Dutch procedures came from ambassadors and since ambassadors are chiefly concerned with two subjects requiring unanimity (i.e., war and treaties), it is not surprising that this one detail was magnified out of all proportion in non-Dutch commentaries on Dutch government. Sir Ralph Winwood, one of the earliest English ambassadors to the Netherlands, complained bitterly that the reluctance of Zealand, occasioned largely by irrelevant commercial rivalry, delayed for long a treaty between the States and James I (Sawyer, 1725, vol. III, pp. 42, 79, 100). Chesterfield, Janicon, and other ambassadors all assert that the unanimity principle delayed business; but whether the delay inconvenienced mostly the ambassadors or mostly the Dutch is a question far too complex to enter into here. Suffice it to say that ambassadors emphasized the unanimity requirements and repeatedly asserted that it caused bad government. The non-Dutch writers on public law and history picked up this point and emphasized it further—often, as with Montesquieu and Raynal, it was the only specific thing they could say about the Dutch government. Other authors who depended primarily upon ambassadors' writings (e.g., Lothian, Williams) emphasized it at the expense of all other features of Dutch government. Not unreasonably, therefore, this half-truth became the one widely known detail about the Dutch constitution, a half-truth remembered because it was a curiosity, just as today the only widely known detail about the Australian government is the equally misinterpreted system of compulsory voting.

This half-truth reached the framers from numerous sources: but it took on special significance when it reached them through the pages of Lord Chesterfield. His essay is the only one of their major sources that deals extensively with the requirement of unanimity. It contains a detailed report of a conversation on the subject between Chesterfield and the Pensionary Slingelandt, in which the Pensionary is reported as agreeing with Chesterfield that in operation the requirement of unanimity almost necessitated a quasi-monarchical stadtholder. (Compare the quotation from the Abbé Raynal above.) It does not take a great stretch of the imagination to visualize the horror that this conclusion must have aroused in all good republican Whigs in the United States. Certainly this conclusion aroused deeper emotions in Americans, who lived with similar provisions in the Articles, than in Europeans like Chesterfield, who were only mildly vexed by Dutch delay. In any event, it seems likely that Chesterfield's essay, which had certainly been read by Wilson, Madison, Gouverneur Morris, and Ellsworth and which, because of its brevity and availability, had probably been read by many others, confirmed and strengthened their convictions on the folly of this requirement. It is thus possible that Chesterfield's essay, written for the wholly private instruction of his son, quite accidentally offered an Awful Example to American constitution-makers. To one who, like the present writer, has always respected the warm humanity and urbane maturity of that great Whig lord, it is pleasing to observe that he had, in this quite unconscious and unanticipated way, some slight influence for the good on our institutions.

V

To say that the framers of the Constitution failed to learn from Dutch history and public law is not to say that they failed to learn from history and politics at all. They were representative men of the eighteenth century and as such they thoroughly believed in the possibility of rational comprehension of human experience and in the possibility of reconstructing institutions on the basis of their comprehension. The experience they comprehended, however, was in this instance only slightly Dutch and mostly American. The discussions of Dutch institutions are to be regarded as an elaborate figure of speech, an extended but not wholly conscious metaphor. The literal reference of the words to the Dutch constitution and the States General are to be understood, I believe, as an intended reference to the Articles of Confederation and the Continental Congress. So understood, the ignorance of the framers about Dutch affairs is irrelevant to the validity of their arguments. And so understood, their disputes have some relevance to experience and are not wholly and irrationally concerned with a myth.

This figure of speech is not to be regarded, however, as merely an ornament of belles-lettres. The framers seized upon this current European half-truth with great eagerness and referred frequently to it in their discussions. What was merely a minor curiosity to Montesquieu and merely a vexation to Chesterfield had deep significance for Madison, Wilson, Ellsworth, and others. This difference in the emotional reaction to the half-truth on the two sides of the Atlantic is clear evidence that the Awful Example was indeed a metaphor for American experience. The metaphor helped to bolster the framers' confidence in the universal validity of their assertions about the Articles of Confederation. In the eighteenth century, when political propositions attained intellectual respectability only under the guise of universals, the service of the metaphor was of some emotional value. Although it really generalized chiefly about experience in the United States and only secondarily and vaguely about experience in the Netherlands, still it assured (doubtless irrationally) the proponents of a strong central government that the requirement of extraordinary legislative majorities hampered the operation of government, not only in the United States, but everywhere.

And so to this conclusion: The framers of the Constitution were influenced neither by the constitution that existed in the Netherlands nor by the history that occurred there. Rather they were influenced—and that only slightly—by the inaccurate descriptions of the Dutch constitution and by the poorly written histories of Dutch events. And on still closer examination it turns out that the framers used this inaccurate description and poorly written history not as foreign experience from which they could learn, but as a metaphor for domestic experience from which they had *already* learned very much. Thus, Dutch federalism is twice and distantly removed from American.

And this conclusion leads to two observations, one of interest to students of the American Constitution, the other of interest to students of the history of ideas. First, in this instance, it has been found naïve to accept at face value the framers' discussions of Dutch public law. If, in this connection, the Constitution owes something to European sources, the debt is not to the Dutch but to the Anglo-French commentaries. And at most the debt is literary, not a debt for an actual transfer of ideas. In this instance, then, the American Constitution has been found to be more indigenous than is usually asserted. (I suspect, without on this occasion undertaking to prove, that the extended references in the conventions to ancient confederations and even to the then contemporary English institutions may be of equally figurative character; if they are, then the Constitution is still more indigenous than the traditional interpretation admits.)

Second, this conclusion suggests that the transmission of constitutional ideas is less direct than might be supposed, were the framers' comments to be taken literally. It has been demonstrated 1) that the existent Dutch federalism had no influence on ours, and 2) that the non-Dutch commentaries served merely to provide a metaphor; but the demonstration has been possible only because, by a happy accident, we can identify all the framers' sources and can trace in precise detail the actual transmission and use of information. For more difficult studies of the transmission of ideas, for studies, that is, where the material is less abundant, the present conclusion suggests a cautionary observation. It suggests that students of the history of ideas ought to be extremely wary—in the absence of clear and irrefutable evidence—about attributing to the institutions and commentaries of one time and place an influence on the institutions of another. Even when those who are purportedly influenced assert, as in this instance they asserted most sharply, that they have been influenced by the example of others, it does not follow that they have actually been so influenced. It may well be that they have been influenced only by poor descriptions of the examples of others. Or it may even be that—as in this instance—the supposed influence is conjured up by those who purport to feel it for wholly rhetorical purposes of their own.

Appendix

In addition to the sources discussed in the text, the following works, listed roughly in the order in which it is most likely that they might have influenced the framers, were also available in English or French. I have omitted from the list translations of Dutch public documents, guide books, and ephemeral pamphlets on public affairs, except for those printed in the 1780s. On the other hand, I have tried to include all major works known to have been in the United States in 1787 or within a generation thereafter. . . .

Notes

1. A list of the substantial discussions of the United Provinces in the Federal Convention of 1787 and the state ratifying conventions:

    a. In Farrand, *Records of the Federal Conventions of 1787:* 1) 2 June 1787, vol. I, pp. 89, 90, 91; Pierce Butler (S.C.); discussion of the executive. 2) 4 June 1787, vol. I, pp. 102–103; Benjamin Franklin (Pa.); epitome of Dutch history. 3) 16 June 1787, vol. I, pp. 254, 261, 266, 272; James Wilson (Pa.); discussion of legislative unanimity. 4) 28 June 1787, vol. I, pp. 449, 458;James Madison (Va.); discussion of Holland.

    b. In Eliott, *Debates on the Federal Constitution:* 5) 21 January 1788, vol. II, pp. 55–56; Rufus King (Mass); discussion of the unanimity principle. 6) 4 January 1788, vol. II, p. 188; Oliver Ellsworth (Conn.); discussion of stadtholderate. 7) 20 June 1788, vol. II, pp. 218–219; John Lansing (New York); discussion of the unanimity principle. 8) 7 June 1788, vol. III, p. 131; James Madison (Va.); discussion of unanimity principle. 9) 9 June 1788, vol. III, pp. 189–190; Edmund Randolph (Va.); discussion of constitution. 10) 11 June 1788, vol. III, p. 268. George Mason (Va.); discussion of prosperity.

    2. Boyd (1951, vol. VI, p. 37; Madison to Jefferson, 16 March 1784). It would be fortunate for our understanding of the transmission of ideas if we knew or could easily guess what titles caught Madison's eye. Unfortunately, no copy of this catalogue has come down to us, according to assurances given me by Mr. Clifford Shipton, Librarian of the American Antiquarian Society, Worcester, Massachusetts. Although the catalogue is described in several bibliographies, the descriptions all stem, so Mr. Shipton tells me, from a Boinod and Gaillard advertisement in the *Pennsylvania Journal* of 17 January 1784. We do know, however, at least two of the titles that must have interested Madison. Washington ordered some books from the catalogue (see: *The Writings of George Washington*, ed. by John C. Fitzpatrick [Washington, 1931 ff.], vol. XXVII, pp. 338–339, 18 February 1784). Among the items he ordered was William Lothian, *History of the United Provinces of the Netherlands* (Dublin, 1780). Quite possibly Washington also thought that light from the Dutch confederacy was of consequence to ours. If he expected light from this work, however, he was probably disappointed, for it is a year-by-year chronicle, based on about 50 French and Latin chronicles, of war, diplomacy, and exploration in the Netherlands and the East Indies from 1598 to 1609. Although it is adequate as a chronicle, it has only incidental material on Dutch political forms and only by laborious inference could one obtain from it a picture of the operation of Dutch institutions. Even the scholarly Madison would, I am certain, have found little light in Lothian. John Williams, *On the Rise, Progress and Present State of the Northern Governments: Viz: The United Provinces, Denmark, Sweden, Russia, and Poland; or Observations...*, etc. (London, 1777, 2 vols.) another item Washington ordered, has 150 pages on Dutch commerce, history, and government and might, thus, be expected to throw more light. Although it purports to contain a traveler's first-hand observations, it is, in the section on the Netherlands, both inaccurate and derivative, since it is mostly an inept reworking of Temple's *Observations*. Williams failed even to note that voting power in the admiralty boards differed from that in the States General; yet he asserted that he had acquired special knowledge about marine affairs in the Netherlands.

    3. The works were Aitzema, *Notable Revolutions* (see Appendix) and De Witt (?) *Political Maxims* (see above: 2). As a further illustration of the difficulties over books, note that Jefferson tried to purchase a French, Italian, or English translation of Grotius, *Annales.* An English translation had been published in the previous century; but Jefferson never found a copy. See E. Millicent Sowerby, *Catalogue of the Library of Thomas Jefferson* (Washington, 1952 ff., 4 vols.), vol. I, p. 125.

    4. According to an estimate made for me by Mr. Edwin Wolf, 2nd, Librarian of the Library Company of Philadelphia, on the basis of the 1789 catalogue and extrapolation of accession numbers, the *Observations* was in the Library Company in 1787. According to the *Catalogue of the Books in the Library of American Academy of Arts and Sciences* (Boston,

1802), it was in the Boston library of that organization in 1802. Since the library consisted almost entirely of the books of Governor Bowdoin, books collected prior to 1786, it was doubtless available in Boston in 1787. According to Henry Adams, *A Catalogue of the Books of John Quincy Adams* (Boston, 1938), John Adams gave a copy of it to his son in 1780, but this volume was probably not physically in the United States until after 1787.

5. Assuming that the board at Amsterdam controlled one-third of naval affairs and that the other boards controlled one-sixth each, and multiplying the fraction of naval authority on each board by the fraction of voting power each province had on the board, then Holland had 42% of the voting power; Zealand, 17%; Friesland, 14%; Utrecht, 9%; Gelderland, 7%; Overissel 6%; and Groningen, 5% — a distribution roughly in proportion to the charges paid to the generality. See: "Instructie, vande Heeren Generale Staten der Vereenighde Nederlanden, voor de Collegien vander Admiraliteyte inde respective Provincien ende Quartieren Opgerecht...13 August 1 1597" in *Groot Placaet Boeck, Vervattende de Placaten Ordonnantien Ende Dicten Vande Doorluchtige Hoogh-Mog: Heeren Staten Generael Der Vereenighde Nederlanden...etc.* (The Hague, 1664), vol. II, folios 1529-31. See also: F.M. Janicon, *État Present Des Provinces-Unies et des Pais Qui en Dépendent* (Hague, 1729), pp. 195 ff.

II THE MEASUREMENT
OF FEDERALISM

The theme that binds these chapters together is the investigation of the thesis of progressive centralization of American federalism. Has it been centralized? If so, in what sense? If not, wherein lies its structural stability? In part I it was shown that centralized federalism was invented at Philadelphia in 1787 and owed very little to previous federations. So, in constitutional outline at least, the present structure is similar to the initial structure.

To investigate the matter further, one needs some measure of variation in constitutional form. Historians of American constitutional law have for long sought to construct a narrative measure of this variation, typically by chronicling changes in legislative and judicial allocations of functions between the nation and the states.

Unfortunately, such measures are badly flawed. For one thing, it is difficult to draw together the vast detail and to discriminate between the significant and insignificant. Furthermore, the subjects of legislation and adjudication are usually marginal, changing the corpus of law at the edges, not reworking it completely. Hence, grand and fundamental reallocations can go on without notice by judges or legislators. Military activity is a case in point. It is the main business of the national government, yet constitutional historians know almost nothing about it. As a result, the narrative histories of reallocations hardly mention it. This neglect is unfortunate, however, because military centralization and decentralization has not synchronized with economic centralization and decentralization. Hence the narrative measure is unfinished. Considering the complexity of the project, it is likely to remain so.

One needs, therefore, some other sort of summary measure that reflects all kinds of centralization. One common measure is income or expenditure by the two levels of government. (Such a measure is developed and reported in the second chapter in this part, Alexander's "The Measurement of American Federalism.") The difficulty with this measure is that it summarizes only administrative detail. Such changes are mainly determined by technological innovation (as, for example, when transportation becomes national, so does it regulation). The important consideration is not, however, technological, but the political relation between levels. Previously there has been no measure of that.

Hence, the first two chapters in this part report the construction and application of a measure of the political relation. In the first chapter the measure is explained in some detail, and empirical evidence is offered of its relevance to politics during the period from 1937 to 1955. In the second chapter, Alexander carried the measure backward to 1837 and forward to 1972. This time series covers about two-thirds of our constitutional history.

In the third chapter we report a wholly different kind of measurement. It concerns the longevity of federations. In *Federalism* I had asked about what conditions are, in general, associated with the formation of federations. I answered in terms of a social law and offered empirical support for its validity. Furthermore, I embedded the law in a theory about the motivation of politicians in the situations in which federations are formed. Hence the law had theoretical as well as empirical support.

In studying longevity, however, it is not as easy to utter necessary conditions nor to relate them to a theory. We know less and we are less able to generalize. So we are constrained to deal with hunches and hypotheses. The third chapter constitutes, therefore, an effort to identify some political features associated with stability or longevity, although we make no claim about a necessary relation.

Nevertheless, the associations we found do make sense. For federations to survive, it must be that the central government be strong enough to overawe the constituents and the constituents be strong enough to resist the center. The constitutional features we identified (numerous states, none disproportionately large) contribute to strengthening the central government relative to the states by rendering them individually unable to resist pressure from the center. At the same time they do not strengthen the central government so much that it can cannibalize the constituents.

4 DISHARMONY IN FEDERAL GOVERNMENT

William H. Riker and Ronald Schaps

Commentary. *In order to maintain the integrity of the constituent states in a federal system, they must be able to dispute, sometimes successfully, with the central government. If the states cannot, they may well become no more than local subdivisions in a decentralized but unitary system, like the local subdivisions in France or in the (dubiously federal) Soviet Union. In effectively operating federal systems, one should thus expect a fair amount of intergovernmental bickering, which is here given the name "disharmony." Conceivably, this disharmony might be moderated in two ways: first, by constitutionally subjecting local governments to the central government (as in France) or, second, by politically reconciling differences through the agency of a political party that simultaneously controls government at both levels (as in the Soviet Union). To moderate by the first method is to abandon federalism explicit, while to moderate by the second is to abandon it implicitly.*

The essence of the federal system is, of course, that bickering continue, although the level of bickering is likely to vary according to the degree it is moderated by partisan unity between levels. We have exploited this potential

Published originally in *Behavioral Science*, 1957, vol. 2, pp. 276–289.

variation to define an "index of disharmony," which we showed was associated directly with amounts of intergovernmental disputes.

In this chapter Schaps and I deprecated the bickering, interpreting it as an unfortunate consequence of the federal form. Today I would take a neutral position, neither deprecating nor extolling. But I would still emphasize that intergovernmental disputes are inherently necessary in federalism. Clearly, if there are no disputes, then either the federal system has been fully unified or it has collapsed. If there are disputes, then federalism is alive and well, though, if they become excessive, constitutional reform or secession will probably follow: as in the calling of the Constitutional Convention itself because of the inability of the central government to govern or as in the secession of the Civil War when the Southerners withdrew rather than allow national Republicans to govern "the peculiar institution."

Unfortunately, the mildly pejorative tone of the conclusion led Roland Pennock to respond with evidence of "harmony" in federalism (Pennock, 1959). Presumably harmony is good and disharmony is bad; so those who approve of federalism ought, apparently, to counter disharmony with harmony, though Pennock agreed with us that the disharmony we described was quite evident. Pennock's harmony was the chance for losers on one level of government to be winners on another. But, of course, this feature is not distinctively federal. All democratic unitary governments (e.g., France or Britain) have local elections that permit losers at the national level to win at the local level.

What is important about federalism is the constitutionally assured potential for local governments to disrupt. This is how they act as a restraint on the federal government. So, if one approves of federalism, one should approve of this disharmony; and, if one disapproves of federalism, one should disapprove of this disharmony. In any case the disharmony is a characteristic feature of federalism while the harmony (or relief from frustration) to which Pennock pointed characterizes all decentralized governments, whether federal or not.

Pennock's error was, of course, occasioned by his ideological intent to reply to the ideology implied in our pejorative comments. This reveals exactly the distorting effect of ideological debate about the characteristics of institutions. Nevertheless, transcending both his and our ideology is our agreement that intergovernmental disputes are an important feature of federalism. This agreement shows that it is possible to discover some things about institutions despite ideological differences.

Modern federalism, which can be regarded as an alternative to imperialism in the expansion of governments, consists essentially of a twofold constitutional guarantee. One guarantee is of the independence and viability of the central government such that its officials are enabled to decide their problems without consulting the officials of the constituent governments. In the United States, as in most modern centralized federalisms, this means that national officials are chosen without the formal aid or intervention of state officials and that national officials govern directly the citizens who choose them (Riker, 1955). It is this independence of the central government from the constituent ones that differentiates modern centralized federalism from peripheralized leagues like the medieval confederations of Switzerland and Suabia, or the Dutch Republic of the seventeenth century, or even the American government under the Articles of Confederation, in all of which national officials were by one constitutional device or another forced to refer decisions on some national questions to the organs of constituent governments (Riker, 1958). (The distinction between centralized and peripheralized federalism is, of course, not so sharp as the naming of the categories may suggest. Even the Dutch Republic had some centralized features [e.g., the Council of State and the Boards of Admiralty] and the United States did not lose one of its severely peripheralizing customs until the notion of instructions to senators from state legislature ceased to have practical effect in the 1840s and 1850s (Riker, 1955).

The other guarantee is of the perpetual existence of the constituent governments such that they are enabled to maintain themselves (in the selection of officials, etc.) independently of the national government. It is this guarantee that distinguishes all federalisms, whether centralized or peripheralized, from unitary states like Great Britain, in which local government is—in legal theory, at least—wholly under the control of the central government.

In political practice, the net effect of the operation of these two guarantees is the existence of two sets of governments in the same place directing the same people. Not surprisingly, conflicts between the two sets have characterized all modern federalisms. There is no necessary reason that such intergovernmental conflict should occur. Indeed, it is theoretically conceivable that constituent and central governments independently pursue harmonious and logically coordinated policies. In actual fact, however, all modern federalisms have at one time or another experienced severe intergovernmental conflicts, such as the American Civil War or the attempt of Western Australia to withdraw from the Commonwealth. And less divisive bickering between the center and the periphery is an almost universal feature of the operation of federalisms. Besides conscious bickering, federalisms constantly suffer from a lack of integration between the policies of the states and the nation. Often this disharmony approaches the extreme instance of fiscal policy in the United States in 1934, when states curtailed expenditures as an economy measure while the nation increased expenditures as a means of combating depression (Hansen and Perloff, 1944). Frequently, as perhaps in this instance, such contradictory policies are adopted without intent to impede or embarrass: they merely occur by reason of differences in ideology and interest among the officials of the two sets of governments. One cannot escape the impression, therefore, that the institutional structure of most contemporary federalisms is highly conducive to intergovernmental conflicts and to a failure to integrate policies. Just how and why the institutions of federalism should work this way is not entirely clear. So it is for the sake of explaining some of the institutional circumstances conducive to conflict that this essay is written.

The Political Party As A Source of Harmony or Disharmony

The one agency that might be expected to harmonize the policies of central and constituent governments is a political party. If the officials of both sets of governments are adherents of the same ideology or followers of the same leader or leaders, then they might be expected to pursue harmonious policies. And in the conventional theory of federalism, it is indeed assumed that exactly this will happen. But in all federalisms which have a relatively free party system with competing political parties, just the converse occurs. In the heat of party struggle, competing parties use the central government against the constituent governments and the constituent governments against the central. The only circumstance in which it is perhaps impossible for intergovernmental conflict to appear as a byproduct of party competition is when one highly disciplined party controls all governments both central and constituent. This is not, however, likely to occur except in dictatorial federalisms like the Soviet Union or Yugoslavia. The motive for establishing federalisms in all instances (except the present German one and possibly the Yugoslavian) has been to attract the adherents of constituent governments into a larger nation without the difficulties of conquest. By reason of this history, in all federalisms there is a residue of localism and sectionalism, which, given an opportunity to flourish in unrestrained party competition, has always resulted in sectionally based political parties. Even in the Soviet Union, where federalism was introduced under a tyranny, much of the opposition to the single party turned out to be sectionally based and Trotskyism found its chief expression in the government of the Ukraine. And sectionally based party competition, whether in a free or dictatorial party system, is certain to make use of the central government to fight some of the constituent governments and some of the constituent governments to fight other constituent governments and the central government. Hence, the very existence of political parties (or in dictatorships, underground factions) seems in a federalism almost certain to call forth intergovernmental conflicts.

If the existence of sectionally based political parties is, as we have argued, certain to occasion intergovernmental conflict, then the degree of party division among the several governments is a rough measure of the degree of possible conflicts between them. Presumably, if one homogenous political party controlled all governments, both central and constituent, there would be no occasion for intergovernmental conflict. If, on the other hand, all constituent governments were controlled by one homogenous party, and the central government by another the degree of federal conflict would be intense. Between these two extremes lie all existent federalisms. The Soviet Union and Yugoslavia have usually attained the former extreme. On the other hand, the United States, Canada, Brazil, and Australia are at present almost in the center of the scale between the two extremes and have at times approached closer to the latter than the former. If one could arrange particular federalisms on a scale between these two extremes, then one would have some rough indication of the probable amount, other things being equal, of intergovernmental conflict and lack of integration in policy. Such an arrangement has heretofore been impossible because there was no way to relate the positions of, for example, governor, senator, and president on the same numerical scale. Hence, when, for example, one party controlled the executive and, by a narrow margin, the upper house and when another party controlled the lower house by a wide margin, it was impossible to say which one controlled—or controlled in what degree—a government as a whole. But by reason of some recently developed mathematical techniques, this difficulty has been overcome. And so in this essay, several federalisms will be placed on such a scale.

To obtain an index of disharmony in a federalism, we will use the so-called power index, devised by Shapley and Shubik (Shapley, 1953; Shapley and Shubik, 1955). This index is based on Shapley's theorem on the value of n-person games. The power index is described thus: Assume a legislature of n members in which each member has one vote and in which a simple majority wins. Assume further that the members can vote in any sequence and that any one sequence is as likely to occur as any other. In any legislature, there are $1 \cdot 2 \ldots \cdot n$ such sequences, i.e., $n!$ (read, "n factorial"). The winning voter, that is, that last voter necessary for a majority in the sequence, is called the "pivot." Thus in a five-member legislature with these rules, c is the pivot in the sequence d, a, c, b, e. The power index with respect to any one member (designated here by "P_i") is this simple ratio:

$$P_i = \frac{\text{number of sequences in which } i \text{ pivots}}{\text{number of sequences (that is, } n!)}$$

In the illustration suggested, $P_c = 24/5! = 24/120 = 1/5$.

This index measures the a priori chances that a member of a legislature has to occupy the marginal or pivot position in a legislative victory. Assuming that the last added member of a minimal winning coalition[1] can more deeply influence the content of the coalition's legislation than the original members, the index is thus a measure of a legislator's power. Although it was developed on the basis of a simple legislature, one of the attractive features of the index is that it can be adjusted to fit a wide variety of constitutional provisions. Thus, it can be applied to the United States government, which consists of a tricameral legislature in which a majority of those voting in two houses is necessary for the passage of a bill, and, if the majority in either of these is less than 2/3, the assent of the third house is also necessary (Riker, 1953). Following the calculations of Shapley and Shubik, the power indices for these several legislators are: for the President, about .166667; for the Vice-President, about .004295; for each Senator, about .004233; for each Representative, about .000958. Similar calculations can be made for any state government, provided that variations in constitutional structure are allowed for.

For both the state governments and the national government the power indices of those legislators who join a particular political party may be summed. Hence, it is possible to speak not only of the power index of a legislator, but also of the power index of a party. If one could assume perfect party cohesion (i.e., such that, if one member of a party votes on one side of an issue, then all members of that party vote on the same side), then, instead of summing the indices of members of one party, the index of the party itself should be calculated, as if the party itself were a player. Thus, the model would be not a simple majority game but a weighted majority game. But in American legislatures, both state and national, party cohesion is not extremely high and over a series of roll calls it is likely that every single member will defect at least once. The unreality of the assumption of perfect cohesion for American legislatures will be at once recognized when it is pointed out that a calculation on the basis of it would produce an index of one for the majority party. Outside of the legislatures of the deep South this is absurd—and in the South the same results are obtained by summation. Hence it seems appropriate in the United States to obtain party indices by summing the indices of the party members.

Furthermore, if the states are considered as a class together, it is possible to calculate the power index of parties in the system of states taken as a whole. If one regards the states as governments of equal authority, as they are regarded in the construction of the Senate, then the power index of a party in the states taken together is the sum, multiplied by 1/48, of the power indices of all the state legislators and governors that assert they belong to the party. If, on the other hand, one regards the states as governments that vary in authority according to their population, then the power index of a party in the states taken together is the sum of the power indices of that party in the states, each state index having been multiplied by the state's percentage of the national population[2]. Whichever method is used, the resulting index is a rough measure of the strength of a party in the states. Once obtained, it can serve for comparison with the strength of that party in the nation as a whole.

The party division that, by our assumption, disturbs the harmony of federalism is that which occurs when states are controlled by a different party from the one that controls the national government. A convenient index that expresses the degree of partisan disharmony between the two sets of governments is then: For any party (or governing coalition of parties) whose power index in the national government is greater than .5, one minus the power index of that party (or parties) in the sum of the states is the index of partisan disharmony in a federalism. Thus, if the power index of the Republican party in the national government is .63 and in the sum of the states (considering the states as equal) is .54, then the index of partisan disharmony is: 1—.54, or .46.

Partisan Disharmony in The United States, 1937–1956

We have calculated the index of partisan disharmony in the United States for the nine bienniums from 1937 to 1956. (The calculation is not for the biennium as a whole, but only for the beginning of the first legislative session of the biennium in each state and the national government. No attempt was made to take account of subsequent changes by reason of deaths, resignations, changes of party affiliation, and special elections.) The particular period, 1937 to 1956, was chosen, not out of a conviction that the most recent is the most interesting or even the most important, but simply because statistics on the party affiliation of state legislators are readily available for that period alone. Most state governments, subscribing to the eighteenth century superstition that parties are inventions of Satan, refused to recognize the existence of parties in state publications throughout the nineteenth century and well into the twentieth. Consequently newspapers and broadsides were the only sources for such statistics until the state manuals became common in the first two decades of this century. While the manuals usually notice the party affiliation of elected officials, in a few states still the superstition is adhered to. Since 1937, however, the Council of State Governments has published presumably accurate statistics on party affiliation in *The Book of the States*, and these we have used for our calculations. Doubtless in other periods (e.g., 1877 to 1896), the index would, if calculated, display more interesting vagaries than in 1937 to 1956. But the labor of searching newspaper files seemed less important than the calculation itself, so we used the statistics at hand, intending, if the results seem significant, to spread the calculations backward in time and more extensively in space.

In calculating the power index of parties in the national government, we used the method described above. In calculating the power index of parties in the states, however, we varied the indices of governors and assemblymen according to the constitutional rules on the governor's veto, the presence or absence of a Lieutenant Governor with tie-breaking powers in the state assembly, the number of state senators and representatives, the number of houses in the state legislature, etc. In the instances of Minnesota and Nebraska we counted all the assemblymen as independents, although, as is well known, many of them cryptically affiliate with a political party. Finally we calculated the power indices of parties in the sum of the states two ways: 1) on the assumption that the states were equal in authority, and 2) on the assumption that the states varied in authority according to their population. Hence we have two indices of partisan disharmony, one designated "equal basis," the other designated "proportional basis."[3]

The results of the calculation are shown in figures 4–1 and 4–2 and also in table 4–1. Figure 4–1 depicts the power index of the Democratic party in both the national government and the sum of the states. (Inasmuch as independents and affiliates of minor parties are a negligible factor in this period, the power indices of the Republican party are substantially the complements of the Democratic indices.) As is apparent, the party in power nationally has in this period done substantially better in national elections than in state elections. We suspect that this has been a characteristic feature of American federalism for a long time, although we do not have the statistics necessary to verify our assumptions. It follows from the pattern of indices for the Democratic party (figure 4–1) that the index of partisan disharmony (figure 4–2) is fairly high. Except for 1937–

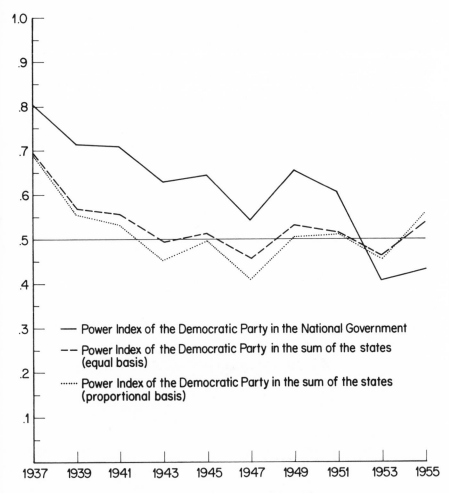

Figure 4-1.   Power index, Democratic party, 1937-1955.

1938 when it was .30, this index has varied between .40 and .60. Interpreting the index as an indication of a serious degree of disharmony when it rises above .50—the point at which the party in control of the national government fails to control the states taken in sum—then roughly half the time in recent years, American federalism has experienced a serious amount of disharmony. If the index is calculated on an equal basis, then in four bienniums out of ten it has risen above .50; if calculated on a proportional basis, there have been five such bienniums out of ten.

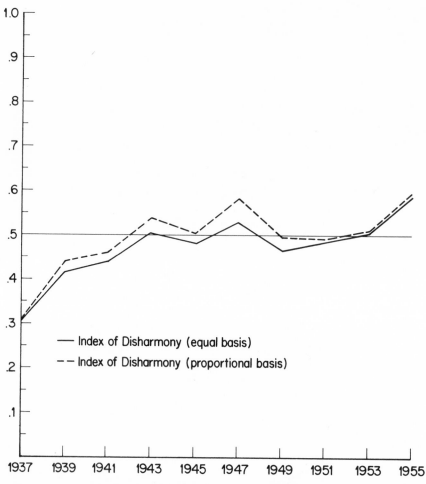

Figure 4-2.   Index of disharmony, United States, 1937-1955.

Assumptions of the Index

If the assumptions beneath the index of disharmony are valid, the
foregoing calculations reveal a disturbingly serious—and, we believe,
heretofore unsuspected—disability in American federalism. But before we
can examine this disability, we must first examine the assumptions of the
index. Some readers will doubtless feel that an index so contrived and so

Table 4–1. Cases considered by the Supreme Court in which United States and state(s) were both involved[a,b]

Biennium	Col. I: Cases in which nation and states(s) opposed[c]	Col. II: Cases in which nation and state(s) aligned[d]	Col. III: Net cases in which opposed Col. I less Col. II	Col. IV: Index of disharmony (equal basis)	Col. V: Index of disharmony (proportional basis)
1937–38	21	13	8	.30	.31
1939–40	29	14	15	.43	.44
1941–42	33	12	21	.44	.46
1943–44	47	14	33	.51	.55
1945–46	24	7	17	.49	.51
1947–48	27	5	22	.54	.58
1949–50	24	6	18	.46	.50
1951–52	30	9	21	.49	.49
1953–54				.50	.51
1955–56				.58	.60

Note.—r Col. III, Col. IV = .789; r Col. III, Col. V = .786

[a] "Cases considered by the Supreme Court..." means not only those cases in which the Court heard argument and issued a decision but also all those cases in which a prayer for a writ of certiorari was refused or an appeal was not granted.

[b] Cases in which both the United States and a state(s) were litigants were assigned to the biennium in which the suit was instituted, whether in a lower court or in the Supreme Court. Thus a case decided in 1947 might be counted as much earlier as 1942. (This is why it has been impossible to carry the correlation further than 1951–52). Cases appealed from an administrative tribunal were assigned to the biennium in which the decision of the tribunal was appealed to the courts. Cases in which either the United States or state(s) appear only as amicus curiae were assigned to the biennium in which the brief was submitted. Cases in which proceedings were instituted or briefs were submitted in the first two weeks of January were assigned to the previous year.

[c] Column I summarizes 1) those cases in which the United States or its instrumentality or agent was a litigant against a state(s) or its instrumentality or agent; 2) those cases in which, when a state(s) was a litigant, the United States submitted a brief amicus curiae against the interest of the state(s); and 3) those cases in which, when the United States was a litigant, a state(s) submitted a brief amicus curiae against the interest of the United States.

[d] Column II summarizes 1) those cases in which the United States or its instrumentalities or agents were litigants on the same side of a case as a state(s) or its instrumentalities or agents; 2) those cases in which, when a state(s) was a litigant, the United States submitted a brief amicus curiae supporting the interest of the state(s). In those special cases in which the litigants were two instrumentalities or officers of a state government and in which the United States intervened either as a litigant or as amicus curiae, we counted the case under column II if the United States intervened on the side of an elected official or if it intervened on the side with the most elected officials. Otherwise, we counted it under column I.

abstract is impossible to interpret and hence of no value in the study of constitutions. Counting, we must all admit, destroys the humane richness of unordered detail. But numerical summaries, although they drown the uniqueness of individual facts, do permit us to comprehend detail that is otherwise beyond our grasp. We count in order to comprehend; yet of every essay in counting we must ask whether or not the counting itself abstracts so far from reality that it precludes comprehension of the things counted. Certainly that question is appropriate here; and so, before proceeding with our main business, it seems proper to say a word about the validity of the assumptions of the index.

The most obvious of the limitations of the index is that it measures unhomogenous things. It measures the division of power (defined as the chance of pivoting on roll calls) among political parties in legislatures. Yet in the United States, the members of a political party are not a homogenous class with respect to their attitudes on public questions nor with respect to their actions in legislatures. Not only is party cohesion rather low in American legislatures; but further, taking a party as a national organization, many members may be diametrically opposed on the public issues of the day. So great is the difference between, for example, a Negro Democratic assemblyman from Detroit, Michigan, and a white Democratic assemblyman from Montgomery, Alabama, that a category subsuming both of them may be utterly meaningless. The assumption of the index is that, if the Democratic party, for example, controls the national government, the Republicans will use the state governments they control to impede the center, while Democratic governments in state and nation will work harmoniously together. It may well be, however, that a dissident Democratic faction in control of a state will obstruct national action far more seriously than Republicans and that the national Democrats will work quite harmoniously with a dissident Republican faction in control of another state. In the United States, where shades of political opinion are expressed in factions rather than in parties, the possibility is considerable of actul situations in violation of the assumption. Such situations are less likely in multiparty systems where shades of opinion tend to be expressed in parties, although in New South Wales in the 1930s the Lang Labour Party seems to have occasioned exactly this sort of factional division.

And yet this limitation of the index is not nearly so serious as it appears to be. All factions of a party, no matter how bitter their squabbles, are agreed at least on the preservation of the party itself. The fact that they continue to associate themselves with it sufficiently indicates that, for example, even the most disaffected Republicans would rather be Republicans than Democrats. In short, intraparty squabbles are moderated by the understood compact to preserve the party in a way that conflicts between parties are not. And in that sense the assumption beneath the index of disharmony is fully justified. The justification can perhaps be realized more vividly if one imagines an index of disharmony calculated for factions rather than parties. Assuming that there were some valid empirical device to identify the factions around which such an index would be constructed, still an index of factional (rather than partisan) disharmony would necessarily involve the assumption that factions are durable and coherently organized. This assumption is even more questionable, with respect to American politics as it is usually described, than the assumption that parties are factionless. It seems, therefore, that an index of partisan disharmony, while not a wholly adequate model of American politics, is yet the best that can now be constructed. The reliability of a model constructed with the perhaps unreasonable assumption that factionalism is less obstructive than partisanship can only be discovered by an empirical test of the results of calculations with it.

A second possible limitation in the index is that in the states taken together all the power of all members of a party is counted, whether the party is in control of the state government or not. Thus conceivably the index of disharmony would be as high as .49 even though one party had a power index greater than .50 in the national government and every state government. In the United States, with its 48 constituent units, such considerable distortion is barely conceivable for the minorities in the states tend to cancel out. But in the federalisms with fewer constituent units, e.g., Canada and Australia, distortion of this sort is less unlikely.

And yet it is not certain that this is in fact a statistical distortion. If the majority party has everywhere only a tiny margin of control, the expectation of factional disaffection is greatly increased. Such factional defection may well lead to using the governments of a federalism against each other—and this is what the index of disharmony is supposed to measure. In the United States in the last two decades, the dissatisfaction of the conservative Southern faction with the liberal Democrats of North and South has seemed to increase as the amount of Republican opposition has increased[4]. Presumably, when the margin between the two parties is narrow, the conservative faction has believed it could successfully carry its disputes much further than when the Democratic party could win without them. It is not at all inconceivable, therefore, that the amount of actual disharmony increases when the index increases, even though the minority party nowhere controls a government. If this is in fact true, then this apparent defect in the index is actually meritorious. Whether it is the one or the other, however, depends upon the result of some kind of empirical test.

A third limitation of the index of disharmony arises from the nature of the power index. In the construction of the latter the notion of power is defined as the chance a legislator has of pivoting in a roll call. It is assumed that legislative rewards, i.e., influence over public policy, accrue in greatest quantity to the marginal legislator. Power in the ordinary sense of the word is, however, much more than the power index allows. It is a vast complex of the institutional and personal ways to influence public policy and governmental action. These ways of influence, power in the ordinary sense, may or may not be related to the chance of pivoting on a roll call. If they are not related, then the greatest rewards may accrue, not to the marginal legislator but to the most advantageously situated. For example, the shape of legislation may more faithfully reflect the opinions of an energetic, persuasive and senior committee member of the minority party than the opinions of any other legislator. And if power in the technical sense of the power index is not in nature closely related to power in the ordinary sense, then the power index may not measure anything at all in natural governments. It does seem likely, of course, that the chance to pivot is a basic sort of power out of which grows nearly every other kind of influence in a representative government. Yet, in the absence of a reasonably impressive empirical test, one cannot be certain that the power index and hence the index of disharmony serves as a model of anything in real governments.

Whether or not these three limitations are extensive enough to destroy the interpretive value of the index of disharmony depends in each instance on some kind of empirical evidence. We have, therefore, sought for some empirical test that would indicate whether or not variations in the index are connected with variations in actual conflict between governments. Such a test is not, however, easily devised. For one reason, federal conflict seldom consists of commensurable events. It is hardly possible to measure on one scale both a civil war and a dispute over the routing of a highway. For another reason, many petty disputes are never publicly reported and are for that reason uncountable. One kind of federal conflict, i.e., formal litigation in courts, is, however, sufficiently recurrent, sufficiently reported, and, we trust, sufficiently commensurable to serve as an empirical indication of disharmony. And so we have constructed a test around it.

We assumed that, when the nation and the states carried their lawsuits as far as the Supreme Court, some actual disharmony existed. In many kinds of litigation between the two sets of governments, lawsuits are a means of amicable settlement of questions over which there is no serious disagreement. When, for instance, the United States acquires land owned by a state, it must pay something for it and one way to arrive at an impartially established price is by condemnation proceedings. If the price set by the district court is accepted by both parties, one can assume that the two governments were simply using the court system as a substitute for the market mechanism. But if land condemnation proceedings are carried up through the court of appeals to the Supreme Court, one can assume that the nation and the state have disagreed seriously either about the transfer or the price. So it is with most other types of federal litigation that reaches the Supreme Court. From a survey of all the cases summarized in columns I and II of table 4–1, it appears that all but two, or perhaps three, involved a genuine controversy between the nation and the states. (The exceptions were cases in which a state was a litigant and in which the Solicitor General of the United States submitted, at the request of the Court and apparently with reluctance, a brief *amicus curiae*.)

Assuming then that federal cases in the Supreme Court reveal the existence of actual federal disharmony, we counted the number of such events and correlated this number, by bienniums, with the index of disharmony. This calculation resulted in a coefficient of correlation of about +.79. Testing this coefficient against the hypothesis that it might have occurred by chance, it appears that the coefficient is just within the 2% level of confidence, which is to say that a correlation this high would occur by chance only in 2/100 of the possible correlations. The coefficient of .79 can hardly be a chance result, and we are, therefore, justified in concluding that there is some positive relationship between the index of disharmony and actual disharmony in American federalism.

High correlations, even correlations within the 2% level of confidence are, admittedly, not especially impressive when only eight items are involved. Still there is a good, nonstatistical reason for believing that the correlation is more impressive than it appears. A large portion of the cases between the nation and the states before the Supreme Court stand as part of persisting and durable controversies not likely to be affected by biennial changes in the relative position of parties. The controversy over state taxation of Indians and Indian lands, the jockeying for control of the natural gas pipeline business between the Federal Power Commission and state utility commissions, the controversy over reciprocal immunity in taxation—these and similarly durable controversies account for about one-third of the cases in table 4–1. Were they eliminated, the variation in the number of cases per biennium would be even more volatile than it is and a much higher coefficient of correlation would result.

It seems fairly certain, therefore, that changes in the index of disharmony are accompanied by positively correlated changes in the actual amount of disharmony as expressed in litigation before the Supreme Court. Unfortunately this positive correlation is not a full test of the reliability of the index. Formally and legally, litigation is instituted by executives alone and in their executive capacity, while executives in their legislative capacity account for less than one-sixth of the total power measured in the index. Still it seems likely that the amount of actual disharmony is dependent upon the political atmosphere of the moment, that, for example, executives find it necessary to institute lawsuits against other governments especially when there is a high degree of partisan disharmony in all branches of government. And if this kind of political atmosphere is important in actual disharmony, then the test, for all its lopsided emphasis on executive action, is still closely related to the index.

Indeed, in light of the test, we are justified in concluding that the index is at least partially reliable 1) even though it ignores factions within parties; 2) even though it ignores the fact that some of the power measured is held by minorities; and 3) even though the power index on which it is based assumes a very special definition of power. Undoubtedly many individual instances can be discovered in which power in the ordinary sense is quite unrelated to the chance of pivoting in roll calls. The fact that a fairly high correlation is obtained between the index of disharmony and actual disharmony suggests, however, that the chance of pivoting is at least an adequate sample of power (in the sense of influence on public policy) in natural legislatures. Thus indirectly—and doubtless tentatively—this test serves also as a test of the validity of the notion of the power index.

Thus, in spite of these limitations, the test shows that to some degree the index of disharmony measures what it purports to measure. The explanation of this possibly curious situation is, we suspect, analogous to the explanation of similar situations in economics. Even though the measure is crude, the fact that it subsumes a vast amount of detail permits conflicting data to cancel out so that we are left with a general statement which, though over-simplified, reliably expresses a gross relationship.

Application of the Index to Other Governments

The index indicates, as we have suggested, the existence of a serious amount of actual disharmony in American federalism. Just how serious this defect is, however, can hardly be comprehended until the index for the past 20 years in the United States is compared with the index in the United

States at earlier periods and with the index for other contemporary federalisms. It would be especially interesting, for example, to discover what effect the passage of the seventeenth amendment had on the index of disharmony. There are good a priori reasons for believing that this amendment tended to increase the index; whether or not it actually did so, however, can be determined only after further data for the calculation of the index are collected. For the reasons previously set forth, we will not here attempt to calculate an index for the United States prior to 1937; but sufficient data are at hand to calculate an index of disharmony for Australia and Canada for the same period as it was calculated for the United States.[5]

By contrast with the index of disharmony for the United States, the indices for Canada and Australia are startling. The Australian index shows extreme variation and extreme disharmony both when calculated on an equal basis and when calculated on a proportional basis. The Canadian index, when calculated on an equal basis, shows less extreme variation than the Australian, and is, except for 1940 to 1944 not vastly different from the two American indices. But when calculated on a proportional basis the Canadian index shows a greater variation than any other (from .09 to .86).

This is an extraordinary result, the more so since for both Canada and Australia it seems reasonable to regard the index constructed on a proportional basis as the more appropriate of the two. In the structure and operation of the United States Senate, the states are theoretically and practically regarded as equal in significance, while in the House of Representatives they are regarded as significant in proportion to population. The Senate also has the same amount of legislative power (in the technical sense) as the House and in addition some so-called executive power the House lacks. Hence it is reasonable, and probably necessary, to calculate the index of disharmony on both bases. In Canada, however, both the Senate and the House of Commons are constructed roughly in proportion to population (the Senate less so, for it is rather heavily biased in favor of the Maritime provinces and against the western provinces). In addition, the Canadian Senate is wholly powerless (in both the technical and popular senses). Hence, an index of disharmony on an equal basis hardly represents the constitutional relationships among the provinces and the center: and one ought probably to regard the index on a proportional basis, as the only appropriate measure of federal disharmony in Canada. In Australia, the Senate is constructed on an equal basis and has somewhat more legislation power (in the popular sense) than the Canadian Senate; but since the Australian Senate is far less important than the House of Representatives, the index constructed on a proportional basis seems the only appropriate measure for Australia as well. Inasmuch as the index on a proportional basis displays for both countries a far greater variation and much more disharmony than the index constructed on an equal basis, figures 4–3 and 4–4 reveal an even more startling result than might at first be assumed.

The extraordinary indices for Canada and Australia suggest that these two federalisms are plagued with much more federal conflict than is the United States. They suggest strongly that constitution-makers in both countries were unwise to copy American federalism as slavishly as they did

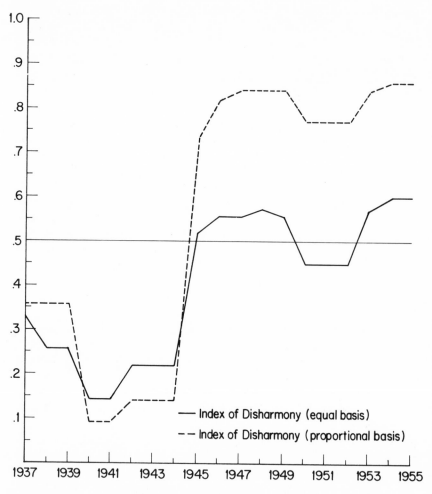

Figure 4–3.   Index of disharmony, Canada, 1937–1955.

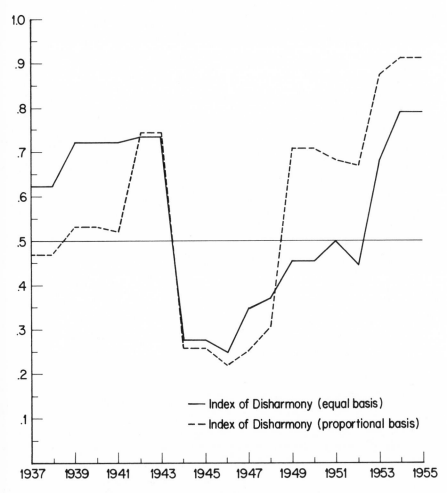

Figure 4-4.   Index of disharmony, Australia, 1937-1955.

and that they might more wisely have adjusted federalism to fit parliamentary as distinct from presidential government. Federal conflicts are disconcerting enough in the United States. If the index is a valid representation of Canadian and Australian reality, such conflicts must be far more disconcerting in these two countries.

Whether or not the index of disharmony validly represents political events in Canada and Australia, we are unable to say. We are quite certain, however, that the extreme variation in the Australian and

Canadian indices is not an accident of the method of computation. It is true that the use of the weighted majority game model is likely to represent the power of a party as much higher or much lower than the popular vote might suggest. Using the weighted majority model, if the party having a national majority wins in every state, the index of disharmony will be zero, even if it wins in each state by only 51% of the vote. But when party cohesion is very high, as in Australia or Canada, this is a fair statement of the political situation: Power is *not* divided among the parties in proportion to the popular vote, but all of it accrues to the winner. That the two kinds of models (weighted majority and simple majority) have here been appropriately applied is well demonstrated by comparing Republicans' very good chances of pivoting in Kentucky with Liberals' very poor chances of pivoting in Queensland or Quebec. However, we leave it to those more versed than we in the details of the operation of these two governments to devise a test of our index. (It seems possible that for Australia a test similar to the one here used for the United States might be devised around the operation of the Commonwealth Grants Commission.) Although we lack a satisfactory test, there are some subjective indications that federalism occasions much greater difficulty in the Commonwealth and the Dominion than in the United States. In *Federal Government* (1953), Professor Wheare remarks (apparently with some surprise) that in "Canada alone of the federations has there been conducted a thorough investigation of the whole working of the federal system." If the indices are a valid representation of the degree of disharmony in the three federalisms, however, it is not at all surprising that Canada, in which the highest degree of disharmony is indicated, should have conducted an elaborate inquiry into federal relations. The Canadian Royal Commission on Dominion-Provinical Relations, which reported in 1937, did not, however, consider abandoning federalism. On the other hand, the minority report of the Australia Royal Commission on the Constitution, which reported in 1929 and which, despite Professor Wheare, conducted a study fully as elaborate although less academic than the Canadian one, did quite seriously propose to abandon federalism (Report, 1929). One can hardly imagine the proposal of so fundamental a revision unless some Australians believed that much federal disharmony occurred. Since Professor Wheare's writing, the United States has also conducted a study of federalism (by the Commission on Inter-governmental Relations). Unlike the Canadian and Australian commissions, however, its studies raised no fundamental questions for they were concerned with techniques rather than public law, its members lacked importance in national politics, its recommendations were hardly noticed by Congress or the press, and its reports created almost no public interest. The contrast between the work and significance of the Canadian and Australian commissions on the one hand and the American on the other clearly suggests that federalism occasions much more difficult problems of governing in Canada and Australia than in the United States—which is what the indices suggest also.

Why federalism should have so much more debilitating effects in one place than in another is not entirely clear. Much more detailed empirical and comparative study is needed before this question can be satisfactorily answered. One possible answer that occurs to us, however, is that federalism operates quite differently in two-party and more than two-party systems. Another is that federalism operates quite differently when the number of states is small and when it is large. A third is that federalism operates quite differently in parliamentary and presidential systems.

As we observed earlier, political parties in a federalism are likely to be geographically based, each one controlling some constituent governments. If there are more than two parties controlling constituent governments, then the likelihood is decreased that the party or coalition with a national majority will have a majority in the sum of the states. In Canada, for example, where there are presently five major parties each with a geographic base (Liberal in the Maritime Provinces and Ontario, Union Nationale in Quebec, Conservative in Ontario and parts of the West, Cooperative Commonwealth Federation in Saskatchewan and British Columbia, Social Credit in British Columbia and Alberta), it is hardly possible that any party have a majority in the sum of the 10 provinces. Although we have no statistical proof of this assertion, it seems likely that the more parties in existence, the greater the likelihood of federal disharmony.

In Canada with 10 provinces and in Australia with six states, the number of constituent governments is much smaller than in the United States. Here, the party with a national majority can lose control of as many as 8 or 10 states without altering the index of disharmony as much as $+.10$. In Australia and Canada, however, if the party with a national majority loses Victoria and New South Wales or Quebec and Ontario (both pairs of which constitute well over half the sum of the states or provinces on a proportional basis), the index can change as much as $+.60$. And, if the index does indicate actual disharmony, this is not a mere numerical change, but represents a sharp reversal in federal relations and the possibility of serious discord between the two largest constituent governments and the center. In short, when the number of states is small, a very few elections can dramatically alter the index, thus leading to an instability not likely to occur in a federalism with numerous constituent units.

In a Presidential system like the United States, it is entirely possible that national and state elections be held simultaneously. Since 1872, Presidential electors and Representatives in Congress have been elected at the same time as governors and assemblymen; and since 1913, Senators have been too. Except for some elections midway in the term of a President, voters are thus forced to decide national and state issues simultaneously and, not unnaturally, they have tended to decide them by plumping for one party. This tendency has kept the index of disharmony below .50 in all the bienniums (1936–1954) following a Presidential election, although it has often risen above .50 in bienniums preceding Presidential elections. In Canada and Australia, however, central and constituent government elections have, so far as we know, never occurred simultaneously. To require that they do so would seriously disturb the theory (although not the practice) of parliamentary government, in which dissolutions can occur at any time. Consequently, voters are able to judge local and national issues by entirely different standards. Thus the voters of Quebec can consistently elect an anti-Liberal provincial government while yet returning Liberals to Ottawa. In Australia the extreme variations in the index result from the fact that, in the period under consideration, the Labour party has usually controlled the sum of the states. Hence the index is low when the Labour party controls the Commonwealth, and high when it does not. In Canada, however, the Liberal party has controlled the Dominion government throughout the entire period under consideration. All the extreme variations in the index result from voters making different judgments on the Liberal party in state and national elections held at different times.

All three of these institutional alternatives (two or more parties, few or many states, simultaneous or temporally separate state and national elections) may thus affect the variations and level of the index. And indeed it is quite possible that other institutional alternatives that have escaped our notice may also affect it considerably. In the absence of detailed empirical evidence, we cannot say what the relationship among these alternatives in their effect on the index may be. It seems likely, however, that a federalism with more than two significant parties, relatively few states, and a parliamentary government is almost certain to experience severe federal disharmony, especially if the constituent governments have anything important to do. The government of West Germany is just such a federalism. Although we have not calculated an index for this government, it appears from casual inspection that the Christian Democratic party has had a majority at Bonn and in the sum of the Länder. There are signs, however, that the majority in the Länder is now slipping away and hence it seems likely that this government will also soon find federalism as uncomfortable as it has been in Canada and Australia. From a German point of view at least, it is unfortunate that the German basic law was so blithely fashioned as a federalism without consideration of the potential disharmony to be faced. Perhaps, if West and East Germany are ever united, German constitution writers will have a second chance.

Even one minor reform might mitigate disharmony in federalisms of the sort here discussed: a provision that all legislatures in constituent governments be elected at the same time as the national legislature. In a parliamentary government, this proviso would require, of course, that a dissolution of the national legislature automatically entail a dissolution of all state legislatures. Lest dissolution in one state force a dissolution on the nation, state legislatures would, of course, be restrained from unseating a state ministry.

Conclusion

In comparison with Canada and Australia the index of federal disharmony in the United States has been neither as high nor as low. In the period under consideration, it has, with one exception, ranged in the area of .50 ± .10. American federalism might thus be described as consistently disharmonious at this level. While it is not disturbed by an index in the range of .80 to .90, it does not experience an index as low as .09. The Canadian and Australian governments, in their occasional periods of proximate harmony, are probably able to bring about necessary readjustments in the federal relation. In the United States, however, such opportunities are probably less frequent. Hence it may well be that, although the index never rises as high in the United States as elsewhere, the effect of consistent disharmony at the level of .50 ± .10 is fully as debilitating as occasional disharmony at the level of .88. It is apparent, however, that before we can discuss the effect of this consistent disharmony we need to project the index farther backward in time, perhaps as far back as the first appearance of the modern party system in the 1830s.

This chapter was undertaken in order to explain some of the institutional circumstances conducive to intergovernmental conflict. We have shown that partisan disharmony between central and constituent governments is (in the United States) related in quantity to one kind of actual conflict and we have set forth what we believe are sufficient reasons for assuming that partisan disharmony as indicated by the index is at the root of most intergovernmental conflict.

For this reason the index of disharmony has significance beyond the actual measurement it makes. Most American students of public law have in recent years tended to ignore or gloss over the amount of actual conflict in American and other federalisms. Perhaps they have unconsciously assumed that, since our federalism is apparently permanent, there is little point in examining its possible inadequacy. (Such an attitude involves, however, the abandonment of the critical function of scholarship and is, of course, ultimately a disservice to the institutions vacuously praised.) We think it likely, however, that the crucial reason our federalism is discussed in unrealistic terms is that political scientists have lacked a precise vocabulary to talk about conflict and disharmony. Still today, the predominant technique in the discussion of federalism is that of speculative philosophy, and juristic arguments devised in the 1780s are still seriously advanced as *descriptions* of federalism.

It is our hope that, by offering this index, some of the discussion may be rendered more precise. For example, in the hands of Professor Wheare, the definition and justification of federalism is reduced to an epigrammatic paradox when he says that federal government "stands for multiplicity in unity." The existence of a paradox is a sufficient indication of imprecise words that have no place in science or philosophy. If this sentence is, however, formulated in terms of the index of disharmony (e.g., "federal government in the United States in recent years has stood for disharmony at the level of .50 ± .10"), then the connotative approbation in the epigram is removed. Whether or not such a level of disharmony is desirable is still a legitimate question for empirical and interpretative inquiry, but the conclusion is at least not forced by the premises. More importantly, however, it is possible to speak precisely of just what unity and multiplicity are (i.e., an index of zero and an index of higher than zero). Once one can speak precisely, it is then at least possible that the vague mist heretofore shrouding discussions of the federal relation might be lifted.

Notes

1. "Minimal winning coalition" is defined as a coalition such that, if one member is subtracted, it ceases to be a winning coalition. In weighted majority games, in which members' votes have different weights, a "minimal winning coalition" is a coalition such that, if the last added member is subtracted, the coalition ceases to be a winning one.

2. In our calculations we have used each state's percentage of members in the House of Representatives, assuming that this percentage is politically more relevant than mere population.

3. In most states the constitutional rules on voting are the same as those in the national government. But these states vary in the following details: These states have no Lieutenant

Governor: Arizona, Florida, Maine, Maryland, New Hampshire, New Jersey, Oregon, Utah, and West Virginia. And in Massachusetts and Tennessee this officer does not preside over the upper house. In North Carolina the Governor has no veto and in the following states his veto can be overriden by a simple majority (rather than 2/3 majority) either of those present or of those elected: Alabama (except for 1945–1949), Arkansas, Connecticut, Indiana, Kentucky, New Jersey (up to 1949), Tennessee, and West Virginia. In Delaware, Maryland, Nebraska, Ohio, and Rhode Island the Governor's veto can be overriden by a 3/5 majority of those present or of those elected. (It was found impossible in the construction of the index to draw a distinction between a requirement involving those present and one involving those elected.)

4. Conservative Southern dissatisfaction has, of course, declined when the Democratic party has ceased to be the majority party in the national government. The observation in the text is limited to the period in which the Democratic party possessed a national majority.

5. In the calculation of the index for these countries an important change must be made in the method of calculation. In Australia, the cohesion of parties on roll calls is said to be exceptionally close (Miller, 1954, p. 92), although we know of no statistical studies of party discipline. In Canada, likewise, party cohesion is said to be quite close (Dawson, 1948, pp. 241ff.), although again we know of no statistical studies. When party cohesion in a legislature is high, then the model of a simple majority game is no longer appropriate. The legislature is more realistically interpreted as a game played, not by individuals but by parties with unequal voting power. Hence the appropriate model is a weighted majority game; and we have thus calculated the power indices for Canadian and Australian parties. (For the method of calculation, see the section by A. W. Tucker in Bradt, 1955). The change of method has this significance: If one party has an absolute majority of the legislature, then it has all the power and an index of one. If a party has less than an absolute majority, its index is less than one, but often quite disproportionate to its membership. In general, the largest and smallest parties have more power per member than their members would have in a simple majority game, and the medium-sized parties less. The effect of this mathematical characteristic is to occasion more violent fluctuations of the index of disharmony than were found in the United States; but as most students of Canadian and Australian federation would agree, this intensification of the movement of the index faithfully represents the temper of these constitutions.

5 THE MEASUREMENT OF AMERICAN FEDERALISM

William Paul Alexander, Jr.

Commentary. *The previous chapter in this part defined the index of disharmony and applied it to the interpretation of three federations. Unfortunately, the time span of the application was brief (only 18 years) which is short relative to the lives of constitutions. In Alexander's chapter, however, the time series has been lengthened to 130 years, about two-thirds of the life of the American Constitution. The index for this longer period permits us to see (and interpret) significant variations in its value, especially since we can compare it with a more conventional index (of expenditures) which Alexander constructed for the same time period.*

Nothing like these two lengthy time series has ever before been available to students of federalism. Their availability now permits a significant reevaluation of American federalism. We can see concurrent phenomena: on the one hand, centralization of administration and, on the other hand,

---

This chapter is based on William Paul Alexander, Jr., "Political Centralization in the Federalism of the United States" (Ph.D. dissertation, University of Rochester, 1973) and on Dr. Alexander's plans to revise it, made before his untimely death in 1974. The chapter in its present form is the work of William H. Riker, under whose direction Dr. Alexander prepared the dissertation.

random variations (neither centralizing nor decentralizing) of the political
structure.

The federal government invented in 1787 was a remarkable innovation
because it was based on a mixture—in about equal parts—of two distinct
organizing principles. One principle was the alliance, wherein important
political decisions are made locally or by agreements among member
governments, and the other was unitary government, wherein important
political decisions are made by the central government alone. Of course,
all federations contain both alliance and unitary features; but up to 1787
the alliance principle was invariably primary. The innovation at Philadelphia was to emphasize the unitary feature. So complicated and original
was the result that some of the framers themselves did not know what to
call it. (See Madison's comments in the Thirty-Ninth *Federalist*.) Since the
mixture was carefully balanced, almost all the great issues of American
politics have generated tension in the federal relation, perhaps affecting
thereby the relative importance of each principle. Hence, a central
question of constitutional commentary has always been whether or not one
principle is gradually excluding the other. The conventional answer is, of
course, that the unitary principle has eclipsed the alliance principle. In this
chapter, however, evidence is presented that the supposed centralization is
neither so certain nor so complete as many have supposed.

Forces Toward Centralization and Decentralization

It is, of course, true that there have been several major constitutional shifts
that seem to have centralized the system. One, which began almost
immediately after 1789, was the transformation of the Senate from its
(probably) intended function of representing state governments to its
modern function of forming simply another house of the legislature (Riker,
1955). By this transformation one main structural embodiment of the
alliance principle became an embodiment of the unitary principle.

Another such shift, possibly of greater significance, was the final
rejection, as a result of the Civil War, of state claims of the right to
overrule national legislation or to secede (e.g., the Virginia and Kentucky
resolves, the Hartford convention, the nullification controversy, and, of
course, the Civil War itself). Perhaps as a result of Appomattox, the only
subsequent such claim (for "inter-position"), raised briefly by segrega-
tionists in the 1950s, was squelched and ignored (Bennett, 1963). Perhaps,
however, the Civil War itself was the only serious effort at nullification,

and perhaps it failed because of the inherently half-unitary feature of the original Constitution.

A third and possibly most important shift toward centralization derived from the 150-year-long controversy over the place of blacks in the polity. Initially, the Construction left this matter up to the states, and surely one of the necessary conditions in 1787 for the retention of some of the alliance principle of the Articles of Confederation was that the South be allowed to deal with its peculiar institution in its own way (Lynd, 1967). Only thus could its politicians agree to the amount of centralization contained in the final document. To the extent, therefore, that the justification of the balanced mixture rested on the necessity of subordinating blacks, each step of the way toward equality for blacks has perhaps weakened the alliance feature and strengthened centralization (Riker, 1964, 1975).

A fourth major shift toward centralization has been the increase in the relative importance of the army and navy at the expense of the militia. The original intention of the framers was that, in true alliance fashion, the military function be divided up among the constituent and central governments, with the *main* authority in the former. (See Article I, Section 8, clauses 15–16, of the Constitution.) But after the disasters of the militia in 1812–1815 (especially the battle of Bladensburg), the states lost their grip on the sword, never to regain it (Riker, 1957).

It seems likely that if there have been major changes in our constitutional structure, these latter two forces are the most important ones, although they cannot be measured by the methods to be used in this chapter. The change in the militia occurred before measurement can begin, and the equality of the blacks has not yet had a chance to make an impact on the measure.

Of course, not all constitutional shifts have been in the same direction. The Tenth and Eleventh Amendments certainly reinforced the alliance principle, as did all the states' rights rhetoric of the nineteenth century and the creation of new states out of national territory. Nevertheless, the bulk of opinion seems to be that the alliance principle has been subordinated to the unitary principle. This is, for example, the overwhelming agreement among students of public law. Even though the lawyers' perspective is far too narrow to be of much value for serious study of constitutional structure—lawyers tend to rely on comments of judges who, however, seldom have occasion to analyze the really profound kind of constitutional change mentioned in previous paragraphs—still, for what it is worth, the legal tradition is to emphasize that the Supreme Court, as the supposed "arbiter of federalism," has expanded the functions of the national government at the expense of the states. It may well be inappropriate, however, to look at the formal allocation of functions as relevant to the political nature of federalism. To say that the central government has the authority to build dams and regulate wages may not mean much if states could not, for technological reasons, do either. Similarly, to say that the central government has the authority to prescribe welfare schemes may not mean much if the day-to-day administration of them is in the hands of the states.

The defect of the argument that the assignment of functions has increased centralization *and hence* diminished the significance of the alliance principle is revealed in the controversy over the interpretation of administrative behavior at the several levels of government. It may well be that the central government has more to do, but that in doing its duties it cooperates with the states rather than overshadowing them. This was the assertion of Morton Grodzins who devised the metaphor of a "marble cake, characterized by an inseparable mingling of different colored ingredients...in vertical and diagonal strands and unexpected whirls" (Grodzins, 1960, p. 265). His point was that "as colors are mixed in the marble cake, so functions are mixed in the American federal system." This theme was elaborated by Daniel Elazar with several case studies of intergovernmental cooperation in the nineteenth century (1962). In the subsequent 15 years, under the influence first of Johnson's "war on poverty" in which federal monies were administered by local organizations and under the "new federalism" of Nixon's revenue sharing, the theme of cooperative federalism has become a more or less constant refrain (Leach, 1970; and Sunquist, 1969). If this interpretation is correct, then the balance between the alliance and unitary principles has perhaps not changed greatly after all.

Still, for all the current enthusiasm for the flow of federal dollars to states in an apparently harmonious giving and taking, it is not at all clear that cooperative federalism is more than a temporary constitutional phenomenon. Certainly not all historians have accepted the Grodzins-Elazar thesis (Scheiber, 1966). And it may well be that all the brave talk about cooperation is no more than a polite gloss over the reality of the central government taking over most of the main functions of government.

An Economic Measure of the Federal Relation

The reason for our inability to decide whether or not the unitary principle has eclipsed the alliance principle is that we lack a measure on the relationship. Indeed, we are not even certain what feature of the relation ought to be measured.

One potential measure—which has seemed reasonable to several writers—is the ratio of expenditures by the central government to total expenditures by all governments (central, state, and local). The significance of this calculation is that it reveals which level of government is performing more duties. As has already been pointed out, however, the performance of functions may reveal very little about the political relation between levels of government. Perhaps one level is assigned a particular task because it has at the moment more readily available resources (as, for example, super-highways were assigned to the national government in the 1950s when the states were otherwise overburdened with educational costs, even though—as indicated by state toll roads—states could have done the job). Or again the cost of a particular task may increase significantly without adding to the political prestige and influence of the level of government doing it (as, for example, the cost of education has increased greatly in the last generation without enhancing the prestige of state and local government).

In short, since who does what may often be a matter of accident or of technological convenience, the measurement of administrative activity may be quite irrelevant to the political relation of federalism. Nevertheless, for what it is worth, we present two estimates of relative expenditures by levels of government. In table 5–1 is an estimate of the federal proportion of *domestic* governmental expenditures for selected years in the period from 1840 to 1962. Domestic (i.e., nonmilitary, noninternational) expenditures are used on the assumption that by 1840 the federal government completely dominated military and international expenditures which were, however, irregular and consequently distorting.[1]

Werner W. Pommerehne has made a similar calculation for the twentieth century, table 5–2, using the same sources, without excluding military-foreign aid expenditures and without including the value of physical grants. Table 5–2 also differs from table 5–1 in that transfers are

Table 5–1.   Federal proportion of domestic governmental expenditures, 1840–1962

Year	Federal proportion	Year	Federal proportion
1840	.16	1913	.24
1852	.22	1922	.34
1860	.13	1932	.30
1870	.33	1940	.49
1880	.28	1952	.45
1890	.31	1962	.49
1902	.27		

Table 5–2. Federal proportion of total governmental expenditures (excluding transfers), 1902–1971

Year	Federal proportion
1902	.34
1913	.30
1922	.40
1932	.33
1938	.46
1950	.58
1960	.58
1965	.55
1971	.48

recorded as expenditures by the recipient government while in table 5–1 they appear as expenditures by the granting government (Pommerehne, 1977).

The remarkable feature of these two series is their similarity up to 1940. Even the different treatment of nondomestic expenditures and transfers makes very little difference.

The tables diverge sharply after 1940, mainly because of the increased amount of military and foreign aid expenditures.

Unfortunately, table 5–2 offers no comparative data for the nineteenth century. Despite the absence of comparison, however, it is easy to see that there are three more or less distinct periods: 1) from 1840 to the Civil War, when the federal proportion varied roughly from one-sixth to one-fifth of total expenditure; 2) from the Civil War to the New Deal, when the federal proportion varied roughly from one-fourth to one-third; 3) from the New Deal to the present, when the federal proportion varied around one-half, or, including nondomestic expenditures, varied from one-half to three-fifths.

If one were to take seriously the belief that the expenditure of money truly represented the power of the purse and that the power of the purse in turn carried with it political control, then one would be compelled to say that political forces favoring the unitary principle have twice permanently reduced the significance of the alliance principle, during and after the Civil War and the New Deal, respectively. It may be, however, that neither antecedent is true. Expenditures may not truly represent functions. Furthermore, the power of the purse may be politically irrelevant simply because fiscal centralization or decentralizaion is not itself politically important.[2] If so, we need a better measure of federalism, and we turn now to that task.

A Political Measure of the Federal Relation

When the Articles of Confederation were centralized into the Constitution in 1787, the main reason for the retention of the alliance element was to make certain the central government could not dominate states. An appropriate measure on the federal relation is, therefore, some kind of indicator of the ability to dominate. If it can be shown that the central government has enhanced this ability, then surely our federalism has in some sense been centralized. But if this ability remains more or less constant, then it may well be that the original mixture of alliance and unitary elements persists.

To measure the ability to dominate is to measure power and, as political scientists know all too well, the notion of power is so confused that it cannot readily be measured. Nevertheless, while we probably cannot measure power in the abstract, we can in some cases perhaps measure power in relation to a particular situation. Such a concrete measure seems possible here.

One necessary condition for the officials of the central government to dominate the constituent governments is for the central officials to be leaders of an all-inclusive national-local group operating governments at both levels. If central officials cannot lead such a group, then they lack a mechanism to run both levels. Of course, various kinds of groups satisfy this condition: the army, political parties, and ad hoc factions. In some federations (e.g., Brazil), national officials use the army to dominate states. At the other extreme, in federations like Canada often the only domination—if it occurs at all—is via some ad hoc alliance, too temporary and issue-specific to be called a faction or a party (Simeon, 1972). In most federations, however, the instrument of central domination is a political party, either more or less in continuous use (as in Yugoslavia, in Mexico, or, until recently, in India) or in sporadic use (as in the United States or West Germany).

Since political parties are formally organized, it is easy to identify and in some sense to measure them. Hence, in those federations where it is appropriate, we can, by looking at the state of political parties, discover whether it is possible or not for central officials to dominate at the periphery. Of course, the fact that, in partisan terms, central officials *might* dominate does not imply that they *do* dominate. In the United States at least parties are often too ideologically diverse and too decentralized organizationally to admit domination. Still, whenever the instrument of domination is a political party, then, by measuring the degree of partisan harmony between the center and the periphery, we can discover whether or not a necessary condition of domination from the center exists, regardless of whether or not the domination actually occurs.

A possible measure, therefore, of the chance for central domination is the degree of partisan harmony between levels of government. If harmony is high, centralization is at least possible, though not necessarily existent. If harmony is, however, low, centralization simply cannot occur in a political system in which parties rather than military force or interlevel diplomacy are the instrument of domination.

An available technique to measure the degree to which a party controls both levels of government is the Shapley-Shubik power index (Shapley and Shubik, 1955).[3] This index is based on the notion that on any particular decision in a constitutional structure in which decisions are made by forming coalitions, the last added or pivotal member of a minimum winning coalition can influence the outcome more than anyone else. The intuitive justification for this assumption is 1) that winners influence decisions more than losers and 2) that, since among all members of a winning coalition the pivotal member is probably the most reluctant to join, he/she is therefore likely to be rewarded with the most influence for his/her accession. (Although this justification ignores many nuances—e.g., leaders seldom pivot and thus may be counted as less influential than followers—still, in a measure as gross as this one, these nuances may well cancel out.) Since constitutions typically prescribe methods for making decisions by voting processes, typically in legislatures (ignoring judicial and administrative decisions except when made by a committee), the Shapley-Shubik index (like almost all others) turns out to be a measure on voting, which means it is most useful as a measure of constitutional power for legislating. Altogether, then, the index is a measure of the expected chance for a particular official to pivot in the coalition formation in, typically, the legislative process of a motion or a committee.

To calculate this expectation, one must know the ways in which a minimum winning coalition may be formed. Conventionally, in this calculation, these ways are all the sequences in which participants both in and out of the minimum winning coalition might be arranged in a coalition forming event. (Thus, for an n-member committee the number of sequences is the number of permutations of n, that is $n!$, which is $1 \times 2 \times \ldots \times n$. Hence for the same winning coalition in the same sequence, the different arrangements of participants after the pivot count as different sequences. For example, if in a five-member body a winning coalition is members 2, 3, and 4, with 4 as the pivot, distinct sequences include, inter alia: (3,2,4,1,5), (2,3,4,1,5), and (2,3,4,5,1).) So the index is simply the ratio of the sequences in which a particular official would pivot to the total number of sequences (which is all possible pivots for all relevant officials). Thus, for an official, i, the definition of the power, P, of i is:

$$P_i = \frac{\text{number of sequences in which } i \text{ pivots}}{\text{total number of sequences (that is, } n!)}$$

As a ratio, $0 \le P_i \le 1$ and $\sum_{i=1}^{n} P_i = 1$. For the government of the United States, and for the assumption that the decision in question is legislation, $i = (1,2,\ldots,537)$, where the President (conditionally a third house if the majority in both other houses is less than two-thirds) is (1), the Vice-President (conditionally a member of the Senate) is (2), Senators are (3) to (102), and representatives are (103) to (537).

To use the Shapley-Shubik index to describe partisan harmony, Riker and Schaps (1957) devised an "index of disharmony," D, where disharmony is the base rather than harmony because of the original constitutional intent to provide for enough disagreement to preclude domination from the center. This index is derived thus: given P_i for officials of the national government, $i = 1, 2, \ldots, 537$, there is for each party, j, j belongs to J: {Democratic, Whig, Republican,...}, a power index, Π_j, in year t, which is the sum of the power of j's members, that is,

where $\Pi_{j_t} = \sum_{i \text{ in } j_t} P_i$. (Throughout, t is fixed; so hereafter it is suppressed to avoid confusion.) Since $\sum_{i=1}^{n} P_i = 1$, $\Sigma_j \Pi_j = 1$. For each state, k, k belongs to K: {1, 2,\ldots, m}, where m varies from 26 to 50 in the relevant time span, there is a value at time t for P_i, where i is a member of the set: {state legislators, governor, and, where appropriate, lieutenant governor}. Hence there is also an index $\Pi_{jk} = \sum_{i \text{ in } jk} P_i$, which is the power of party j in state k at time t. For each j at time t, there is an index of its power in all m states, Π_{jK}, where each state k in K is weighted in the index according to its weight in the national population at the last preceding census, that is, by a factor $\alpha_k = \dfrac{w_k}{\sum_{k \text{ in } K} w_k}$, where w_k is the

population of state k. Hence, the power index of the party as a whole in all
states is:

$$\Pi_{j\ K} = \sum_{k\ in\ K}\ \sum_{i\ in\ jk}\ \alpha_k\ P_i.$$

Finally, at time t, the index of disharmony, D, is: if $\Pi_j > .5$, then
$D = 1 - \Pi_{jK}$, which is, for the party j in control of the national government, the degree to which j controls or fails to control state governments.[4]

Since D is based on P_i, $0 \leq D \leq 1$. If $D > .5$, then party j controls the
national government and other party (or parties) control more than half
the states. Disharmony is "high" and there is presumably a serious barrier
to centralization.

In table 5–3 the index of disharmony is reported for each biennium
from 1837–1839 to 1967–1969, and the same measure is recorded
graphically in figure 5–1.[5] The measurement begins in 1837 because that is
the earliest year in which most officials identified themselves in terms of the
modern party system.

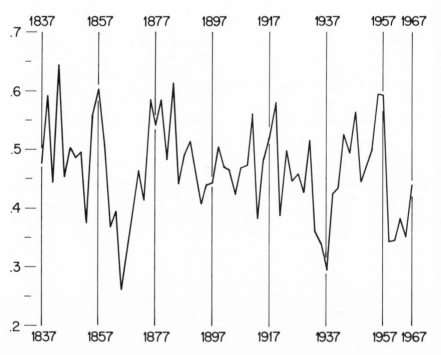

Figure 5–1.   Disharmony index, 1837–1969.

Table 5–3.   Disharmony index, 1837–1969

Year	Disharmony index	Year	Disharmony index
1837	.4771	1903	.4663
1839	.5934	1905	.4246
1841	.4428	1907	.4702
1843	.6434	1909	.4723
1845	.4564	1911	.5607
1847	.5033	1913	.3847
1849	.4875	1915	.4862
1851	.4910	1917	.5255
1853	.3761	1919	.5813
1855	.5561	1921	.3905
1857	.6046	1923	.4986
1859	.5083	1925	.4492
1861	.3681	1927	.4561
1863	.3980	1929	.4293
1865	.2605	1931	.5185
1867	.2660	1933	.3639
1869	.3904	1935	.3408
1871	.4655	1937	.2974
1873	.4167	1939	.4263
1875	.5872	1941	.4363
1877	.5433	1943	.5265
1879	.5868	1945	.4948
1881	.4840	1947	.5660
1883	.6133	1949	.4474
1885	.4419	1951	.4772
1887	.4921	1953	.5030
1889	.5156	1955	.5962
1891	.6530	1957	.5944
1893	.4065	1959	.3445
1895	.4429	1961	.3478
1897	.4456	1963	.3868
1899	.5054	1965	.3540
1901	.4702	1967	.4403

As de Tocqueville remarked, when he visited the United States early in the 1830s, the "great parties" (Federalist and Republican of the 1790s and early 1800s) by which "the nation was divided into two opinions" had disappeared and in their place stood "minor parties" so that the United States "swarms with lesser controversies" (1945, pp. 175–177). But Jackson was, at the very time de Tocqueville wrote, demarcating his friends and enemies into Democrats and Whigs, thereby making possible the use of D from 1837 onwards.

The notable feature of the record of D over 132 years is the relatively high average and the absence of any trend. Although the mean of Π_j is .63, the mean of D is only .47. These facts emphasize that while the party in control of the national government has, on the average, controlled it by over three-fifths, still that same party has, on the average, controlled just over half the states. This difference points up the truism that in a federation, it is a lot easier to get control of the center than of the periphery.

Furthermore, the trend of D is flat. The trend line fitted by ordinary least squares has a slope of $-.0008$ over the whole time span. Even in the recent period (the New Deal and after, with all the technological possibilities for centralization), the slope is only .0016. This fact indicates that despite periods of considerable centralization, such as the Civil War and the New Deal, there is no significant increase in centralization (or decentralization) over this whole era of 132 years. No party has been able to win general control of both levels of government for an extended period. Hence, national officials have lacked an instrument to dominate decision-making in the states. Presumably this is what the framers of the Constitution intended.

Since, unfortunately, this measure goes back only to 1837, it is not possible to know if the political relations of federalism had changed significantly in the preceding 50 years. Still we do know that some dramatic post-1837 events affecting federalism (e.g., the Civil War) have had no permanent effects on the index and that superficial events (e.g., the changing degree of administrative activity at the center) have not been visible in the index at all. If we dare to project backward the irrelevance for federalism of these events both profound and superficial occurring after 1837, we can infer that probably nothing significantly changed the constitutional structure between 1787 and 1837. If so, then the federation of the United States retains today about the same political character as it had in the beginning, namely a balanced mixture of the alliance and unitary principles.

The expenditure-administrative measure shows the central government growing at the expense of the states; the power measure shows the states acting as a persistent brake on centralization. Doubtless each index captures one feature of the federal relationship. The national government almost certainly does do relatively more work today than formerly; but that fact clearly says nothing about the degree of political centralization, which, despite wide swings, probably varies around the same equilibrium point as it did in the 1790s. Since the political relation is more significant for social decisions than the administrative relation, recent students of federalism have probably erred in emphasizing the new centralization and the new harmony. Political disharmony between states and nation seems to be one constant in our constitutional structure. For those who believe, with Madison, that freedom depends on countering ambition with ambition, this constancy of federal conflict is a fundamental protection of freedom.

Notes

1. Table 5–1 is taken from William Paul Alexander, Jr., "Political Centralization in the Federalism of the United States" (Ph.D. dissertation, University of Rochester, 1973), p. 9 and pp. 17–23. For this table, federal expenditures are from United States Bureau of the Census, *Historical Statistics of the United States*, for the twentieth century, series Y484 (federal expenditures) less Y494 (defense and international affairs), and, for the nineteenth century, from series Y350 less series Y351 and Y352. To these federal expenditures are added an estimate of the value of land grants, using as a shadow price the average price per acre of land sold by the United States in the decade surrounding the year of the grant. For table 5–1 the state and local expenditures come from *Historical Statistics* for the twentieth century: series Y536 (state and local expenditures) less series Y519 (federal transfers). Since *Historical Statistics* contains no nineteenth century series (owing to the belief that the data are unreliable), state and local expenditures in this era are estimated (with some heroic assumptions explained in Alexander, *op. cit.*, pp. 19–20) from *The American Almanac* 1842, 1854, and 1861, from *The Eighth Census*, vol. IV, p. 511, from the *The Ninth Census*, vol. III, pp. 11 and 16–27, from *The Report on Valuation, Taxation and Public Indebtedness in the Tenth Census*, pp. 25, 530, 537, 554, and 612, and from *The Report on Wealth, Debt, and Taxation in the Eleventh Census*, part II, pp. 441 and 464–474.

2. The suggestion that federalism is a kind of administrative decentralization and ought to be studied from the point of view of efficient administration derives in the recent literature mainly from Wallace E. Oates (1972), where the malapropism of "federal" as a synonym for "decentralized" is actually used, (p. 12). Oates appears to be wholly unaware that "federalism," both as a word and as a constitutional structure, has a political origin.

3. There are available a variety of power indices, based on different assumptions and not coinciding in measurement. See Riker (1964) for an analysis of the differences among some of the other measures and Nagel (1975) for an effort to reconcile some of these differences. The two indices most relevant for the current study are the Shapley-Shubik index and the Banzhaf index, set forth in Banzhaf (1965). Though it was formerly conjectured that these two indices gave similar results, Straffin (1977) conclusively demonstrates that they can on occasion give startlingly different results (previously unperceived). Unfortunately, there is no good a priori justification for preferring one to another. Hence, it is difficult to defend using any particular index as a measure of power. It is the case, however, that as Straffin observes, the Shapley-Shubik index accords fairly closely with our intuitive understanding of the national government, while the Banzhaf index does not. So, for the application offered here, the Shapley-Shubik index seems better, especially since the large number of situations compressed into one point (from 26 to 51 constitutional structures) and the large number of points measured (66) render it likely that the Shapley-Shubik index produces a credible result.

While it is certain that both indices (Banzhaf and Shapley-Shubik) increase the indicated power of the more heavily weighted of two groups more when one group is especially strong than when the groups are approximately equal, still this feature (which may or may not be regarded as distortion) is at least constant and is, therefore, irrelevant with respect to the use here. With these weak justifications, therefore, power is here measured by the Shapley-Shubik index.

4. The index, D, is constructed for a two-party or mainly two-party system, and for every year t under consideration there is some j such that $\Pi_j > .5$. In multiparty systems, it is necessary to use J as a set of possible coalitions so that D makes sense only if there is a governing coalition, j, such that $\Pi_j > .5$.

5. Data on party affiliation of national officials are from *Historical Statistics*. Data on state officials are in William Paul Alexander, Jr., pp. 56–148. For 1937–1969 those data come from the biennial volumes of the Council for State Governments, *The Book of The States*; for the earlier part of the twentieth century and the late ninteteenth century, they come mostly from official state manuals (e.g., blue books, etc.); for the earliest period, 1837 to the late nineteenth century, they come from local almanacs, newspapers, and other even more fugitive sources.

6 THE RELATION BETWEEN STRUCTURE AND STABILITY IN FEDERAL GOVERNMENTS

William H. Riker and Jonathan Lemco

Commentary. While the evidence in this chapter was initially worked out to investigate proposed reforms in Canada, it is applicable to federations generally. Our question is: What makes federations stable and hence long-lasting. We know very little (and probably can never know anything for certain) about the reasons for stability and longevity for constitutions as a class. But it is reasonable to ask about them for smaller categories of governments, those whose members seem to share a common type of downfall. Such is the case with federations which are prone, on the one hand, to dissolution into their constituent components and, on the other hand, to incorporation into a unitary empire. With respect to federations our question is: What constitutional features prevent either breaking up or complete centralization?

In this chapter we are mainly concerned with preventing dissolution, an emphasis that grows naturally out of our initial interest in Canada. Our first conclusion is hardly remarkable: Centralization (which can be defined only in very general terms) minimizes the chances both of dissolution and of

In 1980 Jon Lemco and I wrote this paper for a conference on Canadian reforms, which had been assembled by Eliot Feldman for the Brandeis-Harvard Seminar on Canada. The conference volume failed of publication. Having excised the topical references to Canada, we now publish it here for the first time.

imperial unification. That is, centralization renders dissolution difficult and further unification unnecessary. Our additional conclusions are more interesting: There is a close association between stability and longevity, on the one hand, and a large number of constituent units, roughly equal in size, on the other hand. We are far from certain that this association is causal, though there is some rationale that this feature encourages stability: A large number of similar constituent units may both remove the possibility that one overweening unit desert or conquer the rest and simultaneously discourage small units from abandoning the protection of a large federation. Still the relation is clearly not necessary (viz., Australia with few units and one very large one seems quite stable). Nor is the relation sufficient: German federalism with many units, none overweening, has been through three incarnations in the last century.

These features seem, however, to have stabilized the United States. It was easy in 1788 for Rhode Island and North Carolina to think of going alone, and in 1861 11 states attempted to secede, but in both cases secession turned out to be impossible. Having survived these tests, this federation, with many roughly equal states, seems quite stable.

Much of the world is ruled by federal governments, but many federations have been quite unstable. Indeed more than half of the federations formed in modern times have fallen apart, and nearly all have had secessionist movements, as, for example, Quebec's proposal to separate from Canada. The world has accumulated so much experience with the survival and dissolution of federations that it is now possible to examine those processes analytically and to formulate generalizations about them. That is what we will do in this chapter.

Our main intention is to identify those constitutional features more or less regularly associated with the stability and instability of federations. An example of the kind of proposition we intend to investigate is: "Stable federations usually have a large number of constituent units while unstable ones do not." Even though we develop and support such propositions, however, we will not then be able to say, *for certain*, that an associated feature, like the number of constituent units, is the *cause* of stability or instability. Macropolitical processes are typically too large and unwieldy for us to isolate cause and effect (Riker, 1959). And mere statistical association does not reveal whether one feature is the cause of another or whether they are joint effects of some other antecedent. Still the association does, at minimum, tell us that a federation is in trouble when it displays one or more features linked with instability—regardless of whether the link is interpreted as causal or merely symptomatic. Furthermore, we can even learn something about the depth of the trouble from observing the number, displayed by the federation, of more or less independent features associated with instability.

This is to be our fundamental enterprise. But beyond the discovery of associations, we can perhaps use the byproducts of the scientific investigation to assess the value of reforms proposed to remedy instability. In order to discover constitutional features associated with stability and instability we need a theory about the nature and operation of federalism. To the degree that our theory leads to (even partially) credible discoveries, we are encouraged to believe that it does indeed reveal essential attributes of federalism. If we are confident about its credibility, we can then use it to discriminate among proposed reforms, selecting those relevant to the essential attributes and rejecting irrelevant ones.

Centralization and Stability

At the outset we examine one feature said to be of overwhelming, though possibly indefinable, significance. This is the degree of centralization about which it is often asserted: the more centralized a federation, the more likely it is to be stable. The notion of centralization is, admittedly, difficult to define because it has come to mean so many different things. We will try to keep it reasonably simple, however, by using it to refer to gross constitutional differences. To do so, we define centralization with respect to a scale on which we order all the constitutional devices for combining constituent governments. At one end we place the most decentralized combinations (like military alliances). In the middle are various kinds of federations in which constituent governments, though continuing to be autonomous in some matters, acknowledge the authority of a central government. And at the other end are unitary governments in which subordinate units have no autonomy at all and are mere administrative agents of the center. Those federations close to the alliance end of the scale we call peripheralized, and those closer to the unitary end we call centralized. Then the proposition under consideration is that federations near the centralized extreme are more likely to be stable than ones near the peripheralized extreme.

There are good theoretical reasons why it should be true. Federations are a step beyond military alliances on the scale of centralization and, invariably, one reason that framers of federal constitutions have taken this step is to improve their capacity to wage war (Riker, 1964, 1975). By analogy, once a federation is formed, the inspiration for further steps along the road toward the centralized extreme is probably also military.[1] The rationale is: To fight war well, even to threaten to fight well, a government must be able to coordinate the goals and direct the actions of the officials of its constituent units. And for this, a centralized federation is better than a peripheralized one. So it is entirely expected that centralized federations be more stable simply because they are typically better able to accomplish what federations are formed for in the first place.

Furthermore, even after federations have lasted so long that the initial conditions and initial motives are no longer relevant, even after the conditions and motives for increases in centralization are no longer relevant, one would expect centralized federations to be more stable. What allows them to remain centralized is the fact that in the initial and centralizing periods they did succeed as centralized federations. They are likely, thus, to have moderated provincial loyalties, which are the main political motive and justification for peripheralized federation.

New or old, centralized federalisms should, by reason of these theoretical considerations, be more stable than peripheralized ones. But the association is not perfect. There are contrary instances such as Switzerland, which, while far more centralized than it once was, is still not nearly so centralized as its neighbors, Austria and West Germany. Yet Switzerland has clearly been more stable in this century than its two federal neighbors. It cannot be said, therefore, that centralization causes stability. Instead, if there is a relationship, it must be that the forces making for stability often also induce centralization. If so, one would expect to find stability and centralization together most of the time in the real world.

This is indeed what we do find, as indicated in the later section, although we are not entirely sure we can define exactly what we have found or that we have explained very much. The problem is that "centralization" and "peripheralization" are very complicated and ill-defined notions. In a very gross way, we can indeed see a clear difference between these categories. For example, very few scholars would disagree that the United States under the Constitution of today is farther from the peripheralized extreme than was the United States under the Articles of Confederation. Still, it is difficult to make finer discriminations. Is the Canada of, say, 1900 more or less centralized than the Canada of 1980? We do not know, and most of our difficulty is that we do not know how to measure federalism (Alexander, 1987). If, for some current federations, one looks simply at constitutional provisions, Canada, for example, seems more centralized than the United States. If one looks simply at administrative structures and taxation and expenditures, then Canada and the United States seem similar—less centralized than Britain or France, more centralized than Switzerland. It one looks simply at ethno-geographic cleavages, then Canada, with a striking division on language and culture, seems peripheralized in comparison with the United States. Comparing Mexico with the United States in the same way, by some standards one seems more centralized and, by other standards, the other. So it is, we think, with many pairs of federations.

Given this ambiguity, we cannot be quite sure what we have asserted when we say that centralized federations are likely to be stable. So it seems worthwhile to analyze the effect on (or association with) stability of less ambiguous and more easily defined features of federal constitutions. Our theory will be less grand, but perhaps more testable.

Constitutional Structure and Stability

Other features of federations that many publicists have believed were influences on the degree of stability are: 1) the presence or absence of exceptionally large constituent units; 2) the number of constituent units; 3) the presence or absence of cultural or ethnic cleavages expressed in language differences, especially when the language differences are regional; 4) the degree of prosperity of the federation; and 5) the degree of political freedom in the federation and its units.

Many other features besides these are conceivably relevant and have been discussed by constitutional interpreters; but we confine ourselves to the analysis of these fairly specific properties of constitutions because they are precisely defined and easily measurable. The arguments offered about each of them and our a priori judgments on the validity of these arguments, are as follows:

1. *Large Units*: One of the main constitutional problems in federations from antiquity onwards has been the disproportionate size (in population or wealth or military power) of one or two units. Many federations exhibit this feature, often because they are a more intimate form of the military alliance built around one leading unit. Whatever the cause, however, differences in size occasion differences in expectations. Large units, by reason of their size, expect to have greater influence on decisions than small units have; small units, by reason of their sovereignty, expect equality of influence. A classic instance of this kind of dispute is the controversy in the Philadelphia Convention of 1787 between the large and small states. In the Canadian federation this kind of dispute is part of the controversy between the West and Ontario (and, in a different way,

Quebec). The differing expectations of large and small units clearly conflict, and often the resulting controversy threatens the stability of the federation. When it is the influence of small units (rather than large ones) that seems impaired by federation, a typical resolution is a guarantee, as in the Constitution of the United States, of equal representation (and territorial integrity) for small units. Alternatively, small units may secede, as happened in the abortive United Arab Republics. When, however, a swarm of small units seems to impair internal authority in a large unit, one typical resolution is for it to separate, causing the federation to collapse (as happened in the British West Indies) and another is for it to conquer the smaller units turning the federation into an empire (as happened in the ancient Delian League and in contemporary Indonesia). Besides Quebec in Canada, we do not know of any other instance in which a large unit has sought special guarantees; but there is nothing in the abstract situation of a large unit that precludes this kind of resolution. Altogether, the variety of resolutions (as well as the occurrence of extreme resolutions like secession and conquest) testify to the intensity of those federal disputes occasioned by the existence of very large units.

Since there are good theoretical reasons for the presence of "oversize" units to be closely associated with instability and since, empirically speaking, the association is ubiquitous, we expect to be able to support the proposition that federations with one or two very large units are more unstable than those with units roughly equal in size.

2. *The Number of Units*: Most federations start out with a few units. Switzerland started with 3, the United Netherlands with 7, the United States with 13, Canada with 4, etc. If a federation succeeds, it often grows by adding new units or at least new territory. But the initial years, before new units are added, are often dangerous ones. As a very close form of military alliance, new federations are subject to the same ills as alliances, namely, their members' conclusion that the combination does not add enough to their military strength to justify the loss of freedom of action. It is easy to come to this conclusion when there are only a few units, especially if the initial military threat or opportunity has receded in importance. And when this conclusion is reached, secession can follow soon thereafter.

But if a federation succeeds enough to attract new members or to conquer new territory out of which new members can be made, then the calculation about secession is quite different. To contrast the calculations, when there are only a few units, the potential secessionists are likely to think they are almost as strong militarily outside the federation as in. Sometimes the secessionists may even think they are stronger outside because by means of secession they can eliminate internal disputes that cause irresolution and weakness. When there are numerous units, however, the secessionists are likely to think that they will be much weaker when standing alone. It was considerations of this sort that, in 1947, drove the native states, especially Kashmir and states in Punjab, into either India or Pakistan. Clearly, with other concerns held constant, the calculation for secession is more likely to be positive in a federation with few units than in one with many units. The War of the Rebellion suggests the contrary, for there were 32 states in 1861; but the isolation of North Americans from the armies of Europe and the considerable military strength demonstrated in the Mexican war doubtless led the secessionists to believe that no foreign government threatened an independent Confederacy.

There is thus a good theoretical reason for federations with few units to be more subject to dissolution than those with many units, though the force of this condition depends very much on the kind of foreign dangers. In the case of a federation like Canada, where there is no perceptible military threat to Quebec (except possibly from Ottawa and Ontario) it is likely that Quebec is in no more danger outside than inside. Hence, holding other considerations constant, it has no military reason to remain in the federation. Since we know by observation that many other secessionist movements have arrived at a similar conclusion, we expect to be able to support the proposition that the fewer the units, the more unstable is the federation.

3. *Language Difference*: The two previously discussed properties of federations are part of their formal, written consitutions. Language differences are part of deeper, unwritten constitutions that have nothing to do with federation as such. No one doubts that language differences are an important source of discord wherever they exist and regardless of whether the countries are federations. Language differences are inextricably related to ethnic, tribal, and religious cleavages, and it is usually impossible to say which cleavage—language, culture, tribe, or religion—is the fundamental source of the discord. Nevertheless language differences, whether a cause of cleavage or simply a convenient sign of cleavage, are clearly related to cleavage and hence also probably related to instability.

Since language differences are a feature of the constitution in the broadest sense, one would expect them to be related to instability in all kinds of governments whether federal or not. Such is the case. Unitary governments like Spain, Belgium, South Africa, etc., are just as plagued with disputes partially expressed as conflicts over language as are federations like Canada and India. Nevertheless, even though not a specific disease of federalism, language disputes might well be expected to exacerbate federal issues. Very likely, federal constitutions are often adopted (or, more accurately, retained) in order to moderate the intensity of disputes represented by language—such is sometimes said to be the case in Switzerland—and federalism may in fact so moderate. Still this does not preclude the possibility that the language differences may be closely associated with instability. One might expect further that when these differences are coincident with provincial boundaries, the federal-linguistic disputes would be intensified and reinforced.

But one should not expect too close an association between language differences and federal instability. Canadians have, we think, falsely attributed their troubles to such an association. They have used the euphemism "bilingualism" (and "biculturalism") to describe the issue between Quebec and the rest of Canada. But to the outsider, this dispute seems to root at least as much in the ancient, unreconciled conquest, which has very little to do with differences in language or culture. If the fundamental issue is a regional hostility, originated in the conquest of 1763 and perpetuated by two centuries of political and economic domination, then the language and cultural difference is at most a superficial rallying cry. To the degree that elsewhere in the world, linguistic disputes are similar, the association between them and instability of federal constitutions is purely accidental and hence unlikely to be close.

Such is what we observe in unitary governments, which are similarly plagued with linguistic, tribal, and ethnic differences. Sometimes these differences occasion civil war; sometimes not. So it is also with federations. We expect, therefore, that we will at best only weekly support the proposition that linguistic differences are associated with federal instability. Too many and too complex forces are at work in this relation to be summarized accurately into either a literary or a statistical one-sentence generalization.

4. *Degree of Wealth*: It has often been suggested that wealthy countries, whether federal or unitary, are more stable than poor ones, presumably because in a rich society, people are both happy with the status quo and unwilling to disturb it, while in a poor society, people are exactly the opposite. The converse proposition, that rich societies are unstable, is just as defensible, however, presumably because the very fact of prosperity may well encourage revolutionaries to believe that revolution is worthwhile.[2] The empirical evidence is just about as equivocal as the arguments: witness the vast and inconclusive literature on revolution and rising expectations. We expect, therefore, to support only weakly the proposition that poverty or wealth is associated with federal instability. Nevertheless, since some such relation has often been posited, we feel obliged to investigate it.

5. *Freedom*: A final assertion about stability, commonly met within the popular press but seldom in the professional literature, is that governments of free societies are more stable than oppressive governments. Casual inspection of political experience leads one to doubt this assertion. For every free country with a stable government there seems to be an equally stable despotism. The stable United States is matched by the stable Soviet Union. Or the stable Malaysia is matched by the stable Burma. Conversely, for every unstable free government, there seems to be an equally unstable despotism, as exemplified by the five relatively short-lived Brazilian regimes in the last half-century. Since there seems little association between freedom and stability in governments generally, we do not expect to find it in the subclass of federations. Nevertheless, since the assertion is often made that freedom and stability are related, we feel obliged to test it out.

The Analysis of Evidence

In order to examine these possible relations between institutional structure and stability, we need to measure the effect of structures on stability in a variety of federations. To do so we have looked at the 40 federations that have existed, even briefly, from 1798 to the present. (We chose 1798 as the beginning point in order to include the United Netherlands which existed, officially, from 1577 to 1798.) The other 39 include nations in North America (Canada, pre- and post-Civil War United States, and Mexico), Latin America (Grand Columbia, Venezuela, Argentina, and Brazil), Africa, Europe (Switzerland, United Netherlands, Germany, Austria, Yugoslavia, Soviet Union) and Asia (India, Pakistan, etc.). See the Appendix for a complete list.

The dependent variable, "stability," is measured by dividing the degrees of stability of federations into three classes: 1) stable, 2) partially stable, and 3) unstable. All failed federations (which do not now exist because they were, like the British West Indies or the United States of 1787–1861, broken up into their constituent units, or because they were, like Nigeria or Indonesia, transformed into unitary governments) are included in the unstable category. Federations still in existence are categorized as either stable or partially stable according to whether or not they are at this time (1980) threatened by separatism, secession or civil war. Stable was coded "0," partially stable "1," and unstable "2."

The independent or structural variables, with which we will attempt to explain stability, include centralization, size and number of units, etc., as suggested by the theories of federalism set forth in previous sections. The most important independent variable, "centralization," was analyzed separately from the others because of its all-inclusiveness and because of our inability to measure degrees of centralization precisely with the available evidence. We distinguished between centralized and peripheralized federations, mainly by our own rough judgment, and thus generated a dichotomous variable which could be related in both a bivariate and multivariate analysis to degrees of stability. Centralized was coded "1" and peripheralized "0."

Our other independent variables included:

1.   The number of constituent units, as measured by counting units in each federation and dividing the federations into three groups: those with 2–5 constituent units (coded "1"), 6–11 units (coded "2"), and 12–50 units (coded "3"). A trichotomous rather than dichotomous categorization was used in order to minimize the influence of especially large or especially small federations on the entire analysis.

2.   The presence or absence of "oversized" constituent units, as measured by whether one or two constituent units were large enough (in terms of population) to attempt to dominate the federation or secede from it. The dichotomous variable "oversize" (coded "1") or "not oversize" (coded "0") was defined precisely as oversize if one or two provinces had twice the population of the next largest province; and otherwise, "not oversize."

3.   Language cleavage, as measured by the existence of two or more significant language groups. This is also a dichotomous variable, defined as a cleavage (coded "1") if two or more languages are widely spoken, otherwise not (coded "0"). If a majority speaks one language, a second language is defined as "widely spoken" if 20% of the population uses it. If no language is spoken by a majority, then a language cleavage exists.

4.   The degree of "wealth" of federations as measured by defining a "rich" federation (coded "1") as one in the top half of the countries of the world ranked according to income at the time the federation existed, and by defining "not rich" (coded "0") as one in the bottom half of the same list. In part the categorization for this dichotomous variable could be derived from easily available data (e.g., gross national product (GNP) as collected by the United Nations); but in part also the categorization was subjective and tentative. Evidence for the categorization of the United Netherlands, for example, was sketchy at best.

5.   The degree of freedom, our final independent variable, as measured by the definition of freedom and the categorization of nations as "free" (coded "2"), "partly free" (coded "1"), or "not free" (coded "0") by

Freedom House (Gastil, 1978). Since the annual survey by Freedom House covers only those federations now in existence, we followed the Freedom House methods to categorize federations that had failed. We arrived thereby at a trichotomous variable.

The first technique of analysis was a simple cross-tabulation of each of the independent variables and stability. As is apparent from an inspection of table 6–1, there is a positive association between each variable and stability.

It is worth noting that Tau B or Tau C is significant at least at the .01 level for all the variables and, most importantly, our cross-tabulation of the number of units and stability revealed that 9 of 10 of those federations with between 2–5 provinces failed entirely, while 13 of 19 with 12–50 units are stable or partly stable. Similar results were realized for our independent variable "oversize." Those federations that had no oversized constituent unit were far more likely to be stable than those with an "oversized" one.

It must be noted, however, that in such a pairwise analysis as this, excessive bias is a real hazard. Some independent variables may appear to contribute to stability only because other variables, which might supercede them, are not included in the comparison. Hence, impressive as the cross-tabulations are, further statistical analysis seems appropriate. To reduce the inherent bias, we conducted a discriminate analysis on our variables other than centralization. Discriminate analysis tests the ability of a set of independent variables to predict correctly the classification in the trichotomy (or groups) of the dependent variable for each of our 40 countries. A canonical discriminant function, a multivariate analysis, revealed that the independent variables could discriminate to at least the .0066 level and explain 91% of the variance between groups. In addition, our analysis was able to predict or classify 30 out of the 40 federal cases on its first try and 6 of the remaining 10 on the second. Only 4 of the remaining 40 cases were not accurately classified on the basis of the discrimination functions extracted.

The standardized canonical discriminant function coefficients (as indicated in table 6–2) are important because each coefficient represents the relative contribution of its independent variable to the discrimination into categories on the dependent variable. The interpretation is analogous to the interpretation of beta weights in multiple regression. It is clear that the number of constituent units and "oversized" units are the most important discriminating variables.

A test of significance, appropriate, of course, only for samples and not, as here for entire populations, is Wilks Lambda, which we offer as an

Table 6-1.   Bivariate associations with stability

Centralization:[a]	Centralized	Not centralized
Stable	11	2
Partly Stable	1	4
Not stable or ended	5	17

Kendall Tau B significance level: .0003.

Number of constituent units:	2-5	6-11	12-50
Stable	0	3	9
Partly stable	1	4	4
Not stable or ended	9	4	6

Kendall Tau C significance level: .0016.

Oversized units:	No	Yes
Stable	7	5
Partly stable	2	7
Not stable or ended	2	17

Kendall Tau B significance level: .017.

Language cleavage:	No	Yes
Stable	8	4
Partly stable	2	7
Not stable or ended	4	15

Kendall Tau B significance level: .009.

Rich:	No	Yes
Stable	5	7
Partly stable	5	4
Not stable or ended	17	2

Kendall Tau B significance level: .002.

Free:	No	Partly	Yes
Stable	3	3	6
Partly stable	2	5	2
Not stable or ended	11	4	4

Kendall Tau B significance level: .002.

[a] While this table concerns an entire population rather than a sample, so that significance tests are inappropriate, still an informal way of appreciating the obviously high degree of association between centralization and stability is to note that, were this a sample, the Kendall Tau B level of significance (that is, the probability the association is by chance) would be .0003.

Table 6–2.   Standardized canonical discriminant function coefficients (A) and level of significance of Wilks Lambda (B)

	(A)	(B)
Number of constituent units[a]	−0.59233	.008
Oversized units[b]	0.42337	.011
Language cleavage[c]	0.37429	.021
Rich[d]	−0.30190	.013
Freedom[e]	−0.19417	.126

[a] Since the values for stability increased with instability (0,1,2) and the values for constituent units increased with the number of units, the negative sign means that the smaller the number of units the greater the instability.

[b] Since values for oversized units were coded (0) no, (1) yes, the positive sign means that stability is associated with no oversized units.

[c] The positive sign represents an association between increasing instability and increasing number of languages.

[d] The negative sign represents the inverse relation between instability and becoming rich, i.e., prosperity and stability are associated.

[e] The negative sign represents an inverse relationship between increasing instability and increasing freedom, i.e., stability and freedom are (slightly) associated.

informal suggestion of the meaning of the association. It showed that all of our independent variables, with the exception of freedom, could discriminate between groups to at least the .02 level. Clearly freedom is not a useful variable for discriminating degrees of stability, although the others, especially the number of units, probably are, when taken together.

Discrimination analysis does not isolate the effect of individual independent variables on stability, however, and with that in mind we conducted a regression analysis on the variables. (See table 6–3.) An analysis of centralization alone resulted in this relationship:

$$\text{Stability} = \alpha + \beta x_1$$

or $Y = 1.68 - 1.03x_1$

(0.24) . . . . Standard Error

Where Y = Stability on a scale from 0 (stable) to 2 (unstable):

x_1 = Centralization on a scale from 0 (not centralized) to 1 (centralized)

β = the normalized coefficient of x_1

α = a constant.

Thus a unit change in x_1, for example, decentralizing by going from 1 (centralized) to 0 (peripheralized), would lead us to expect a 1.03 negative

Table 6–3. Regression analysis of variables

Name of variable	Beta	F-score	Significance[a]
Centralization	0.56253[b]	18.517[b]	.001[b]
Number of units	−0.28836	6.521	.01
Oversize units	0.27057	2.696	.05
Language cleavage	0.15110	1.735	Not significant
Rich	−0.18121	1.396	Not significant
Freedom	−0.05392	0.476	Not significant

[a] If the analysis had been conducted on a sample rather than a whole population, an F-score of 3.61 would be significant at the .01 level.

[b] This equation related only centralization, and not the other independent variables, to stability.

change in Y, that is, a change from stable (0) to partly stable (1) or from partly stable (1) to unstable (2). This inverse relationship is obviously very strong (almost one to one) and r, the correlation coefficient between the variables, is −.56. Were this the analysis of a sample rather than a universe, the association would be significant at the .001 level. As centralization is so difficult to measure, however, we conducted a regression analysis on our remaining variables, some of which are doubtless features of centralization, and found a close association between stability and the number of constituent units (an association that would be significant at the .01 level), and between stability and "oversized" units (an association that would be significant at the .05 level). The remaining three independent variables were not closely associated with stability.

Our evidence suggests, therefore, that the more centralized a federation the more likely it is to be stable, that the more units it has, the more likely to be stable, and that without an exceptionally large province it is likely to be stable. Presumably, a small federation (in terms of units) with a large province is likely to be unstable. It is vital to stress, however, that this strong association is not necessarily a causal relationship.

There is, however, one extremely strong and important negative result: Language cleavage, prosperity, and freedom are *not* important for stability. From now on these variables ought to be ignored in discussions of stability.

Finally, we conducted several tests to detect multicollinearity and determine the degree of bias. (See table 6–4.) The most notable test was a measure of the partial r_j^2 (where r_j^2 is defined as the squared multiple correlation coefficient of the jth independent variable on all other independent variables, which was intended to discover if any pair of the

Table 6-4. Test for the presence of multicollinearity

Variable	r_j^2
Number of units	.163
Oversize units	.235
Language cleavage	.376
Rich	.336
Freedom	.204

several independent variables were measuring the same thing (Lemieux, 1978). Omitting centralization (which is, of course, a summary of many variables) our remaining variables had partial r^2 ranging from .163 to .376, which by any standard are fairly low degrees of correlation and hence low degrees of multicollinearity. Since none of the scores appears to distort the analysis severely, we infer that we did not measure the same thing with our several independent variables other than centralization (Deegan, 1979).

Altogether, we have observed clearcut evidence of an association between stability and centralization, between stability and numerous units, and between instability and "oversize" units. Our results are thus especially illuminating for the case of Canada, because it has the exceptionally large provinces of Ontario and Quebec within a comparatively small number (10) of constituent units. Canada has had, of course, its periods of intense instability. Perhaps what has saved it from collapse is that it has two large units balancing each other, rather than just one large unit.

Conclusion

The statistical investigation on the whole confirms our expectations. Centralization and stability are indeed closely related, though our estimate of centralization is so subjective that we are not quite sure what the relationship means. Despite our uncertainty, however, the association means something because our scale for measuring centralization is macroscopic. Surely very few observers would dispute that the Soviet Union is more centralized than Canada and that Canada is more centralized than the West Indian Federation was. Since many of the judgments in the analysis are as indisputable as these, the high degree of association of stability with centralization cannot be lightly dismissed. Canada has had, of course, its periods of intense instability, even though only in the middle of this triple. Perhaps, as we just observed, what saved it is two large units balancing each other, rather than just one. Nevertheless two large units (Jamaica and Trinidad) did not save the West Indian Federation.

More significant, perhaps, is our discovery about particular constitutional features. While our conclusion about centralization combines 40 observations in one regression equation, thus summarizing a huge amount of constitutional experience into one sentence, it may be that some readers will reject our criticism because, as we freely admit, our judgments on centralization are subjective. For that reason, therefore, we have looked at other, more objectively measurable properties of constitutions. And from that observation—also of over 40 federations—we derive similar criticism. Small numbers of units and oversized units indicate real dangers for federations. On the other hand, language cleavages, poverty or wealth, and political freedom or repression do not have much to do with longevity.

This fact premits us to conclude with some comments on the current revision of federal constitutions. The great effort in Canada to placate Francophones, while immediately successful, is probably misdirected. They may have moderated, for the moment, Quebeckers' disillusionment, but there is no reason to suppose that the long-term stability of the regime has been strengthened. Perhaps Canadians should seize the current opportunity to break up Ontario and Quebec into several provinces each. By contrast, Nigerians, whose federation is near collapse and who are therefore more desperate, have perhaps reformed correctly for the long run. They are dividing up states and increasing the number of them rapidly. If the Nigerian federation, which lacked a very good military-diplomatic reason for existence, survives at all, this increase in the number of states may be what saves it.

Appendix

A Listing of the Federations

1. Argentina (1853–)	7. Burma (1948–62)
2. Australia (1901–)	8. Cameroon (1961–72)
3. Austria (1919–)	9. Canada (1867–)
4. Austria-Hungary (1867–1918)	10. Central African (1953–63)
5. Brazil (1946–)	Federation
6. British West Indies (1958–62)	(Rhodesia and Nyasaland)

11. Chile	(1826–27)
12. Colombia (Grand)	(1819–1830)
13. Congo (Leopoldville)	(1960–69)
14. Czechoslovakia	(1938–)
15. Ethiopia	(1952–62)
16. Germany-Prussia	(1867–1919)
17. Germany-Weimar	(1919–1933)
18. Germany-Federal Republic	(1949–)
19. India	(1950–)
20. Indonesia	(1949–50)
21. Iraq and Jordan	(1958)
22. Libya	(1951–63)
23. Malaya	(1957–63)
24. Malaysia (Singapore)	(1963–65)
25. Malaysia (Without Singapore)	(1965–)

26. Mali	(1959–60)
27. Mexico	(1917–)
28. Nigeria	(1960–)
29. Pakistan	(1947–)
30. Switzerland	(1848–)
31. United Arab Republic (2 units)	(1958)
32. United Arab Republic (3 units)	(1958–61)
33. United Netherlands	(1579–1798)
34. Union of Soviet Socialist Republics	(1918–)
35. United States	(1776–1861)
36. United States	(1865–)
37. Uganda	(1962–67)
38. Venezuela	(1860–)
39. South Yemen (South Arabia)	(1959)
40. Yugoslavia	(1946–)

Notes

1. This appears to be the case for the United States. Assume that an appropriate measure of centralization is in terms of the proportion of governmental income received by central government as distinct from constituent and local governments (that is, the larger the proportion of total income for central government the nearer to the centralization extreme of the scale). Since the 1830s there have been two notable long-term and permanent increases in the central government share of total governmental income: in the decade of the Civil War and in the decade of World War II. Each involved a large increase, which was maintained in subsequent decades. See the chapter by Alexander, "The Measurement of American Federalism."

2. Many Quebeckers have said to us, in explanation of their extreme position: "This is the first time in its history that Quebec has been rich enough to go it alone." If what they say is more than a local wisecrack, we would expect to find some association between wealth and instability.

III FEDERAL INSTITUTIONS

The primary problem in this book is to estimate the amount of change in American federalism. Has the initial federal balance between alliance and empire been self-perpetuating and fairly stable or has it been progressively centralizing?

As reflected by our treatment of the United States in chapter 6, where we categorized it as unstable prior to 1865 and stable thereafter, American federalism has gone through one searing test. The justification for treating it as unstable prior to 1865 is that the threat of dissolution was almost continuously present from soon after the end of the War of 1812 until the end of the Civil War. A profound military threat from abroad initially occasioned federalism in 1776 and was one main rationale for the Constitution. This threat continued throughout the period 1790 to 1815, as partisan division over the choice of allies (i.e., French or British) led ultimately to the War of 1812 and the second British invasion of the United States. Throughout its 30-year duration the British threat stabilized the American federation, repressing all thoughts of secession.

But the War of 1812 ended inconclusively: While the British

dominated militarily, they were not able to win decisively. Thereafter, as the United States continued to grow in wealth and population, the threat from Britain receded. Hence also, the military necessity of federation declined, and by the time of the nullification movement of 1830, it was possible for reasonable men to adopt a position that implied secession. From then until secession actually occurred in 1861, the threat of secession was always in the background. Consequently, we labeled American federalism unstable in that period.

In so doing we may well have erred. As it turned out the attempted secession failed, mainly because the national government was strong and determined. This suggests that, despite the appearance of instability, this centralized federalism was constitutionally endowed with the authority to maintain itself.

Regardless of the interpretation, the failure of the Southern confederacy effectively prohibited future secession, so that the system has since surely been stable in the sense that it could not dissolve. But, of course, it might become unitary, as did Britain in the Act of Union. And on this point the evidence is equivocal. On the one hand, the system has centralized administratively; on the other hand, politically and constitutionally it had remained about the same.

We have two kinds of evidence of centralization. The data of the federal proportion of governmental expenditures show considerable increase from 1840 to the present. There are two considerable jumps upward: first, in the period just after the Civil War and, second, just after the New Deal. These upward jumps reflect the centralizing reality of new federal functions. In the first jump, the military activity was permanently centralized (as described in the excerpt from *Soldiers of the States*), and many new regulatory and support activities were undertaken (in agriculture, internal improvements, and territorial administration). In the second jump, the federal government took over most welfare from the states and invented much new economic regulation.

A second evidence of centralization is more literary. Chapter 8 contains an analysis of the transfer of the military function from the states to the nation. Since the military function has to do with the survival of the national government as an organization, it is by far the most important of national political and administrative activities. Its transfer to the central government must mean considerable administrative centralization, at least, and perhaps political centralization as well. Chapter 9 contains my estimate of the total effect of all such transfers over the course of the 190 years up to 1964. This estimate is highly subjective, of course, but, lacking anything better, I have reprinted it here.

If one looked only at the allocation of functions and the expenditures on them at each level, it seems that American federalism has progressively centralized, becoming something much different from what it was in 1789. Were that indeed true, then one would infer that our federalism has not been self-perpetuating, but has been repeatedly reshaped by surrounding circumstances. While that inference might be difficult to understand theoretically, it would at least be clear.

As a matter of fact, however, we also have much contradictory evidence about centralization, both literary and statistical. Much of the supposedly progressive centralization was actually embodied in the Constitution itself. In chapter 2, on the origins of the present system, I showed that the tone of the Constitution was deliberately very close to the unitary end of the scale. If so, then the progressive centralization is not a change of constitutional structure, but rather just the progressive revelation of features already present in 1787. A concrete demonstration of this fact is contained in chapter 7 on the Senate and in chapters 10 and 11 on the Presidency and political parties. In the chapter on the Senate I showed that, while the actual divorce of the states from the Senate was not legally recognized until the Seventeenth Amendment in 1913, still the marriage itself was for practical purposes barely consummated because the Constitutional provisions did not admit state legislators' control of Senators. By this evidence, then, our federal system has not changed. In 1787 it was about as centralized as it was going to be.

Furthermore, this degree of centralization is fixed. If American federalism had progressively centralized, one would expect that the system become fully centralized or unitary at some time, perhaps indeed by now. (The federalist dual monarchy in Britain lasted slightly less than a century before full centralization.) But there seem to be constitutional features in the American system that preserve the states, not just in name, as in the Soviet Union, but as real centers of political control.

The evidence for this proposition is both literary and statistical. The statistical evidence is in chapter 10 on the Presidency. In a progressively centralizing system, one would expect the chief political officer to concentrate political authority in his office. Yet the American President has only briefly been able to do this. Why? The answer presented in chapter 11 (on political parties) is that the effect of the federal structure on political parties is to forestall the imperial Presidency. No one in the system can get control of a political party at both national and state levels. This prohibition effectively prevents the use of parties as instruments of centralization.

All of this effect is summarized in the index of disharmony (described and used in chapters 4 and 5). That this index has varied more or less randomly since 1837 reveals the stability of American federalism. The fact that parties never control both states and nation means that both they and the government itself can never be centralized.

Bringing together the detail on centralization, I summarize the interpretation of the history of our federalism thus:

- The framers created a highly centralized federalism verging on unitary government.
- The full potential of their creation has been revealed by the facts that, for example, state legislatures never really controlled the Senate and that administrative centralization took place without political centralization.
- So profound was this centralization in 1787 that it was in fact self-perpetuating, training succeeding generations to accept its implicit values. Thus, the potential for dissolution, ever-present from 1815 to 1865, was nevertheless too weak for successful revolt.
- Nevertheless, the framers did not centralize fully. They retained a role for the states, which is why the system remains just as federal as it was two centuries ago.
- With fixed limits at both the alliance and imperial ends of the scale, the federal system can neither centralize completely nor dissolve.

7 THE SENATE AND AMERICAN FEDERALISM

William H. Riker

Commentary. This essay, along with chapter 2 (on the invention of centralized federalism), provides the essential data for the proposition that the main centralization of our federalism occurred in 1787. Casual observation suggests that the Senate was progressively detached from state legislatures' control until the final separation in 1913. But the evidence here assembled indicates that the connection was always tenuous. State legislatures, ostensibly Senators' constituents, were actually never more than convenient electors. Hence the real centralization was the change in 1787 from state delegates to Congress to United States Senators. The framers, intent on reducing the role of the states, reduced it so much that the Senate, despite appearances, was, from the beginning, a national body.

At Philadelphia in 1787 the authors of the Constitution invented a new kind of federalism. In previous federal governments, the participating states were no more intimate than permanent allies, and citizens retained a primary loyalty to local governments. The federalism of 1787 achieved a converse effect, however, for it subordinated the member governments

Reprinted from the *American Political Science Review*, 1955, vol. 49, pp. 452–469.

and created a nation. Likewise, while the earlier federalisms were notoriously prone to muddles in policy and stalemates in action, the American form turned out to give reasonably effective government, even in the short run. For both its nationalism and its effectiveness, therefore, it found favor with constitution makers elsewhere: in the larger Latin American states, in most of the new nations of the British Commonwealth, in the Germany of Weimar and Bonn, even, on paper at least, in the Soviet Union and Yugoslavia. Probably the clearest demonstration of the prestige and utility of the American invention was the revision (in 1848) of the Swiss Confederation into a federalism patterned after the United States. The cantons thereby abandoned the one remaining survivor of the alliance type of federalism, represented in the middle ages by the Swabian, Rhenish, and Lombard leagues, as well as by the Swiss. And so it happens that about half the earth is presently ruled by federal governments—all of them reminiscent in one way or another of the Philadelphia invention.

What was the secret of this new federalism? Why was it so effective, so nationalizing that half the world has seen fit to borrow it? If the inventors themselves had understood exactly what they had invented, we could hope to answer these questions more easily. Unfortunately, however, the inventors were not quite certain what they had done, and their confusion has been transmitted to scholars and jurists even in our generation. Many of the delegates were, of course, fully conscious that they had created a new political form. In the thirty-ninth *Federalist*, for example, Madison demonstrated that in the proposed Constitution the alliance type of federalism was systematically infused with devices borrowed from unitary governments. What resulted from this infusion was, he observed, something unique, so unique indeed that he had no word to name it. But although he and other delegates were proud of their invention, they could not state with adequate generality how their federalism improved on others. Even Hamilton, whose utterances usually displayed the systematic coherence of the doctrinaire, left diverse rationales unreconciled. In the fifteenth *Federalist* paper, for example, he implied that the essential merit of the new Constitution was its provision that the central government should rule persons as well as states. In the seventieth *Federalist* paper, on the other hand, he suggested that the essential merit was a single executive, as against the collegiate form hitherto usually characteristic of federations.

Looking at the Philadelphia invention with the historian's advantage of hindsight, it is now possible to perceive the advantageous feature of the new federalism. After 165 years, it is clear that the Constitution was effective and successful because, in contrast to all previous federalisms, it made the central government formally independent of the states, leaving the states no effective constitutional means to control national decisions. By this standard we can distinguish two major types of federalism: one in which federal decisions are made exclusively through the machinery of the central government (this type we can describe as centrally directed or centralized), and the other in which federal decisions are made, partially at least, through the machinery of local governments (this type we can describe as peripherally directed or peripheralized). Centralized federalisms are, it turns out, just about as capable of effective action as most unitary governments and certainly as capable of creating a citizen loyalty. But in peripheralized federalisms, like the old Swiss Confederation or contemporary international organizations, where local governments by constitutional right take part in central decisions, direct the voting of their delegates to the center, form suballiances to control its policy, confirm federal decisions, and influence federal policy as much as does the federal government itself, there these local governments usually retain the primary loyalty of the citizen.

To say that the federalism of 1787 was centralized subsumes the statement of the fifteenth *Federalist* paper that the national government was to rule persons as well as states; one of the reasons the state governments could not, under the new form of federalism, control the federal government was that the states did not control the relation of citizens to the nation. Some peripheralized federalisms have permitted the federal government occasional direct contact with citizens (e.g., in military affairs and, rarely, in judicial affairs); but the American federalism allowed the central government to do almost all its business directly with persons—its taxing, its recruiting, its policing, its judging, etc. Hence the state governments were deprived of that middleman position which in peripheralized federalisms permits them to control the policy of the center. Similarly, to say the federalism of 1787 was centralized subsumes also the assertion of the seventieth *Federalist* paper concerning a single executive, for the collegiate executive in peripheralized federalisms has always been one major device by which the federated governments have controlled the federal.

In a variety of others ways, too, the new Constitution centralized federalism. For example, by the provision (Article I, Section 10) that "No State shall, without the consent of Congress,...enter into any agreement or compact with another State...," it isolated state governments from each other. Thereby it forestalled formal factions among states, one of the most frequent occasions in earlier federalisms for devolution of authority to local governments. (Such factions were, incidentally, the characteristic defect of the Swiss Confederation.) Again, by the provision (also Article I,

Section 10) that "No State shall enter into any treaty, alliance, or confederation...," it forestalled formal intrigue with foreigners, intrigue which might force the whole federation into an undesired position. (Incidentally also, such intrigues were the characteristic defect of the Dutch Republic.) Both these provisions were copied, almost verbatim, from the Articles of Confederation (Article VI), but in a centralized federalism they had a special force. They did not, it is true, prevent the Civil War, which involved a formal faction of states, or the Hartford Convention, which contained the threat of intrigue with foreigners; but they did enable the United States to surmount those difficulties in a way that centralized its federalism even more.

Altogether, therefore, the Constitution provided for a national government largely independent of the federated governments. It contemplated, of course, that the people of the states would control the national government. But it contemplated also that the control would be direct, not through the agency of state governments. Naturally, it did not forestall sectionalism; no constitution, federal or unitary, could do that. But it did arrange things in such a way that state officials had to use the political party, not state governments, to make their influence felt in Washington. Thus, although the constitutional system was undeniably federal, although the state governments continued to pretend to a vague sort of "sovereignty," still it was federalism with a difference: state governments, as state governments, could not hope to control national policy.

While we, with our longer experience and larger vocabulary, can thus identify the achievement of 1787 as a centralization rather than a peripheralization of federalism, the authors of the Constitution themselves were not aware that they had really shut off all circuits for states to direct the nation. Indeed, they thought that the Senate, at least, retained the peripheralized character of the Articles of Confederation. With two members from each state, members chosen indeed, by state government, it embodied half of the so-called Great Compromise. It was the most important national institution so constructed,[1] and the founding fathers evidently believed that it was sufficient to maintain the principle. The delegates from the small states signed the Constitution as eagerly as did the delegates from the large and then went home to urge its adoption. Hamilton, much as he yearned for a unitary state, reconciled himself to the form of the Senate and rationalized it concisely and drearily in these words:

...the equal vote allowed to each State is at once a constitutional recognition of the portion of sovereignty remaining in the individual States, and an instrument for preserving that residual sovereignty (*Federalist*, p. 62).

The Senate did not, however, have quite the anticipated effect. Except for the few occasions when sectionalism has been organized by state governments, the Senate has not been a peripheralizing institution. This failure of the Senate to represent state governments is a crucial constitutional development, for thus was achieved the centralizing purpose of the Convention of 1787 in spite of the miscalculation of the delegates. Indeed, this failure of the Senate is of equal and similar significance to the failure of dissident factions to carry through such states' rights programs as the Virginia and Kentucky Resolves, the Hartford Convention, or the Civil War—any one of which, if successful, might have peripheralized or entirely destroyed American federalism. But, although constitutional practice so significantly diverges here from constitutional form, the divergence has never been systematically examined. And so this paper is devoted to an examination of the development of the role of the Senate from the representation of state governments, which was the role initially intended, to the representation of the people of the states, which was the role finally played.

This change of role has two chronological phases. The earlier phase— and for that reason probably the more important—is the gradual failure of state legislatures to enforce their instructions to Senators. The second phase is the gradual transfer of the power to elect Senators from legislatures to the people, a transfer that starts with the public canvass and culminates in the Seventeenth Amendment. By the completion of these two changes, the Senate was divorced wholly from state governments and could not possibly have the effect that the founding fathers expected.

I

The Senate seemed in 1787 to be a peripheralizing institution because it was to be elected by state legislatures. Election by state legislatures implied accountability to them. And if that accountability had in fact come to exist, then the governments at Boston and Albany, Philadelphia and Trenton, Richmond and Charleston might very easily have forced the national government to refer its problems to them. State legislatures and the parties that preferred them to the national legislature did indeed try to enforce accountability by means of the doctrine of instructions. Hence that doctrine was, next to the method of election itself, the main avenue through which state legislatures pushed themselves into national affairs.

The idea that Senators ought always to obey their immediate constituents is now almost forgotten. Only scholars still know that it was ever acted upon, and few of them have studied the action systematically enough to recognize its significance. (But see Haynes, 1938, vol. II. pp. 1024–1034, for examples, and Dodd, 1902, for analysis.) State legislatures did indeed continue until 1913 to instruct their senators according to the traditional formula ("Be it resolved that our Senators in Congress are hereby instructed, and our Representatives are requested, to vote for..."). But by 1860 few Senators felt bound by instructions; and, under the Republican centralism thereafter, they regarded them as mere expressions of opinion. Hence by long disregard the doctrine of instructions passed into obscurity, and in so passing freed the national government from the peripheralizing influence of the Senate.

The doctrine of instructions followed naturally from political institutions prior to the Constitution. Town meetings in colonial New England regularly instructed state representatives and continued to do so until the disappearance of the Federalist party in New England (Colegrove, 1920). Elsewhere, voters occasionally instructed by petition; and as late as 1835 Thomas Ritchie, one of the great Jacksonian editors, attempted to revive the practice in Virginia (Ambler, 1913). Delegates to the Continental Congress were often instructed; and since the Articles of Confederation (Article V) explicitly provided for the recall of delegates at any time, the instructions were easily enforced.

We have no clear indication as to the attitude of the delegates at the Constitutional Convention toward the practice of instructing, for the subject is not mentioned in any of the records. On the one hand, many delegates seemed to expect that the Senate would resist the democratic folly of more popular bodies; and this expectation implies that they did not anticipate that the popular bodies would regularly instruct and thus control the Senate. On the other hand, nearly all of them anticipated that the Senate would protect state rights; and it is hard to visualize any practical system of protection that did not include the doctrine of instructions. Regardless of the attitude of the founding fathers, however, state legislatures, accustomed to both giving and receiving instructions, continued to instruct Senators after 1789.

But from then on instructions were less effective—and that is the reason why the Senate did not peripheralize American federalism. State legislatures lost the sanction of recall and the first Congress definitely approved the loss. The House refused by a large majority to add "the right to instruct" to the First Amendment, apparently because it seemed too "democratic" for the representative system and smacked too much of the localism of the Articles (*Annals of Congress*, August 15, 1989, vol. I, pp. 733–747). Seventeen state constitutions, mostly in New England and the Midwest, did eventually come to guarantee the right to instruct (Colegrove, 1920, p. 443); but, of course, this guarantee meant nothing if the national government refused to recognize it. Similarly, when senators of the first Congress had occasion to discuss some of their many instructions, several Federalists argued that instructions "amounted to no more than a wish" and that legislatures were "only the machines to choose" senators, possessing no more right to instruct them "than the electors had. . .to instruct the President." On the other hand, William MacClay, a proto-Republican, who had already tried to control the vote of his fellow Senator from Pennsylvania by getting the state legislature to instruct them, argued that responsible representation required obedience to instructions (MacClay, 1927, pp. 188, 382–389). The Federalists, in the majority, clearly won the debate and thereby not only discouraged instructions then but also aligned themselves and their descendant parties against the principle of instructions forever.

State legislatures and the Jeffersonian Republicans, however, held tenaciously to the doctrine of instructions. The North Carolina legislature, for example, intending to rebuke Samuel Johnston's disobedience, invited him to render an account of the first Congress. He refused to attend and report to them and they refused to reelect him (Wagstaff, 1910). With a strong sense of particularism, legislatures continued to expect that Senators would obey frequent and detailed instructions. It was altogether appropriate, therefore, that the Kentucky Resolves of 1798, the great pronouncement of Jefferson's party, should take the form of instructions to Senators.

Republicans were eager to make the doctrine of instructions work, for they believed that without it "the power of electing would be. . . incomplete, and the Senator, instead of being a servant, would be the uncontrollable sovereign (John Tyler in Tyler, 1884, vol. I, p. 274). But instructions were freely violated even then and needed a new sanction to substitute for the sanction of recall, which had so effectively peripheralized the federalism of the Articles of Confederation. So compelling was the need for a substitute that the whole subsequent history of instructions can be written in terms of the search for, the discovery and application of, and the ultimate disillusionment with, a substitute for recall.

In the absence of recall the most obvious sanction was refusal to reelect, as in the case of Samuel Johnston. But it was weak: New majorities in state legislatures could not threaten a Senator who, chosen by the old majority, knew he would not be reelected anyway, or who, with a longer term than theirs, might hope for reelection and vindication from their successors. So, sporadically and in floundering fashion, Republicans and state legislatures alike searched for a better substitute. When several Senators violated instructions in voting "not guilty" on the impeachment of Justice Chase, a constitutional amendment was introduced to rebuke them:

> That the legislature of any State may, whenever the said legislature shall think proper, recall, at any period whatever, any Senator of the United States, who may have been elected by them...(*Annals of Congress*, vol. 14, p. 1214, March 1, 1805).

"Whenever...at any period whatever"—the redundance testifies to the passion, but the motion was tabled. Several years later the Massachusetts legislature (ironically Federalist) invented a better sanction. John Quincy Adams provided the occasion: Though elected as a Federalist, he voted for the Embargo Act, whereupon Timothy Pickering, Adams' colleague and the leading Federalist senator, roused Massachusetts Federalism to win the spring elections in 1808 (Adams, 1902, p. 240). The new Federalist legislature promptly censured Adams and, adding indignity to the rebuke, elected his successor six months ahead of time. Sensitive to the "accumulated personal malignity borne me...by those who rule the State," Adams felt compelled to resign (Adams, 1928, p. 57).

This was, so far as I can discover, the first instance of a forced resignation, the only substitute sanction ever used with any success. But it too was not nearly so effective as recall, for it worked only against men with a quick sense of personal honor and, even then, only when there seemed to be mitigating circumstances of party advantage. Explaining to Senator Anderson of Tennessee that he indulged his sense of honor only because Jeffersonians were five-sixths of the Senate, Adams wrote:

> If then I did abandon you, it was from the perfect conviction that you were too strong to need any assistance of mine. For be assured, if the odds had not been so unequivocally decisive,...highly as I reverenced the authority of my constituents, and bitter as would have been the cup of resistance to their declared will, I would not have yielded up my trust until the moment when it was taken from my hands.... (Adams, 1914, vol. III. pp. 269–270).

The next instances of censures and forced resignations, involving David Stone of North Carolina and William Branch Giles of Virginia, occured at the end of the War of 1812. These resignations signified little in the politics of the period, for neither was submitted until after the people ratified the censures by reelecting Madisonian majorities to the state legislatures (Anderson, 1914, pp. 166 ff.; Tyler, 1884, vol. I, pp. 273–275; and Hoyt, 1914, vol. II. pp. 1–6). But they counted much for developing the sanction, and Giles especially, publicly disavowing instructions even as he obeyed them, placed the subject in the forefront of party controversy. In the South, where forced resignation was most important, these two cases formed the tradition, thereby aligning conservatives against instructions entirely and setting a precedent on which radical Jacksonians could rely.

In the interim of incoherent issues and disorganized parties between 1815 and 1832 there were, so far as I can discover, no forced resignations. But they occurred often in the 1830s, when politics polarized around such events as Clay's motion of censure for the removal of deposits from the United States Bank, Jackson's extraordinary message in reply, and Benton's motion to expunge the motion of censure. As Jackson pointed out in his reply to the motion of censure, it would have failed if four Whig senators had obeyed instructions to oppose the restoration of deposits (Peleg Sprague of Maine, Theodore Frelinghuysen and Samuel Southard of New Jersey, and Thomas Ewing of Ohio). He might have added that it would have failed by one vote more had not Rives of Virginia resigned rather than obey instructions to support restoration. Jackson's emphasis on disobedience, however much he disclaimed any design "to interfere with the responsibility due from members of the Senate to their consciences, their constituents, and their country," was in fact intended to encourage state legislatures to instruct or instruct out of office every doubtful senator (*Congressional Globe*, April 16, 1834, vol. 1, p. 316). A Whig in Tennessee described the local agitation over Benton's motion thus, and his words concretely reveal the importance of the doctrine of instructions in a time and place of great Jacksonian influence:

> The "expunging resolutions" had been suffered to sleep in quiet in the legislature for the space of near a five-month. Meanwhile . . . no means were left untried to gain friends indoors and without. The people were invoked, and Gen. Jackson's reputation, like Caesar's pierced and bloody mantle, was held up before them. Public meetings were called and private memorials circulated. They sought to seduce the ignorant by misrepresentation, and to allure others by promises and flatteries. Gen. Jackson . . . did not think it out of the way to address himself personally, and by strong appeals, to many members of the legislature, and among them to some who must have been designated by some shrewd friend at Washington (the Speaker of the House [Polk], we suppose here), for they had never had the honor to see or be seen by the President, and were surprised—not flattered off by the distinction (Scott, 1856, pp. 337–338).

Although the Democrats failed there, Tyler and Leigh of Virginia and Mangum of North Carolina resigned rather than obey instructions to vote to expunge, and were replaced by Jackson men. Since Benton's resolution passed by a vote of only 24 to 19, the three forced resignations provided the margin of success. This vote has often been derided as a "tinsel victory," but in fact it finished shaping the disciplined Democratic party which Jackson bequeathed to Van Buren and Polk. That instructions and forced resignations were crucial for the shaping testifies to the significant role they played in that era of American politics.[2]

But it testifies also, at the high point of instructions, to the inadequacy of their sanction. Although forced resignations, along with other Democratic victories, helped to expunge, they still were only half effective. The New Jersey legislature, for example, having instructed their Senators to expunge, then requested them "to resign their seats...in case they should not think it proper to vote as above directed" (*Congressional Globe*, February 1, 1836, vol. III, p. 159). The Democrat, of course, obediently voted to expunge; the Whig disobeyed and refused to resign; yet two years later he was reelected by the expanded Whiggery at Trenton. So it seems that resignations were not easily forced when Senators sat for six years, state legislators for one or two. Nevertheless, in the South—where the people generally and even some Whig leaders thought that instructions were vital to popular rule—the substitute sanction worked fairly well. Consider what lies back of this advice given by J. H. Pleasants, editor of the Richmond *Whig*, to John Tyler when he and Leigh were instructed to vote for expunging:

> If you obey, dishonorable motives, the love of office...will at once be ascribed. A great clamor will be got up, with design to influence the elections in April, and they will be most perniciously influenced by it. If you *disobey*, and retain your seats, I do not hesitate...to say, that our hopes of carrying the State, spring and fall, will be annihilated at once. The cry of violated instructions is raised; false issues will again be made, and the true issues merged in them.
>
> You correctly say that, before that cry, false or fair, no man has been able to stand, let his popularity have been what it may. It overthrew us last spring, and will do it the next;...if you relinquish your seat, you give us the argument of obedience... always influential....You disarm the enemy and inspirit our friends...[with]...a sentiment of indignation.
>
> ...Success in Virginia is the first thing to be considered. Success is secured by your resignation—defeat is entailed by your retaining your places. I am very sensible that, by resigning, you countenance dangerous heresies...but you are powerless to sustain...[our]...principles by holding on. You but strengthen the hand of the enemy... (Tyler, 1884, pp. 524–525).

Only in the South, however, did instructions thus influence elections and hence only there was forced resignation really effective.

Jackson's use of instructions was both the high point of their life as a custom and the beginning of their obsolescene. Always fertile in the generation of political devices, always convinced that custom was not a rope that bound him but the raw material for a whip that would fit his hands, Jackson transformed instructions into a device by which he, as a national leader, could control both state and nation. Instructions and forced resignations were too fragile to endure for very long after the transformation. The purpose that had formed them and encouraged their development was thoroughly peripheralizing. When Jackson made them serve a national, centralizing purpose, the political circles that had previously fashioned the theory and practice of instructions lost interest in them. Thus Jackson—who usually stood in theory for localism in government, but who in practice almost always centralized—here, typically, occasioned the decline of the one major instrument for state control of national policy.

Hence, after the flowering of forced resignations in the climate of the expunging resolution, the sanction was less used, perhaps because Jackson's successors lacked his prestige to manipulate state legislatures. Even in retirement, however, Jackson himself still made it work. Outraged by Tennessee's defection to the Whigs in 1836, he schemed to redeem it for the Democracy. He induced Polk to run for governor and after Polk's victory wrote exultingly to Van Buren:

> ...of course Mr. Foster [the Junior Senator] and his gagg law will not any more trouble the United States Senate—Judge White must resign, or he will feel the weight of instructions and a Senator elected over his head—the precedent set by our last Legislature [which instructed Grundy, a Democrat, to vote against the sub-treasury] will justify this procedure. My own opinion is, White will resign— Bell being disappointed in going into the Senate to fill White's vacancy, which was the price of his apostasy, if he is disappointed in getting into the Speaker's chair will resign or *cut his throat* in despair and disappointment; and this catastrophy will end the existence of bluelight federalism in Tennessee (McCormac, 1922, pp. 152, 165–169).

Bell's throat remained intact, but White and Foster were indeed instructed out, by being required to support the entire Van Buren program.

Still the Jacksonian device of humiliating instructions did not catch on. It was never again successful in Tennessee and was used elsewhere only reluctantly. Thus the North Carolina Whigs, theoretically opposed to instructions, tried to force out Bedford Brown and Robert Strange with a resolution asking them to "represent the wishes of a large majority of the people of this State" (Hamilton, 1916). Although Brown and Strange refused to treat this as an instruction, they did resign in 1840 to seek re-endorsement from the people—and did not get it (*Congressional Globe*, January 14, 1839, vol. 7, pp. 110–111; Hamilton, 1916).

This was the last important case of forced resignation. Hence also it began the end of the doctrine of instructions, although some Southern senators did continue to regard even unpalatable instructions as binding. Senator Jarnagin of Tennessee, for example, voted under instructions for the tariff of 1846, but only after great pressure from President Polk himself and several of his emissaries (Polk, 1910, vol. II, pp. 24, 49). Polk recorded his worries in his Diary:

> ...My Private Secretary...informed me that the Bill...to reduce the tariff had been [re-] committed to the committee on Finance...by a majority of one vote, Mr. Jarnegan [sic] having disregarded his instructions and voted with his Whig friends. Jarnegan holds the fate of the bill in his hands and there [is] no reliance to be placed upon him. He declared on Saturday last in the presence of the Cabinet...that he would vote for the Bill, and yet today he voted to embarrass and defeat it (Polk, 1910, vol. II, pp. 51–52).

Still, Jarnagin's reluctant "yes" on final passage carried the bill.

Even this obedience—in letter if not in spirit—could not last if the sanction disappeared; and that is just what happened. There were no clear cases of forced resignations after 1846. In 1849 Thomas Benton, Jackson's aide in organizing forced resignations, received and ignored unpalatable instructions. In the same year Lewis Cass, then the titular chief of the Democracy, was instructed to support the Wilmot Proviso; he not only disobeyed without resigning, but even persuaded the legislature to rescind its resolutions. Not surprisingly, therefore, John Bell of Tennessee remarked in justification of his disobedience on the Kansas question in 1858 that he found even "Democratic Senators obeying or disobeying instructions at their discretion."[3] In 1878, L. Q. C. Lamar of Mississippi disobediently voted against the Bland silver bill. A great outcry was raised about the violation; Jefferson Davis even broke the silence of his retirement to denounce Lamar and defend instructions as a principle of the old Democracy. Lamar stumped his state in 1879 and again in 1881 defending his course and was triumphantly reelected (Mayes, 1896, pp. 330–364, 345–411, 441–442). Thereafter instructions were obeyed if palatable and unconcernedly ignored if they were not.

Instructions failed, I believe, through lack of a dependable substitute for recall. Forced resignations, the only available sanction, required that elections turn on the issue of obedience and that senators love honor more than office. By mid-century, neither requirement could be met. Voters quite reasonably refused to consider form more than substance; and the Democratic party that asked them to do so had for a time lost those states in which the technique was most popular. By mid-century, also, the

Senate's prestige had risen so high that no man could lightly resign from it. From 1792, when Charles Carroll resigned, preferring to sit in the Maryland Senate, even from 1842 when Franklin Pierce resigned an office without a future in a city his wife disliked (Nichols, 1931), the Senate's prestige rose steadily, as the statistics on resignation show: from 1790 to 1819, 89 Senators resigned; from 1820 to 1849, 91; from 1850 to 1879, however, only 34, exclusive of the seceders, who were also expelled; from 1880 to 1909, only 23; from 1910 to 1939, only 21. Also, a change had come about in the motives underlying resignations. The prestige of the Senate had at first been little greater than that of high state office, but this was no longer the case from about 1850: from 1790 to 1849, 48 Senators resigned to take state office; from 1850 to 1949, only eight. From 1850 to 1949, 50 out of 90 Senators resigning took high office in the national government, while 20 more resigned for ill health or financial reasons. How could instructions be enforced when neither political principles nor personal honor could compel men to resign a valuable property?

Localistic sentiments were extraordinarily strong in the first half of the nineteenth century. Had they had adequate institutions, they might have succeeded in peripheralizing American federalism. It is, therefore, crucial good fortune that no effective sanction for instructions was ever developed. In the absence of a sanction, the device of instructions gradually ceased to operate; and only the constitutional method of electing Senators remained as a method by which the Senate might peripheralize federalism. To the gradual obsolescence of that method also, we now turn our attention.

II

At the same time as instructions lapsed into obscurity, a new device began to appear for further separating national and state legislatures. This was the public canvass for seats in the Senate, a canvass, that is, of voters rather than of state legislators, a canvass in which candidates for the Senate helped elect those state legislators who were more or less formally pledged to vote for them. Prior to the 1830s, candidates for the Senate did not usually campaign until after the state legislature was elected, at which time they canvassed not the voters but the legislators. A master-servant relationship was thus established, except when, as rarely happened, the majority of the legislature chose a Senator not of their own party. The Senator, the servant, necessarily owed the legislators gratitude; but they owed him nothing—perhaps this explains why they felt free to instruct him so peremptorily. The rise of the public canvass for the Senate subtly changed this relationship. When a candidate for the Senate stumped the state in a campaign for the state legislators, he urged voters to vote for those candidates who were in turn pledged to vote for him for Senator. Gradually, voters came to choose between rivals for the state legislature, not on the basis of their capabilities as lawmakers but rather on the basis of the vote they would cast in senatorial elections. When this happened, each state legislator then owed his office less to his own merit and more to the merit of the candidate for the Senate with whom he was aligned. As a result, Senators earned gratitude as much as they owed it. And, when gratitude flowed in both directions, Senators depended less on state legislatures and in turn national government depended less on local government.

The system of public canvass for the Senate, both the product and the cause of popular excitement in campaigns, probably originated in the party turbulence of the 1830s. It received a fillip from the free-soil agitation of the 1850s, and matured with the development of rigid parties after the Civil War. Although possibly some candidates canvassed publicly earlier, the first instance I can find is the Walker-Poindexter campaign in Mississippi in 1834. Friends of Senator Poindexter, a Republican turned Whig, arranged for him to castigate Jackson at a series of outdoor banquets. At the first one, Robert J. Walker replied so effectively that the assembled crowd passed a resolution asking him to run for Poindexter's seat. Both candidates then canvassed the state, and, in striking anticipation of the Lincoln-Douglas campaign, met occasionally in debate (Foote, 1874, pp. 217–79). The struggle between Democracy and Whiggery intensified the public canvass for the Senate, as well as all other sorts of campaigning. By 1841 the public canvass was so well established that Polk, as governor of Tennessee, refused to call a special session of the legislature to fill a Senate vacancy because "the members elected to the legislature in 1839 had not been chosen with the selection of Senators in view" (McCormac, 1922, p. 183). Doubtless this was merely a polite and politic way of saying that the Democrats were in the minority; but it is still significant that Polk could rationalize his interest with a reference to the public canvass.

It was the Lincoln-Douglas campaign, occasioned like earlier ones by a new minority and a split in the majority, that popularized the public canvass over the whole nation. In order to quell the Buchanan Democrats in Illinois, Douglas arranged for the state convention to endorse his reelection. Similarly, the Republicans endorsed Lincoln lest some of their legislators vote for Douglas in order to embarrass Buchanan (Sparks, 1918, p. 19). Each candidate had, therefore, a pledged slate of electors. This was entirely new, for even the public canvass had not heretofore turned legislatures into mere electoral colleges. The correspondent of the New York *Evening Post* said it was "without a parallel" because:

> ...another instance can [not] be shown where two individuals have entered into a personal contest before the people for a seat in the United States Senate—an office not directly in the gift of the people, but their representatives (Sparks, 1918, vol. III, p. 540).

Inaccurate history, perhaps—but good evidence of the impression the campaign made. Some journals, like the Boston *Daily Advertiser*, were disturbed:

> It would be unfortunate for the social and industrial interests of the States, if this mode of electing legislators, solely and chiefly from regard to their votes for U.S. Senator, were to become general (Sparks, 1918, vol. III, p. 536).

And the Cincinnati *Commercial:*

> It is difficult to conceive of anything more illegitimate...the Senator...is the representative...of the state, as an independent polity, and not...of its individual citizens; and any attempt to forestall the action of the Legislature, either by party action or personal appeal to the people...is...an offense against the sovereignty whose freedom of action they thereby seek to fetter and control (Sparks, vol. III, p. 540).

Conservative disturbance did not, however, prevent the spread of the canvass, especially in states where the parties were in balance. The mechanics of reelection also encouraged it. Regularly, from 1790 to 1913, about 40% of the Senators won reelection and an even larger proportion sought it. Hence, gradually, most sitting Senators came to be considered candidates for reelection. Once the public canvass operated, the parties solidified behind and against these presumptive candidates: thus, John Sherman, for example, said that near the end of his fifth term in 1892, "I considered myself a candidate, without any announcement, and entered into the canvass as such" (Sherman, 1895, vol. II, p. 1118).

The combined effect of popular excitement and presumptive candidates is indicated by the history of elections in Indiana, one of the states really marginal in party attachment at the turn of the century. In the two decades, 1891–1910, there were seven regular elections. In every case the public clearly understood that the incumbent Senator was a candidate. In three other cases—in 1896 when the Republican, Fairbanks, beat the venerable Voorhees, in 1908 when the Democrat, Shively, beat Hemenway, and in 1910 when the Democrat, Kern, beat Beveridge—the party out of power had clearly (if not always officially) nominated a candidate long before

November. Thus in five-sevenths of the opportunities a candidate was in effect nominated before the state legislature was elected.

The endorsement of candidates in convention, the other new aspect of the Lincoln-Douglas campaign, was not, however, so readily accepted elsewhere. The Massachusetts Republican convention, fearing that conservative legislators would not vote for Sumner, did indeed copy the Illinois technique in 1862 and 1868 (Storey, 1900, pp. 233, 356). But not until the mid-eighties, when the public canvass was quite frequent, did formal pledging again become popular. Then it spread widely and soon seemed an extraconstitutional means for popular election of Senators.[4] In the election of William E. Borah in 1906–1907, both Republican candidates organized campaigns in every county of Idaho to elect a slate of county convention delegates though Borah himself had opposed the pledging of delegates in 1894 (Johnson, 1936, pp. 63–68).

These devices, the public canvass and pledged legislators, were at their height soon after 1900. How well they worked is shown by the idiom: people spoke of the "election" of Senators in November, when in fact only state legislators were then elected. Sometimes, of course, even candidates who had not campaigned tried to get elected by combining the minority with malcontents of the majority. Sometimes, as in Turpie's election in Indiana in 1887, the coalition succeeded; more often, as in Hanna's election in Ohio in 1898, it did not. And prolonged deadlocks—G.H. Haynes (1906, pp. 180–181) counted 45 between 1891 and 1905—could often be broken only by ignoring the voice of the people. But despite these aberrations, the public canvass did work to free the Senators from deep dependence on legislatures in at least half the elections in the turn of the century era.

The public canvass occurred, however, only when there was a sufficiently high degree of political excitement. If the excitement was lacking, as for example in Massachusetts, where the overwhelmingly dominant Republicans were wholly blind to any defect in the characters of Senators Hoar and Lodge, then Senatorial elections reverted wholly to the legislature. The direct primary, however, formalized and generalized the public canvass. This device, which originated in South Carolina in 1888 and which spread rapidly through the Populist and Democratic South, was widely copied after 1903 (when Lafollette instituted it in Wisconsin) in the Midwestern and Northwestern states most deeply touched with progressivism. By 1910, 44 out of the 46 states had primary election laws, and 28 of these provided in one way or another for the nomination of party candidates for the Senate at the party primary (*Congressional Record*, 1910, vol. 45, pp. 7113–20). More than half of the Senators could assert proudly, with Cummins of Iowa: "I was selected by a primary vote in *my state*" (*Congressional Record*, 1911, vol. 47, p. 1742. Emphasis added). The constitutional method of election could hardly serve a peripheralizing purpose when many senators believed they owed their seats, not to the state legislatures, but to the people.

Legislatures were not, however, formally bound by the primary results. The dominant party could, and occasionally did, ignore the primary in choosing the Senator. But even this gap in popular control was closed by the invention of the Oregon system. It provided not only for Senatorial nomination in primaries but also for a test of popular sentiment between the nominees at the November general election. Candidates for the state legislature could, if they chose, subscribe to a promise to vote for the candidate who won the test vote in November. In 1909 the Oregon legislature, a majority of which had subscribed to the promise, actually elected a Democrat, George Chamberlain, because he had won in November 1908, even though the legislature was overwhelmingly Republican. (Eastern Republicans were inclined to regard this as the best.possible argument against direct election.) Finally, fearing that even this method of "solemn promise" would not work—the fear indicates the extent of bribery in state legislatures during Senatorial elections—Oregon amended its Constitution to require the legislature to elect the people's choice. Thus, the Oregon system instituted a rigid pattern of popular election and excluded the state legislature from the selection of Senators as far as could be done under the Constitution. It was copied in Nebraska and Nevada and would probably have been more widely copied had not the Seventeenth Amendment· made imitation unnecessary.

III

The Seventeenth Amendment completed the centralizing process that the public canvass began. The canvass had started to make the decision of the people a guide for the legislature. The system of pledging legislators, the direct primary, and finally the Oregon system had each formalized the role of the voters a little more, until finally it seemed likely that the legislatures would select Senators as mechanically as the electoral college selected the President. Thus these earlier reforms both occasioned the Seventeenth Amendment and anticipated its effects.

From the time that the public canvass became a fairly regular feature of Senatorial elections (i.e., from the 1880s), there had been widespread agitation to amend Article I, Section 3. In the Forty-eighth Congress

(1883–1885) there began a flood of proposals for popular election, in the form of memorials from state legislatures, petitions from private groups, and resolutions from congressmen. The agitation reached its high-point in the first session of the Fifty-second Congress (1891–1892), which received 7 memorials, 54 petitions, and 25 resolutions on the subject. On January 16, 1893, the House actually passed a resolution to submit an amendment to the states—but the resolution never got out of committee in the Senate. The agitation leveled off thereafter, but persisted until the Amendment was finally and formally proposed in 1911. The House indeed resolved to submit an amendment in 1894, 1898, 1900, 1902 (unanimously), and 1911. On the last occasion, the Senate concurred.

It concurred because there was little point in holding out any longer. Thirty-seven state legislatures (more than the three-fourths necessary to adopt an amendment) had, by memorial to Congress or by institution of senatorial primaries, indicated that they no longer wanted to elect Senators. Observe this colloquy, which occurred not long before the Senate gave in, between Senators Cummins of Iowa, a Republican progressive, and Heyburn of Idaho, also a Republican and by far the most dogged opponent of direct election:

> Mr.   CUMMINS. . . . the Senator from Idaho is insisting. . . that if the voters of the United States be permitted to say who shall be their Senators, then this body will be overrun by a crowd of incompetent and unfit and rash and socialistic and radical men who have no proper views of government. I am simply recalling to his attention the fact that the people of this country, in despair of amending the Constitution, have accomplished this reform for themselves.
>
> Mr. HEYBURN. Like a burglar.
>
> Mr. CUMMINS. In an irregular way, I agree, but they have accomplished it.
>
> Mr. HEYBURN. Like a burglar.
>
> Mr. CUMMINS. And they have accomplished it so effectively that, whether the Constitution is amended or not, the people in many or most of the States will choose their own Senators (*Congressional Record*, June 7, 1911, vol. 47, p. 1734).

The accomplishment was a fact; hence Heyburn could not argue, he could only sneer. Like the Nineteenth Amendment—and possibly also the Eighteenth—the Seventeenth simply universalized a situation which a majority of state legislatures had already created.

Since the Seventeenth Amendment thus simply acknowledged an already existing situation, scholars and citizens alike have been unaware of its exact significance. Senatorial resistance to the doctrine of instructions was deliberately nationalistic. The opponents of instructions wanted to expand the role of the national government and to curtail the role of the states. The advocates of instructions were the states' rights parties. The failure of instructions was, therefore, a planned victory for centralized federalism—although not a conscious victory, for it came too slowly to be recognized by the participants. On the other hand, the Seventeenth Amendment, another very real victory for centralization, was hardly a deliberate one. Throughout all the agitation for the Seventeenth Amendment and its preceding reforms, no one—so far as I can discover—ever advocated them as a way to centralize federalism. The public canvass for the Senate was so natural a development out of other and earlier public campaigning that no one thought it needed justification. But if anyone had ever felt called upon to justify it, he would, I am sure, have described it as a democratic or popular device, which, intrinsically, it was. The same remarks hold for the extensions of the public canvass: presumptive candidates and pledged legislators. They were not justified; they were merely used, first because they were a new and effective way to win elections, later because they were simply a part of the procedure of campaigning. The direct primary for Senate seats and the Seventeenth Amendment were, however, elaborately justified. These were the dearest inventions of progressives to bring about a democratic utopia; these were the devices on which progressives in practical politics and progressives in universities thoroughly agreed. In consequence, they produced mountains of words in exhaustive and usually naive justification. But none of these justifications interpret them as devices to centralize federalism. It was, on the contrary, frequently asserted that the direct election of Senators would peripheralize federalism, strengthening state legislatures by forcing them to concentrate on state business. It is difficult to understand how even the progressive propagandists imagined that depriving legislatures of their only control over national affairs would strengthen houses that were already decadent for want of a significant agenda. Instead, the reforms were justified simply but voluminously as extensions of democracy and as methods of avoiding deadlocks and bribery in Senatorial elections.

Only the opponents of the Seventeenth Amendment understood its effect on federalism. In quite graphic terms Elihu Root, for example, described the control that state legislatures would lose. In 1911 the New York legislature still retained more power than most over the election of senators. Doubtless, therefore, the intimacy suggested was typical of other states only in an earlier era:

> Mr. President, this change [the popular election of Senators] would take the direct responsibility of Senators for their actions from the States [sic] legislatures

to the people at the polls. The members of the State legislature...are familiar with the incidents and difficulties of legislation. They know how necessary it is that in order to accomplish beneficent results mutual concession shall be made. They know how impossible it is that any one man, or any one locality, or any one State can have all of its own way. When members of this body have to explain to the State legislature the reasons for their action, they meet minds that are competent and trained for the appreciation of their explanation. The people at large have far less understanding upon the subject that I am now speaking of than their legislature...This will cease to be a deliberative body if every Senator has to convince, to explain to the great body of the people of his State every act he performs and every concession he makes (*Congressional Record* 1911, vol. 46, p. 2244).

And he drew from his remarks a warning to the states' rights Democrats of the South, who provided the bulk of the votes for the Amendment:

Let me tell the gentlemen who are solicitous for the preservation of the sovereignty of their States that there is but one way in which they can preserve that sovereignty, and that is by repudiating absolutely and forever the fundamental doctrine on which this resolution [to amend the Constitutional] proceeds (*Congressional Record*, 1911, vol. 46, p. 2243).

But Root's understanding is not typical. Most opponents did no more than quote with pseudo-scholarship what the founding fathers had said about the Senate. Hence for all of its supporters and for most of its opponents, the centralizing effects of the Seventeenth Amendment went entirely unnoticed.

They were unnoticed because, by 1911, the state legislatures had lost all touch with national policy. By reason of the failure of the practice of instructions and by reason of the gradual mechanization of their part in the electoral process, the legislatures had been increasingly confined to the particular problems of their states. Hence the Seventeenth Amendment only formally excluded them from participation in national government. The actual exclusion, which the Amendment recognized and ratified, was the result of a constitutional evolution in process for the preceding 120 years.

IV

By reason of the development described in this essay, the main peripheralizing feature of American federalism was excised from the Constitution. And that very excision had a centralizing effect, for it allowed other centralizing forces to operate with a minimum of restraint. The state governments of course remain to peripheralize federalism by means of their influence in political parties; but at least these governments cannot by constitutional right interfere with national policy. And considering that, compared with the national government, they have on the whole turned out to be far less efficient in action, far less competent in decision, and far less democratic in spirit, this change in the role of the Senate was surely good fortune for us all. Although we received it unconsciously, it seems important now to comprehend it rationally. Not only may we then defend our centralized federalism against the contemporary resurgence of peripheralizing measures but also we may more wisely advise our imitators, especially in international organizations.

Notes

1. The electoral college should probably be interpreted as another peripheralizing institution, inasmuch as its authors probably expected that state legislatures would choose the electors. But it was largely accidental that the electoral college had this peripheralizing form; indeed the framers adopted it only because they thought there were worse disadvantages in all the other forms suggested. Although the state legislatures did usually choose the electors in the early years of the Republic, still the Constitution did not formally invest them with the duty. It merely said: "Each State shall appoint, in such manner as the legislature thereof may direct, a number of electors..." (Art. II, Sec. I). Hence, because the form was accidental and the wording imprecise, the electoral college was quickly deprived of whatever peripheralizing character may have been intended. Another part of the Constitution that might have turned out to be peripheralizing was the ambivalent provision on state courts in the supremacy clause. But the series of decisions, beginning with *Martin v. Hunter's Lessee*, 1 *Wheat.* 304 (1816), which deprived state courts of any authoritative role in interpreting national law, eliminated that danger. The Second, Ninth, Tenth, and Eleventh Amendments were also quite clearly intended to peripheralize. They were not, of course, the framers' work and are not, indeed, in harmony with the original Constitution. By reason of the disharmony, perhaps, they (especially the Tenth and Second) have been more effective for peripheralizing than provisions of the original Constitution itself.

2. As the vote on the resolution to expunge indicates, the substitute for recall did sometimes work. Aside from the forced resignations already mentioned (Adams, 1808; Stone, 1814; Giles, 1815; Rives, 1834; Tyler, 1836; Leigh, 1836; Mangum, 1836), these resignations were also forced: Tazewell of Virginia, 1832; King of Georgia, 1837; Foster of Tennessee, 1839; White of Tennessee, 1840; Brown of North Carolina, 1840; Strange of North Carolina, 1840; Preston of South Carolina, 1842; Haywood of North Carolina, 1846. Several other resignations, submitted in similar circumstances, should be classed as "almost forced": Sprague of Maine, 1835; Porter of Louisiana, 1837; Black of Mississippi, 1838; Rhett of South Carolina, 1852; Berrien of Georgia, 1852; and Everett of Massachusetts, 1854.

3. Benton's instructions: *Congressional Globe*, vol. 21, p. 98; Cass' instructions: *Congressional Globe*, vol. 20, p. 432; rescinded, *Congressional Globe*, vol. 21, pp. 702–703;

Bell's instructions: *Congressional Globe*, vol. 27, p. 805. Bell's speech and Andrew Johnson's reply well summarize the arguments for and against instructions.

4. Haynes, "Popular Election of United States Senators," *Johns Hopkins Studies* vol. 11, Haynes mentions especially the Democratic convention in Illinois in 1890 and the Republican convention in Minnesota in 1892, to which should be added as another outstanding example the Republican convention in Indiana in 1886. In the 1890s, these precedents were widely followed, and county conventions frequently pledged candidates for state legislator to a particular senatorial candidate. See Sherman, vol. 2, p. 1118, and Mayes, pp. 433-434 and 446. In 1911, Senator Brown of Nebraska could say: "...it has been the frequent custom in States without primary election laws, as well as in States with them, to nominate candidates for the legislature, and in the nominating conventions pass resolutions instructing the nominee when elected to vote for some man for Senator" (*Congressional Record*, vol. 46, p. 2493).

5. Details of the Oregon system are set forth in *The Code of the People's Rule*, S. Doc. 603, 61st Cong., 2nd sess., pp. 33 ff. Details on its operation are readily available in *Congressional Record*, May 5, 1910, vol. 45, p. 5827, in a speech by Senator Jonathan Bourne, which is reprinted under the title "Popular Government in Oregon," *Outlook*, October 8, 1910, vol. 96, pp. 321–330.

8 THE DECLINE AND RISE OF THE MILITIA

William H. Riker

Commentary. The significance of this chapter is that, for one function, it reveals the dynamic of administrative centralization. In the Constitution, the administration of the militia is discussed in more detail than any other administrative function. As with no other function, the framers specifically divided the militia between the central government and the states; and, in order to ensure that the appropriate division be maintained, they devoted two clauses, one quite lengthy, to prescribing a role for the states. Yet in spite of their care, the militia is now governed almost entirely by the United States. Indeed, most people who are not actually members of the National Guard think it is merely a national military reserve and are not aware that it is in fact the state militia.

How this change came about is explained in Soldiers of the States, *three pertinent chapters of which are reprinted here. The states gradually abandoned the militia in the period 1815–1860 in a process described in the section entitled "Degeneration of the Militia, 1792–1860." Concurrently, the*

From William H. Riker, *Soldiers of the States* (Washington, Public Affairs Press, 1957), portions of chapters 1, 3, and 4.

United States developed a small professional army and navy with a relatively large officer corps. Consequently, the national government fought the Civil War with the army and navy, and enlisted volunteers and ignored the militia. Beginning in 1877, the states began to revive the then moribund militia, wholly for purposes of internal police, a process described in the section entitled "Revival of the Militia, 1877–1903." The militia was an expensive police, however, so the states sought federal aid. The regular army and navy were, of course, loath to see national military expenditures diverted to support domestic police. So the compromise, beginning in 1903 and continuing to this day, has consisted of a trade of national financial support for national control of the militia. As a result, the states still have a militia to use for some restricted police functions, while the training and most of the personnel selection is under national control.

In 1787 almost the entire military force of the United States was in state hands. The states abandoned it after the War of 1812 and when, from 1877 on, they tried to regain some military functions, they found that they could do so only by accepting national control. Thus the function carefully divided in 1787 is almost completely centralized in 1987, an impressive and apparently radical change. This is the best possible evidence for the claim that our federalism has been progressively centralized.

Soldiers of the States

Every kind of government has its own characteristic problems. Empires, both ancient and modern, have been especially plagued with colonial discontent. Feudalisms have been especially plagued with petty civil wars among constituent units. Monarchies and dictatorships have been especially plagued with the personal vagaries and bad judgment of the autocrats. Democracies and other governments in which competition for leadership is institutionalized into a permanent feature of political life have been especially plagued by, on the one hand, indecision (as in contemporary France), and by, on the other hand, too hasty decision (as has occasionally happened in the United States). Federalism also has its characteristic problems, problems that grow out of the double government, both halves of which are guaranteed to exist so long as the constitution lasts. By reason of one guarantee, a presumably sovereign national government is unable to control directly the organization and operation of its supposedly subordinate units. By reason of the other guarantee, the once sovereign or putatively sovereign constituent governments are unable to control their own destinies. . . . . On both levels, in short, the guarantees of federalism lead to uniquely federal problems, problems that are not faced by any other kind of government.

One such characteristically federal problem is that occasioned by the division of functions between the central and constituent governments. So that the constituent governments might have enough important things to do to retain the loyalty of their citizens, the framers of federal constitutions have often divided up functions that elsewhere belong exclusively to the central government. But in thus guaranteeing the federal system, this division of functions has also guaranteed constant haggling between the politicians and administrators engaged in the joint operation of a divided duty. In this sense, therefore, it often happens that the guarantees of federalism turn out to be guarantees of inefficiency as well. Hence, of every federal system, one may legitimately inquire whether or not federalism is worth the inefficiency it may occasion.

That is the central inquiry of this book. But such a question cannot be asked in a vacuum. It must be asked in relation to some specific function that is divided up. Here it is asked about the militia.....

A review of this particular military experience promises to illuminate the problems of joint administration especially brightly because, on the one hand, the militia is the only area in which the nation and the states have attempted to work together throughout most of our history, and because, on the other hand, the militia is one of the most important functions so divided. Many of the functions now divided have only recently been so, but the framers of the Constitution divided authority over the militia in specific detail; in more specific detail, actually, than they divided any other authority. In 1792 the national government began to exercise the duties the framers had assigned to it. And as early as 1808 Congress gave the militia the first grant-in-aid in the history of this or any other federalism. Clearly, this experience with joint administration covers, in military affairs more than any other governmental function, a longer time and more varied political circumstances. One of the faults in recent studies of divided functions and joint administration is that they have concerned only twentieth century examples and are thus too temporally circum-scribed. This fault can be corrected by a review of experience with the militia.

Although today the National Guard, which is the organized militia, is far overshadowed by the Army, the Air Force, and the Navy, early in the nineteenth century the militia was popularly regarded as the most significant part of our military force. In the beginning of the Republic, it was indeed regarded as one of the most important governmental functions. In the Virginia ratifying convention of 1788, for example, the militia was discussed in more detail and more fervently than any other aspect of the proposed federalism. And, for another example, the Second Amendment to the Constitution was intended to guarantee the permanence of the division of control over the militia. Even as late as the second decade of the twentieth century, when the militia had long since ceased to rival the regular army, textbooks on state government still commonly devoted more space to the militia than to any other state administrative function. Today the National Guard is not regarded as important even to the states—recent textbooks on state government commonly dismiss it in a page or two. The Commission on Intergovernmental Relations which existed from 1953 to 1955, and which undertook to examine and generalize about 25 functions jointly administered by the nation and the states, entirely overlooked the National Guard. Whether this oversight was simply accidental or whether it was deliberately designed in order to permit the Commission to draw the conclusions that it wished to draw, still no one has yet criticized the Commission's oversight—and this lack of criticism clearly indicates that most citizens and indeed most political scientists no longer think the militia is worth talking about. But even though the militia has thus lost its hold on the popular consciousness, still the United States spends more money on the National Guard than on any other jointly administered program—except highway construction and old age assistance. Thus, although the National Guard may have diminished in popular estimation, it still has a secure and lucrative position in the national budget. And in the course of American history as a whole, there can be no doubt that the militia has been regarded as the most significant of the jointly administered functions.

Degeneration of the Militia, 1792–1860

The essential principle of the Militia Act of 1792 was the liability of all free white male citizens, aged 18–45, to militia duty. Allowing for local variations in age and occupational classes, this was the seventeenth and eighteenth century version of universal military training. Deep-rooted as this institution was, however, by the middle of the nineteenth century, the states had, through incompetence and inaction, utterly abandoned the principle, although they did invent a new and more easily administered system of volunteer militia, the forerunner of the National Guard.

The failure of the states to maintain the essential principle of the militia system cannot at all be blamed on the national government or on any national administrative policy. Military historians, displaying more military than historical judgment, have often condemned the Act of 1792 as unrealistic and unworkable in its universality. Wholly unappreciative of the political, social, and military circumstances of the United States in 1792, they have castigated the First and Second Congress for ignoring Knox's (and Washington's) proposal of a system of age classes with intensive training for the youngest class. Yet the Act of 1792 simply incorporated the principles of the several militia laws of the states, principles that were inherited from English and colonial militia systems, and thereby asked the states to keep on doing well what they were then doing and what, if the furor that led to the Second Amendment is to be credited, they presumably wanted to keep on doing. The Knox plan, an innovation a hundred years ahead of its time, was appropriately ignored in the interest of maintaining state freedom of action. A few years later, moreover, the national government gave the states substantial financial help in administering the system. As has already been pointed out, the Militia Act imposed a special tax on militiamen in that they were required to provide themselves with muskets and other accouterments. Initially this was the most expensive part of the system, inasmuch as no money was appropriated to pay militiamen (except when they served in the field or sat on courts martial). And so the national government tried to help, first by an Act of 1789 permitting states to purchase muskets at national arsenals and thus ensuring them a supply in what was then a seller' market. When the states indifferently ignored this offer, the Tenth Congress enacted a permanent annual appropriation of $200,000 to buy muskets for distribution among the states in proportion to their militia enrollments.

This was the first grant-in-aid in our history and for that reason it is notable in the history of federalism. For its day, it was a sizable grant. I believe, though I cannot prove, that it was more money than all the states then spent annually on the equipment, organization, and maintenance of the militia. Furthermore, there were no strings attached to the grant—no national supervision of, for example, the care of the muskets—an unwise oversight as it turned out, for many a countryman used his ramrod as a poker and thus rendered his musket useless except for parade. Like most subsequent grants-in-aid, it was intended to help the states to do what they were supposed to do but were not in fact doing. Unfortunately, however, neither Congress nor the War Department undertook any supervision of the use of this grant until near the end of the century. Consequently, although the national government did considerably more than was proper for it to do in the constitutional theory of the authors of the Second Amendment and the Act of 1792, it was unable to forestall the failure of the militia system.

I

When and where the militia system failed are easily demonstrated by precise numerical evidence abstracted from the annual returns on the militia, presented to Congress annually from 1803 to 1863 by the Secretary of War. These annual returns were based on reports made by the Adjutants General of the states under the Act of 1803. The raw data for the returns, that is a count of men and officers by companies and by branch of service and a count of equipment and ordinance, were collected by militia captains at the annual or semiannual musters. The brigade inspectors compiled the raw data into reports to state Adjutants-General who in turn reported to the governors and the Secretary of War. In this connection, the interesting fact about these state reports is their irregularity, both over time and among states. When a report exists, it indicates that the reporting state maintained at least the minimum militia organization and that it was at least pretending to obey the regulations of the Act of 1792 on universal military training. It does not follow, of course, that the absence of a report indicates that a state had abolished its militia. The absence may simply indicate that the Adjutant General of the state (usually underpaid and often unpaid) neglected his duty. Nevertheless, in most instances the absence of a report does indicate that the enrollment system, the chief physical manifestation of the principle of universal liability, had temporarily or even permanently broken down.

The states had substantial inducements to report: The distribution of arms under the Act of 1808 depended, until 1855, on the proportion of each state's enrolled militia to the national total. In an era of swiftly increasing population, failure to enroll and report then meant that the delinquent state received a smaller amount of arms than it might otherwise have received.

In his report of 1844, the Adjutant General of Indiana, whose militia had not been fully mustered for 12 years, remarked: "In consequence of the entire failure of the major generals to return to me the strength of the militia composing their several divisions, it will be impossible for me to lay before your Excellency any statement of the *number* of men, within the State, subject to the performance of militia duty.... [T]he military organization is almost entirely abandoned. Offices have been vacated and not filled; and hence it is, that the few officers who hold commissions are unable to report the strength of the militia under their commands." Adjutant General Reynolds then calculated that Indiana was losing about $5320 per year in muskets because of its failure to muster and report (*Report*, 30 November, 1844, p. 1).

Even in a state as comparatively well organized as New York the same inducement operated. In his report of 1845, the Adjutant General of New York remarked that the effect of disorganized divisions, infrequent parades and numerous exemptions was that the state lost its fair share of arms from the national bounty. He compared New York with Pennsylvania and Ohio thus (Report, *New York Assembly Documents, 1846*, 1: #6):

	Population in 1840	Militia in 1841	Muskets Received in 1841
New York	2,428,921	173,599	1556
Pennsylvania	1,724,033	236,171	2116
Ohio	1,519,467	180,258	1616

If New York had reported militia in the same proportion as Pennsylvania, New York would have received, *ceteris paribus*, at $14 per musket, roughly $20,000 more than it actually did receive—no mean sum in 1841. Clearly, the grant-in-aid was a substantial inducement to report.

But in spite of the inducement states failed to do so. Often state Adjutants General apologized to the Secretary of War for their failure, explaining, for example: "No doubt the militia of this State is 30,000 strong [although only 23,000 were reported], as no returns have been received from the 3rd, 4th, and 9th brigades, as well as some regiments in the 2nd division" (*American State Papers, Military Affairs*, 3: 690).

Even in Virginia whose Adjutants General filed returns quite faithfully, the accuracy of the reports was suspect. In his annual report for 1847, the Adjutant General of Virginia complained: "The annual return of the militia of this state which I now have the honor to lay before you, is as accurate as it can be made from the imperfect and sometimes incomprehensible materials of which it has to be made up.... No efforts of this department can overcome the negligence or incapacity of many of the adjutants, whose duty it is to make the regimental returns" (Report, Virginia Public Document #11, September 30, 1847).

On one occasion the Adjutant General of Delaware explained his failure to forward a militia return in this agonized letter: "In obedience to the above recited Act of Congress [i.e., Act of March 2, 1803], I have the honor to inform you that the Legislature of Delaware passed an act at Dover, February 2, 1816, entitled 'An act to repeal military fines for non-attendance on days of parade'...., rendering entirely inoperative 'An act to establish a uniform militia throughout this State'.... The consequences naturally flowing from that law have been a total neglect of every appearance of military duty: for, in removing the obligation to muster, on the part of the private, every incentive having a tendency to urge the officer to the performance of his duty ceases to exist: if, in addition to these causes, we take into consideration the circumstances of the vacation of almost all of those officers by death, resignation, or the expiration of the term of office, and no new appointments being made by the executive authority, the utter inability of the Adjutant General to comply with the requisition contained in the above act of Congress will appear clear and evident" (*American State Papers, Military Affairs*, vol. 2, p. 320). Incidentally, Delaware Adjutants made no report from 1811 onward except for an obviously spurious report in 1832 for 1827.

Assuming, as seems reasonable in light of these comments, that most failures to report indicate the failure of the state to maintain even a skeletal militia organization, then the number of returns for each year is a rather good index of the existence of the militia. If an army cannot count its men and guns, it probably cannot readily put men in the field. Figure 8–1 shows the percentage of states submitting reports for each year from 1802 to 1862 (except for 1813, 1814, 1817, 1818, 1846, 1847, when the Secretary of War did not submit a report to Congress). This chart shows a high percentage of reporting states in the years from 1802 to 1812 and a gradual decline

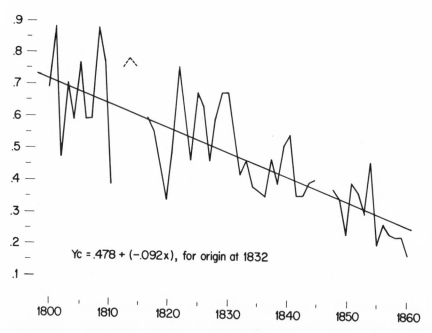

$$Y_c = .478 + (-.092x), \text{ for origin at } 1832$$

Figure 8–1. Percentage of states submitting militia returns, 1802–1812, 1815, 1818–1845, 1848–1860.

thereafter until by the time of the Civil War only a few states were interested in or capable of reporting. (The experience of the whole period, exclusive of the years not reported to Congress, is a straight line on figure 8–1 originating at 1832, with the equation, $Yc = .478 - .092x$.)

The figure clearly demonstrates that the states, by their indifference, destroyed the traditional militia system during the first half of the nineteenth century. In a careful study of the militia from 1846 to 1860, Paul Tincher Smith concluded that the system was destroyed in the era between the Mexican War and the Civil War (Smith, 1919). The statistics in figure 8–1 indicate, however, that the system started to degenrate much earlier. If one must have a date for the inception of decadence, it is clear that during the 1820s the states were only with difficulty maintaining the system and that during the 1830s many of them abandoned the effort.

That the system failed is not surprising. That it lasted as long as it did is a remarkable tribute to the hold that the notion of a citizen-soldiery, the image of Cincinnatus, had on the thought of Amercian politicians. Here is expressed the spirit of sentimental democracy at both its best and worst: At its best in the high confidence in the mass of men, in its faith that the ordinary farmer might easily switch roles from ploughman to rifleman; at its worst in the ideological determination to ignore the reality the militia presented. Thanks to this spirit, the system that died in the 1830s was not officially interred until 1903, even though the Mexican War, the Civil War, and the Spanish War had to be fought without the use of it.

II

The odds against the system were tremendous. It depended for its success on effective state government. Yet few state governments were efficiently organized then. Most of the original states were not rich enough to pay a militia and the new states, which had all they could do to establish a minimum of civil governments on the frontier, had even less money and energy to devote to one. It depended for its success on the enthusiasm of citizens. Yet, increasingly, citizens evaded militia duty, condemned musters as vulgar, and laughed at those patriots who tried to be part-time soldiers. It depended for its success on the enthusiastic support of politicians. Yet politicians were as indifferent as the citizenry. For both political and ideological reasons they refused to create an effective system. In light of these difficulties, the surprising fact is not that the original militia system failed, but that some people at least continued to have faith in it.

The first of the just-mentioned difficulties, the inefficiency of state governments, especially of frontier states, is clearly indicated in table 8–1, which shows the relative frequency of state militia returns. In this table the states are arranged in descending order of the frequency with which they submitted returns. Thus Massachusetts, which submitted returns 52 times in the 54 years that returns were published, stands at the top of the list, while Mississippi, which submitted returns only twice during the 42 years of its statehood that returns were published, stands near the bottom. The 13 original states are printed in italic type. Inspection of the table thus indicates that the original states were, on the whole, more conscientious about submitting returns than the new states. Over one-half the original states submitted returns in over one-half the possible years. Only two, or roughly 10%, of the new states submitted them that frequently: and both those had had a militia before the Act of 1792. The frontier states lacking cash for military expenses, in some cases (e.g., Illinois, Mississippi) made almost no effort to organize a militia. Furthermore, they had no military tradition from the Revolution to live up to. (Incidentally, it is worthy of note that the original states most conscientious about reporting were, generally, those that made the greatest contribution to the Revolutionary cause.) Lacking both military traditions and money, the new states shirked their responsibilities under the Act of 1792. Such shirking had consequences beyond the borders of the delinquent state: No national military officials dared to place much reliance on the militia when only New England, Virginia, New York and perhaps Pennsylvania had the rudiments of militia organization. Thus, the neglect of duty on the part of some states acted as a drag on the militia system as a whole.

The inefficiency of most of the new states and of almost half the original states is probably but a reflection of citizen hostility toward militia service. That hostility is reflected in a variety of ways, for example, the constant increase in the number of exemptions, outright evasion of service, passive disobedience, and positive displays of contempt.

Throughout the period after the War of 1812 until the breakdown of the system, there was a constant pressure for exemptions from militia service, a pressure so effective that in some states the exempt were almost as numerous as the liable. By the Act of 1792, Congressmen, customshouse clerks, seamen, ferrymen on postroads and others believed to owe special duty to the national government were exempted. Most states exempted in addition all state and local officials, all clergymen, all teachers, and all students in colleges. In addition many states exempted millers, ferrymen, conscientious objectors, smiths, members of volunteer fire companies, those who had served five or seven years in the uniformed militia, etc. And then there were other devices for quasi-legal exmption, one of the most

Table 8–1. Percent of years of statehood from 1802 to 1862 for which states submitted militia returns*[a]

State	Percent	State	Percent	State	Percent
Massachusetts	96	Ohio[c]	43	Vermont[c]	26
Connecticut	91	Michigan	39	Indiana	17
Virginia	87	Missouri	36	Tennessee[c]	13
New Hampshire	76	Wisconsin	36	Illinois	13
New York	76	Louisiana	34	Arkansas	13
Maine[b]	75	South Carolina	32	Delaware	7
Kentucky[c]	69	New Jersey	30	Texas	6
Rhode Island	65	Georgia	30	Mississippi	5
North Carolina	59	Alabama	28	Florida	0
Pennsylvania	44	Maryland	26	Iowa	0

[a] Years in which the Secretary of War submitted no returns to Congress are not counted in the base for the percentage. California and Minnesota, which were states for only 12 and 4 years prior to 1862, are omitted on the ground that the base for calculating percentage is too small for reliability.

[b] Maine, as a part of Massachusetts prior to 1820, had the Massachusetts militia organization from before the Revolution.

[c] Vermont, Tennessee, and Kentucky were states before the system of militia returns was instituted. Ohio became a state the same year.

popular of which was brief service as a commissioned officer. The operation of this device is nicely described in one of the exhibits attached to the report of the Militia Board in 1826:[1]

> That the object in accepting a commission is exemption from duty; and that this object is effected, is evident from the rapidity with which exemptions are made. In the last twelve years, eight or ten...different individuals have held the office of colonel of the regiment composed of the militia of this county. This regiment...is thus officered: one colonel, one lieutenant colonel, one major, six captains, seven lieutenants, and six ensigns, twenty-two in the whole, and I think it will not be far from the truth to say that all of these officers have been vacated with nearly the same rapidity that the office of colonel has (*American State Papers, Military Affairs*, vol. 3, p. 476).

If the above testimony by N. Howland of Rhode Island is to be believed, in a regiment of approximately 300 men about 180 earned exemptions in 12 years in this simple way. The testimony continues thus:

> ...in 1823 General Collins was appointed to the command of this brigade; he appointed a Mr. Northern as his aid; in 1824 there was no general; thus Mr. Northern was exempted; in 1825 General Diman took the command of the brigade, and appointed a Mr. West as his aid; in 1826 General Muenscher succeeded...and appointed Mr. Richman as his aid; General Muenscher will resign at the expiration of the year, and his successor appoint some other aid; and thus three individuals, the oldest not more than twenty-six years of age, are exempted from further duty merely by holding a commission a single year.

It might be added that the duties of an aide were not arduous.

The exemption thus achieved in some states by occupational or political privilege was in others achieved by financial privilege, whenever the state allowed exemption on the basis of a commutation fee. In other states exemptions were generalized to all men, even without a commutation fee, under the pressure of democratic agitation. Colonial militia systems invariably contained quite severe fines for absence from musters; and states followed this example in the early years of the Republic. The fines were a considerable source of public revenue, at least enough to pay the expenses of the courts-martial that imposed them, and in some instances even enough to support the militia system. More significantly, the fines were the only method then known of enforcing the principle of universal liability. In the first quarter of the nineteenth century, however, the effectiveness of the fines declined because courts-martial and civil judges reduced the dollar amount and because, with inflation, the dollars cost less. Consequently, for the prosperous the fine came to be regarded as a fee to avoid the vulgarity of musters. Poor men not unnaturally resented the evasion as a plutocratic special privilege. Hence, one of the standard reforms on the list of democratic agitators was equality of exemption by abolition of the militia fine. In states with weak military traditions, e.g., Delaware, this reform was effected quite early in the century by legislative action. Elsewhere, as in Indiana, it was effected somewhat later by lax enforcement. In states with stronger military traditions, the fine was removed only with some struggle.

In the constitutional conventions of Rhode Island in 1842, of New Jersey in 1844, of Iowa in 1846, of California in 1849, of Michigan in 1850, and of Ohio in 1851, the fines were attacked on much the same grounds as imprisonment for debt, an evil to which they were in fact closely related. In 1840 this kind of attack resulted in the complete abolition of militia fines and the invention of the volunteer system in Massachusetts. Maine and Vermont copied Massachusetts in 1844 and New Hampshire did the same in 1851. In New York, on the other hand, in 1846 this attack resulted in changing the fine into a small commutation fee (50 cents per year), which was supposed to be used to support the rest of the militia. Connecticut, Pennsylvania, and Ohio at least, copied the New York device before the Civil War (London, 1957). As table 8–1 indicates, New England, New York, Pennsylvania, and Ohio were among the states that preserved the minimum of militia organization. Yet the consequence of the abolition of fines or of transforming them into commutation fees was in fact the destruction of the traditional system. Equality of exemption was substituted for equality of service and thus the principle of universal liability was clearly negated.

Those who believed in the militia system had to contend not only with the indifference that led to illegal and legal evasion; they had to contend also with active hostility. Militia service was usually regarded as a kind of extra tax, especially as the danger of foreign invasion—which had proved unsuccessful in 1812–1815—receded. Farmers and mechanics, who in all states but Massachusetts lost a day's work and pay by parade, naturally resented the loss. And for those who lost the work and pay, the loss was psychologically the more depressing when many other persons obtained exemption on less and less valid grounds. Against this burdensome system, the ordinary citizen had two weapons, passive disobedience and humor, both of which turned out to be remarkably effective. The increasing degree of passive disobedience is suggested by these figures from New York state: In 1822, 73% of the infantry privates, artillery matrosses, and cavalry troopers were present at the annual muster. In 1835, 57% were present. In 1841, only 47% were present. Thereafter, shamefaced Adjutants General did not publish attendance figures. Some of these absentees paid fines, of course; but the fines in New York were collected by civil officials who were anxious to be reelected. Little was collected and much of what was collected was, because of the opportunities presented by the primitive accounting methods of the era, misappropriated (*Report*, 1843, 1852).

One of the chief reasons few fines were collected was the popular displays of resentment, terrifying indeed to elected persons. In Albany in 1831 there was much agitation of this sort. Several times during the autumn musters burlesque parades followed the militia parade: "The annual military parade of the 89th regiment, Col. John Osborn, and the 246th regiment, Col. A.V. Fryer, took place, when a considerable number of privates appeared in the most ludicrous and fantastic costumes imaginable. The object of the persons engaged in this affair was to bring the militia system into contempt; it gave the officers much annoyance."

Not infrequently, disgusted militiamen elected the town fool their captain in order to display their contempt for the whole business. Perhaps one of the most delightful instances of spoofing the militia system is set forth in the memoirs of O.H. Smith, a Whig Senator from Indiana. The incident apparently occurred in the late 1820s or early 1830s:

"In the early history of Whitewater, the military spirit ran high and all aspirants for honors and places were solicitous to make stepping stones of militia offices. But in time the military spirit began to abate, and officers to resign.... The whole system seemed to be on its last legs, when all at once arose to public notice, in the county of Wayne, the man for the occasion in the person of Major Lewis. He was a young man, like Julius Caesar, of a weak body, but with the military ambition of a Charles II. Although but a lieutenant he became a candidate for major, and having no opposition was triumphantly elected. The first step of the Major was to provide himself with a splendid blue uniform coat, covered with gold lace and large gilt-eagle buttons; a coat that Napoleon himself might have worn while commanding at Austerlitz; a chapeau, in imitation of the one worn by Gen. Jackson at the battle of the Horse Shoe, surmounted by a towering red plume, with a white tip; epaulets that might have graced the shoulders of Blucher as he led the Prussian army to the aid of Wellington at Waterloo; a true Damascus blade in its brilliant scabbard, reaching to the feet; boots of the Suwarrow order, reaching up to his seat, with a pair of gold-plated spurs with shanks a foot long. The great military parade which was to revive the spirit of the revolution, was soon to come off, near the east fork of Whitewater, under the command of Major Lewis in person. Captains were required to be early in the field, with their respective commands, 'armed and equipped as the law directs.'

"The great and memorable day at last arrived. The parade-ground was early filled with waving plumes and crowds of anxious citizens. The aid-de-camp of the Major came galloping into the field in full uniform, directly from head-quarters, and halted at the marquee of the adjutant. In a few minutes the order from the Major was given, in a loud military voice, by the Adjutant mounted on a splendid grey charger: 'Officers to your places, marshall your men into companies, separating the barefooted from those who have shoes, or moccasins, placing the guns, sticks, and corn-stalks in separate platoons, and then form the line ready to receive the Major.' The order was promptly obeyed, in true military style, when at a distance Major Lewis was seen coming into the field, with his aids by his side, his horse rearing and plunging, very unlike old 'Whitey' at the battle of Buena Vista. . . . The line was formed; the Major took position on a rising ground, about a hundred yards in front of the battalion; rising in his stirrups, and turning his face full upon the line—'Attention the whole.' Unfortunately the Major had not tried his voice before in the open air, and with the word 'Attention' his voice broke, and 'the whole' sounded like the whistle of a shrill fife.

"The moment the sound reached the line, someone at lower end, with a voice as shrill as the Major's, cried out 'Children, come out of the swamp, you'll get snake bit.' The Major pushed down the line at full speed. 'Who dares insult me?' No answer. The cry then commenced all along the line, 'You'll get snake bit, you'll get snake bit.' The Major turned and dashed up the line, but soon had sense enough to see that it was the militia system that was at an end, that it was not Major Lewis that was the main object of ridicule. He dashed his chapeau from his head, drew his sword and threw it upon the ground, tore his commission to pieces, and resigned his office on the spot. The battalion dispersed, and milita musters were at an end from that time forward in the Whitewater country" (Smith, 1858, pp. 44–46).

No institution could survive such jeering. But it was not only the city mechanics and rough frontiersmen who condemned musters. The more respectable and prosperous elements of society were equally hostile and it was they who created the stereotype of the militia muster as a drunken display. As early as 1826, in the report of the Militia Board of that year, disdain for the muster is one consistent theme throughout the answers to the questionaire, e.g., "assemblies of the idle and dissipated," "a *red-letter day* or day of dissipation," "the worse than useless musters, . . . instead of schools of practice, schools of insubordination and vice" (*American State Papers, Military Affairs*, vol. 2, pp. 399–400, 435). The motives that a century later led to the Eighteenth Amendment here led to a condemnation and discontinuance of musters.

Besides the inefficiency of state governments and the indifference and hostility of citizens, the militia system faced almost insurmountable administrative problems. From the beginning skeptics recognized these problems clearly. Here speaks Ebenezer Huntington, Revolutionary hero and for long Governor of Connecticut, in answer to a query from his Congressman about how to improve the militia (*American State Papers, Military Affairs*, vol. 2, pp. 263–265):

> The song which has been incessantly sung, ever since the Constitution was adopted, that the militia are the sure bulwark of our nation, the safe guardians of our liberties, is now in the mouth of every one, and he who doubts the truth of it is deemed a political infidel: yet with all the odium attached, I acknowledge myself no convert to such a doctrine. Let the government proceed to regulate the militia to the utmost length...it will be just so far as to make them food for powder in the day of battle; and death, or what is worse, loss of honor, must be expected by every officer of spirit connected with them.

And he concluded with what appears to a later generation as an all too accurate observation: "It is our parsimony which makes us too highly estimate the militia; if the militia were more expensive than enlisted troops, there is not an American but would reprobate the idea."

Huntington expressed his views in 1810, when faith in the militia was still almost universal. After the War of 1812, however, few could deny the lesson of the war, which was, that the system, in aiming at universal preparedness, achieved only universal unpreparedness. Having thus awakened to the inadequacies of the system, politicians increasingly recognized the crucial reason for the failure, that is, the shortage of professionals competent to train militiamen.

The only reforms suggested in Congress from 1792 to 1817 were versions of the Knox plan of 1790—that is, a scheme of several age classes with special and intensive training for the youngest class.[2]

While versions of the Knox plan continued to appear after 1817, those who most carefully and extensively analyzed militia problems offered proposals more directly aimed at alleviating the shortage of officers. William Henry Harrison, as chairman of the House Committee on the Militia in 1818, offered a notable reorganization plan, which, while it proposed age classification and national financing for encampments, emphasized especially a sort of ROTC, that is, national financing for and army supervision of the training of militia officers in schools and colleges (*Annals of Congress*, vol. 23, pp. 609 ff). In 1826 an ad hoc Militia Board, which included in its membership Winfield Scott, Zachary Taylor, and William H. Sumner, the Adjutant General of Massachusetts and much the most imaginative milita officer of the era, proposed nationally financed annual training encampments for militia officers and non-coms (*American State Papers, Military Affairs*, vol. 3, pp. 338–428). This plan was, in the judgment of the present writer, much the most reasonable reform ever suggested while the principle of universal liability was yet retained. Its cost was not excessive, considering what was then spent on the regular army, and it offered genuine promise of producing a reasonably efficient militia. Perhaps it is needless to say that it was never considered by Congress, although most discussion of the militia in the next 20 years relied heavily on it.

The shortage of officers, which is so clearly indicated by the change in the kind of militia reforms discussed in Congress, grew out of many circumstances: Citizen indifference and hostility was, of course, a significant factor; population was growing far more rapidly than the list of graduates from military colleges; internal migration, which was carried on mostly by men of military age, constantly depleted the junior officer class. But, whatever the circumstances that occasioned it, there can be no doubt that the shortage was acute. In the early 1820s Connecticut replaced about one-fourth of its officers annually. While Connecticut could so replace and yet maintain the appearance of a militia, states with fewer human resources could not. In state after state the marginal factor in the failure of the system was vacancy in the Table of Organization and incompetence in such officers as were commissioned. These were the crucial defects which Harrison and the Militia Board tried to remedy.[3] Lacking a good supply of officers, the musters failed, and with the failure of the musters—which were the chief institutional embodiment of the principle of universal liability—the failure of the whole militia system necessarily followed.

In view of these difficulties it is not surprising that the militia system failed. The story of its failure has already been roughly sketched: the transformation of musters from serious military exercises to carnival occasions, the development of methods to evade militia duty, the inglorious record of the militia in the War of 1812. Apart from these broad developments, however, two incidents from the 1830s nicely epitomize the end of the system of 1792:

In 1832, conscious of the shortcomings of the system, Pennsylvania militia officers assembled in extraordinary convention at Harrisburg. After three days of debate, the convention petitioned the national government to reform militia organization. At no point in the record does it appear that anyone thought of asking the state of Pennsylvania to carry out the duties that the Anti-federalists of 1787 and 1790 and 1792 so carefully preserved for it. And what did the national government do? In 1840, at the request of the House Committee on the Militia, which had been bombarded with requests like the one from Pennsylvania, Van Buren's Secretary of War, J.R. Poinsett, submitted a plan for the reorganization of the militia. Poinsett echoed the Militia Board plan and in so doing made no original contribution to militia reform. Unfortunately, however, his plan was offered in an election year, one of the most hotly and irrationally contested elections in our history. Whigs seized upon the proposal for nationally financed encampments of 200,000 men and, as Senator Clay of Alabama said, it "was sent out in all the Whig papers from Aroostook to the Sabine" as a plan for a standing army. Democrats tried to defend themselves with a *tu quoque*. They printed 20,000 copies of the report of the Senate Committee on the Militia, a report that contained the original source of Poinsett's plan, that is, the report of 1818 written by William Henry Harrison who in 1840 was the Whig candidate for President. That the whole issue had ceased to have any relevance to national defense and had come to concern only the Presidential election is clearly demonstrated by the vote in the Senate on printing the report. All the Whigs voted against printing and 90% of the Democrats voted for it—a clear party vote on both sides (*Congressional Globe*, 14 June 1840, vol. 7, p. 462).

Thereafter no nineteenth century Congress ever seriously discussed militia reform. Indeed, in 1855, the Congress officially—though indirectly —recognized that the militia system of 1792 had failed. The occasion was this: The Act of 1808 had provided for the distribution of $200,000 worth of muskets to the states in proportion to the numbers of militia in each state. The army appropriation of March 3, 1855, provided that the distribution be according to the number of representatives and Senators from each state. The pressure for this change came from all those states—a considerable majority—that neglected their duty under the Act of 1792 to enroll the militia and that were therefore getting only a small share of the grant-in-aid. So long as most of the states did their duty under the Act of 1792 there was no reason to change the basis of the calculation of the grant; but, when a large majority neglected their duty, the neglectful ones could change the basis of the distribution.

Examination of figure 8-1 will show that the agitation about militia reform in the 1820s was accompanied by sporadic but rather general submission of returns; that in the years 1840 and 1841, the years of agitation over Poinsett's plan, a number of neglectful states were encouraged to submit returns; that in 1854 in connection with the agitation that led to the new formula of 1855 a large number of neglectful states submitted returns; and finally that in 1855, after the change in formula, fewer states than ever before submitted returns. This point can thus be regarded as the informal demise of the system of 1792, although we continued to pretend that the system existed until 1903.

Revival of the Militia, 1877–1903

Although the states failed to maintain the traditional militia system, they did not entirely neglect their duty under the Constitution. They invented a cheaper and more easily administered substitute, the system of volunteers. While the substitute clearly abandoned the principle of universal liability, which had been the distinguishing characteristic of the militia system in both England and America, this substitute did produce a few companies of organized troops, which is something that the original system no longer provided. It did not, of course, produce enough men to fight a war; but it did keep the notion of a militia alive until, in the late 1870s, the states found a new use for it.

The last significant use by the national government of the militia organized under the Act of 1792 was in the Seminole War (1836–1842). A few militiamen were, it is true, used in 1846–47 against Mexico. (More than "a few," perhaps, for there were 12,601 out of a total force of 104,285; but the militia were only 12% of the total and the rest were national troops, either volunteers or regulars. Although the absolute number of the militia in 1846–1847 is fairly large, the proportion is small, especially in comparison with the War of 1812 when the militia was 88% of the total force, Upton, 1917, p. 221.) A much smaller proportion of militia was used in the Civil War. According to a compilation by the Adjutants General of the states in 1893, only about 47,000 militia were used during the entire war. Most of these were for one or three month tours of duty; and over 80% of them came from New York (*Congressional Record*, 12 January 1983, vol. 24, pp. 514–516). In 1861, militia companies were often, after fairly extensive changes in personnel, transformed into companies of volunteers; but when this happened they lost their distinctive character as a force partially under state control. In 1898, following the precedent of 1861, such militia as were used were transformed into volunteers. Not until 1916 were the militia again used by the national government; and then they were the product of the volunteer system, not the product of the old system of universal military service under the Act of 1792.

Thus, in summary of the history of the militia in the latter half of the nineteenth century, it may be said that when the states abandoned the principle of universal military training, they could not be relied upon to furnish soldiers. Hence for 100 years after 1815, the militia was not extensively used by the national government, even in time of war. Nor was the militia used by the states. As a consequence, it fell into desuetude and was only saved from complete disintegration by the system of volunteer companies which can be regarded as a kind of expiatory substitute by the states for the system of universal service. In the late 1870s, however, the states, suddenly and for wholly domestic purposes, revived the dying volunteer system.

Once revived, the militia was again available for inclusion in the national military system. State governments and militia officers alike were eager to see the revived militia put into military use—for only thus could they justify financial assistance from the national government. This assistance and the integration of the revived militia into the defense system were forthcoming in 1899 and 1903. Hence, the chief developments in the history of the militia system in the latter half of the nineteenth century are the spread of the volunteer system, the revival by the states of the militia in this volunteer form, and the grooming of this revived militia for a place in the national military force.

I

The Militia Act of 1792 did allow for the existence of volunteer companies. Its section 8 permitted states to incorporate private companies that would be attached to the militia but not organized on the territorial principle set forth in the Act. This was, as the debate on the clause clearly demonstrated, a device to preserve some of the notable and socially prominent companies then in existence. (For example, the Ancient and Honorable Artillery Company of Boston, the 1st troop of Pennsylvania Cavalry in Philadelphia, etc.) What was then permitted as an afterthought and as a concession to an already existing institution—even though somewhat inharmonious with the institutions contemplated by the Act— turned out to be the most viable portion of the militia.

The volunteer militia—so called because its members volunteered for service in special companies, often called the uniformed militia because its members provided themselves with uniforms, often called also the active militia because its members undertook to receive more frequent training than the annual or semi-annual parades—was by 1826 beginning to supplant the militia contemplated in the Act of 1792. If one can believe the estimate of the numbers of volunteer militia in the answers to the Militia Board questionnaire, they were something between 10% and 15% of the total militia, that is, something like 100,000 or 150,000 out of a full force of about 1,000,000.[4] The states did much to encourage volunteers. In most states, service in volunteer corps for five or seven years exempted a man from further militia duty. Since by the Act of 1792 all free white males were liable to 27 years of duty, this provision saved at least 20 years, and, what is more, 20 years of fines which might amount to well over $100. Of course, the volunteers had to provide their own uniforms, but, especially if the uniforms were furnished by one who wished to be elected colonel or captain, this was not usually a personal expense. Today a group of village merchants may in a burst of civic pride buy uniforms for the softball team. In the early nineteenth century the same impulse in the same class resulted in a uniformed militia company. One state, Massacuhetts, paid its uniformed militia and had, therefore, the most impressive parades of any state in the union at this era.

The questionnaires sent out for the Militia Board in 1826 contained the question, "Are the regular or volunteer militia most efficient?" The militia officers who replied were almost unanimous in their belief that the volunteers were superior to the regulars. Here follows some typical testimony. "I commanded a militia regiment many years, and I suspect no one ever strove harder to make them respectable, but with little effect. I published a proposition to raise a volunteer regiment, to be clothed in the simplest uniform, viz: a plain blue coat, white pantaloons, and a black cockade. I turned out, one parade, 750, rank and file, and I had the satisfaction to see them respectable and respected" (*American State Papers, Military Affairs*, vol 3, p. 445).

A few doctrinaire Republicans, like General Henry Dearborn, Jefferson's Secretary of War and commander of the disastrous Niagara campaign in 1812-1813, did, it is true, cling to their notion of a citizen soldiery and universal service (*American State Papers, Military Affairs* 3: 475). But they were a small minority among those who had actual experience with militia commands. Not surprisingly, therefore, militia officials tended to rely more and more on the uniformed militia. In Massachusetts in 1840 (Act of 24 March) the state formally abandoned the principle of universal liability and established a system of paid volunteers. Within the next decade, most of the New England states followed suit. In New York, when the musters failed to attract as many as half the enrolled militia, Adjutant General Rufus King (grandson of the Senator) undertook to lend state owned arms to volunteer companies as an inducement toward organization (*Report*, 1842). As a result of this policy, adopted in 1841 and followed by his successors, uniformed companies steadily increased in number, while the militia as a whole declined. In 1846 and 1848, New York devised a new system, already mentioned, of taxing the inactive militia to buy uniforms and arms for the volunteers. Other states followed the lead of New York and Massachusetts, so that by the time of the Civil War, the only real militia were the volunteer corps.

II

In the decade or so after the Civil War, the militia was at its lowest ebb in our history. Only a few Northern states attempted to maintain a militia organization; and during Reconstruction, Southern states could not do so. It is true that in the North the state staffs expanded in the postwar era, but the expansion was solely for the purpose of keeping records of volunteers and militia in the Civil War, not for managing an existent militia organization.

The Adjutant General of Indiana in his report of 1872 explained his work with admirable brevity: "The militia of this State is wholly unorganized and it has not been deemed expedient to attempt the organization of any part of the militia under the present defective law on the subject. . . ." But he did ask for more help because "soldiers look upon the office as a 'Military Intelligence Office' [i.e., office of legal advisor], and the Adjutant General is expected to fully inform himself upon the subject of all laws affecting the interest of soldiers or their heirs or dependent relatives." Much the same condition existed in Iowa, and even in New York, with a much larger militia than any other state, the chief business was the maintenance of historical records (Iowa: *Report*, 1870, p. 41; New York: *Report*, 1868, p. 38).

One indication of the state of the militia in the postwar era is the care that states took of United States ordnance issued them during the Civil War. In the Army Appropriation Act of 3 March 1875, it was enacted that the loyal states be credited for the amount of money they owed the United States for this ordnance, provided that states should receive no credit for those arms that the Secretary of War found had been misapplied or sold. In a report of the Chief of Ordnance 6 February 1878, it appears that only one-third of the states and territories took good care of the material, that is, only 10 of the 29 states and territories were given full credit. Over one-half received either no credit or an insignificant amount. Table 8–2 (offers full detail on the credit given.) Those states that received no credit presumably either sold or lost or gave away the arms. Manifestly, a state that took no better care of military property than this was not the least interested in maintaining a militia. It is not conversely true, however, that

Table 8–2. Credits given to states for ordnance issued by the United States, 1861–1865, and preserved by states until 1877

States given full credit:	
Connecticut, Iowa (only $923 worth issued), Kansas, Maine, Maryland, Massachusetts, Michigan, Pennsylvania (only $1,327 worth issued), and Wisconsin	9 states
States given about 98% credit:	
New York	1 state
States given about 80% credit:	
California, Delaware	2 states
States given about 55% credit:	
Minnesota, Ohio	2 states
States given about 4% credit:	
New Hampshire, Vermont	2 states
States given no credit:	
Illinois, Indiana, Kentucky, Missouri, North Carolina, Oregon, Rhode Island, Tennessee, Arizona, Dakota, Nebraska, New Mexico, District of Cloumbia	
	13 states and territories
	Total: 29

Note. State balances in 1875 varied from $923 (Iowa) to $638,358.37 (Vermont). The average was $57,244, and the mode appears to be about $7,000.

Source. "Letter of the Secretary of War...4 February 1878," Senate Executive Document No. 22, 45th Congress, 2nd Session, Part I, p. 11.

preservation of the arms implied a healthy militia. Indeed, several of the states that saved rifles faithfully had no militia to use them.

The table of credits given for the preservation of Civil War ordnance sets the maximum number of Northern states that might be said to have had an organized militia in the postwar decade. A similar maximum can be set for the Southern states. The Army Appropriation Act of 3 March 1873 directed the distribution to the 11 Southern states of the arms that were due under the grant-in-aid of 1808 but that had not been drawn by these states during the period of war and reconstruction. Then the Army Appropriation Act of 3 March 1875 repealed this provision of the act of 1873 and provided that all undrawn balances be covered into the Treasury. Five of the 11 states (Alabama, Florida, North Carolina, South Carolina Tennessee) thereby lost most or all of what was due under the 1873 appropriation. Presumaby the militia of these states was so disorganized that no officer could even in a two-year period carry out the simple action of ordering arms.

On the basis of these two indications, a maximum of 20 states could keep or order arms, which are among the most rudimentary acts of a military organization. Not all of these 20 had, however, an active militia. Iowa, for example, had only a few companies and these short-lived, although it had a perfect record of preserving arms (Upham, 1920, pp. 13–18). When by order of Congress in 1877 the Adjutant General attempted to revive the militia returns under the Act of 1803, which returns had not been submitted since 1862, many states were totally unable to report, among them a number of states that show up well by the standard of keeping and ordering arms. Thus, Delaware, Georgia, Louisiana, Arkansas, and Virginia, all of which were among the 20, failed to report. In others, for example, Minnesota, there was no organization higher than the company level. On the basis of all the foregoing indications, I estimate that at most 12 states had a militia consisting of permanent and regularly trained volunteer companies with some sort of coordinating organization, however slight, i.e., Maine, Massachusetts, Connecticut, New York, New Jersey, Pennsylvania, Texas, Ohio, Michigan, Wisconsin, Kansas, and California. Thus, at very most, less than one-third of the states kept a militia going during the postwar decade.[5]

This postwar indifference to the militia is quite understandable. Few taxpayers could sympathize with large militia appropriations when there was almost no likelihood of foreign war, when it was apparent that the regular army could easily cope with the death throes of Indian culture, and when the nation already possessed a vast number of unorganized, but campaign hardened, veterans, who could, presumably, be drawn upon in the unlikely event of a military emergency.

Although citizens were thus understandably indifferent and although the militia of over two-thirds of the states was wholly disorganized, still in the late 1870s and early 1880s the volunteer militia suddenly blossomed. Summer training camps, which Massachusetts and Connecticut—and these states alone—had held from the 1850s onward, became a standard feature of the militia system. States began to petition for inspection and training from regular army officers. State military budgets increased rapidly. New York and a few other states began an extensive armory construction program. After preparatory conferences in 1878 and January 1879, the National Guard Association of the United States convened at Saint Louis in October 1879. Fourteen states were represented, six of which clearly had no militia earlier in the decade. The compelling motive for the convention seems to have been a desire to plan strategy for lobbying for an increase in the grant-in-aid under the Act of 1808. Bills for the increase appeared in every subsequent Congress until one passed on February 17, 1887.

III

Considering that by reason of its prewar decadence and its postwar neglect the militia of over two-thirds of the states had wholly decayed by the early 1870s, the revival so soon thereafter is, on the surface at least, utterly inexplicable. Yet the revival occurred; and, if one assumes that men are at all rational, it must have some explicable reason—as indeed it did.

The reason is to be found in the growth of the labor movement in the late 1870s. As the economy recovered from the panic of '73 and as giant and impersonal corporations came to dominate transportation and steel and mining industries, labor unions, which had long been only a minor feature of our economic life, suddenly assumed new roles and somewhat larger proportions. The numerically most sucessful of these in this decade was the Knights of Labor. It had about 5,000 members in 1877 and about 50,000 in 1879. The Knights terrified the propertied classes, not only by its size (though small, in the total working force, it was the largest union the country had yet seen) but also by its secrecy. (by reason of which those who feared it were enabled to magnify their fear). Much more terrifying than the mere organization of labor, however, was the great railroad strike of 1877, which was the first major demonstration of the progress of the labor movement and which was crucial in the history of the militia as well.

The strike was spontaneous and unplanned, though it spread like wildfire to all the major roads of the country. In several cities, notably Pittsburgh and St. Louis, the strikers displayed the violence and vacillation of a *jacquerie*. In the traditional American ideology, a *jacquerie*, downtrodden and disaffected, is not supposed to exist. Perhaps that is why the propertied classes and their politicians—rendered uneasy and resentful by this wholly unexpected event—put down the strike so ruthlessly.

The strike was brief. On most roads it lasted only from the sixteenth or nineteenth of July to about the first of August. Even the Pennsylvania Railroad which suffered by far the greatest amount of property damage, was back in full operation by mid-August. To put the strike down, 11 states used about 45,000 militia. New York and Pennsylvania together spent almost $1,000,000 to suppress the strike.[6] In addition about 2,000 United States troops were used for patrol, while almost the entire army was alerted. About 100 strikers were killed and several hundred more were wounded (Yellen, 1936). The credit for breaking the strike probably belongs to the Army and President Hayes, although undoubtedly the militia killed more strikers[7].

Although the strike was a brief spontaneous eruption, thousands of men were involved on each side and the violence deepened the involvement. Since it was in the transportation industry, it affected at least indirectly even the remotest parts of the country. Consequently, as has often been remarked, this strike developed class consciousness in the hitherto fairly docile American workingman and served as the prelude to the endemic strikes of the next decade. What is less seldom realized, however, is that the strike developed class consciousness in the owners and managers of corporations as well. They could no longer conceive of themselves exclusively in the idyllic role of master craftsman or even in the politically irresponsible role of entrepreneur, assigned to them in classical economics. They were forced to think seriously of physical means of controlling their employees. Thomas A. Scott, president of the Pennsylvania, described the strike as an "insurrection" and, even after the strike was well broken, seriously likened it to the beginning of the Civil War (Scott, 1877). When economic relations are discussed by businessmen in terms such as these, then the captain of industry cannot well avoid becoming, at least indirectly, a captain of armies also. With this new role for businessmen, there followed a new function for the military and a new opportunity for the militia.

Businessmen and politicians decided almost instantaneously that the strike was to be broken by force. Even before the strike was several hours old and while it was a minor *contretemps* in one small town, the governor of West Virginia, at the request of officials of the Baltimore and Ohio Railroad, called out the militia—an action that probably contributed much to the subsequent violence on both sides. But it was not clear for some months what military organization would be assigned the function of strike-breaking. That the militia finally received the assignment is indeed the crucial circumstance in the development of the National Guard.

Initially, the regular army seemed most likely to receive the assignment. In numerous states the militia failed to cope with the strikers until backed up or superceded by the Regulars. One thousand Regulars finally broke the strike in Pennsylvania, where it was most violent and prolonged, where 9,000 militia out of one of the best systems in the country failed. Not only was the army objectively superior here but also it was available in all states, something that could not be said of the militia. President Scott of the Pennsylvania, whose authority in this matter doubtless deserves respect, thought that only five states had militia adequate for "suppressing riots." Furthermore, some businessmen at least wanted to give the army the function and some army officers wanted to get it. In the essay just cited, Scott proposed that Congress empower the federal courts to grant, on the mere application of employers, injunctions against strikes in interstate commerce, injunctions that, he expected, the army would regularly enforce. Such a system would, of course, tend to place individual employers in the position of army commanders, a position not a few seemed to covet. The Secretary of War also seemed to welcome it. Apparently he thought frequent riot duty would help wring from Congress increased appropriations for the army; and so he urged the army's case for the function of strike-breaking:[8]

> The army is to the United States what a well-disciplined and trained police force is to a city....Those who oppose any increase in the Army do so upon the theory that the local militia is sufficient for all purposes of preserving the peace and suppressing local uprisings....[But] Our fathers who framed the Constitution...doubted the wisdom of relying upon the militia, and so provided for the employment of Federal troops for this purpose. If this seemed necessary to them,...how much more necessary is the same thing now? As our country increases in population and wealth, and as its great cities become numerous, it must clearly be seen that there may be great danger of uprising...; and it is a well-known fact that such uprisings enlist in greater or less degree the sympathies of the communities in which they occur. This fact alone renders the local militia unreliable in such an emergency. Besides, it is known that few of the States have any permanent or well-drilled soldiery, and the recent troubles have strikingly illustrated the value, in such an emergency, of the discipline, steadiness, and coolness which raw levies never possess, and which characterize only the trained and experienced soldiery.

In the famous Burnside report (1878) on the organization of the Army, General Sherman, then the commanding general, included numerous quotations from Washington's writings, tending to demonstrate that Washington distrusted the militia.[9] The clear inference, which, however, the Senate committee did not formally draw, was that the army ought to be used for all military functions, including, presumably, police duty. Shortly thereafter (in 1880) General Upton wrote his penetrating history of American military policy, one of the central themes of which was the persistent inadequacy of the militia. Upton urged the repeal of the grant-in-aid of 1808, which would, of course, have resulted in the complete collapse of the militia and the inheritance by the army of its police functions.

Superior as the army was in both action and availability, eager as both captains of industry and generals of the army were for the army to assume police duty, still the militia was gradually recognized to have the assignment, and with it the militia prospered.

Probably the chief reason the militia was settled upon as the solution to "labor troubles" was that it proved loyal in 1877. In his report for the year of the strike, the Adjutant General of Pennsylvania remarked, in some astonishment, that the Guard obeyed orders (Report, 1977): "Composed as it is, not of capitalists, but largely of men who are employed, it is surprising that, under the circumstances, there was not more real and permanent disaffection. What little there was, was only temporary, and the speedy return to duty, which was thereafter performed with courage, zeal and fidelity, entitle the citizen soldiery to the confidence and support of the people." If the militia could be relied on to protect property in Pennsylvania, where feeling ran highest in 1877, then certainly it could be relied on elsewhere. And indeed, except for West Virginia, such was the experience of all other states that called out the militia.

The volunteer form of organization favored this display of loyalty. Had the traditional system of geographical enrollment been in force, most units would have contained men in sympathy with the strikers and would not therefore have been trustworthy. But under the volunteer system, recruits tended to be only those who were willing to perform strike duty. In numerous instances groups of businessmen formed volunteer units during the strike. In that way the militia of, for example, Iowa, doubled in size. Though no more than chance posses, they acted as if they were organized militia, a fact that doubtless accounts for the excessive bloodiness of the strike-breaking. These ad hoc volunteers were, of course, persons with an ideological or even pecuniary interest in breaking the strike. Thus in Indiana in 1877, 11 companies were organized in Indianapolis during the strike. Of them the Adjutant General said: "They were composed of our best citizens, and commanded by some of our most distinguished men..." (e.g., S. K. Flecther, a leading banker; Benjamin Harrison, subsequently President of the United States; Lewis Wallace, son of the noted author-politician; etc.) (*Report*, 1878). When the politico-economic opinions of militiamen were suspect, they could easily be discharged, something that would have been impossible under the old system of universal military service on a geographic basis. The Adjutant General of Indiana described exactly how the process worked. After telling of his inspection of a company in a coal-mining county where there had recently been strikes, he said: "I found that some of the company had been miners, and deeming it better that none who were in any [sic] interested in the mining troubles should belong to the company, I so directed, and one officer and 37 men were mustered out....The remaining portion of the company being composed of farmers, and seeming satisfactory to all parties, were permitted to remain as a militia company."

It is somewhat overstating the case to attribute the revival of the militia to the railroad strike of 1877. The strike was, however, a crucial event. It awakened in the substantial taxpayers a sense of need for a large internal police and made them willing, even eager, to pay for it. While they could not persuade Congress to enlarge the army, they could and did persuade state legislatures to appropriate money for the militia. Militia officers, who were delighted with the opportunity to do something, quite eagerly pointed out their value. "Now that the importance of a good militia has been so fully demonstrated," said the Adjutant General of New York in his report for 1877, "it may be confidently expected that the Legislature will hereafter increase the appropriation...for the National Guard." By the confluence of these two interests, corporate managers and owners and national guard officers, who were of course overlapping classes, state support for the militia did suddenly increase in 1878. New York began its great armory building program. Iowa for the first time began to spend money on the National Guard, etc., etc. Any proper statement of the cause of the revival of the militia would mention, of course, the fact that it had never completely died, that the constitutional tradition assigned the police function to the states, and that Congress clearly preferred to let the states spend money to break strikes, etc.; but any statement of the cause must necessarily also mention extensively the strike of 1877 and all the reactions to it.

IV

For some time after the revival of the militia, strike duty continued to be its primary function. In a compilation based on reports from state Adjutants General and admittedly incomplete, it appears that at the very minimum 30% of the instances of active duty for the militia from 1877 to 1892 were in connection with strikes. And, of course, most such duty involved longer active service and a larger number of militiamen than any other kind. Table 8–3 contains a compilation of these instances. Thirty percent are in some way clearly labeled as strike duty, while many others called "suppression of riots," "preservation order," "repression of a mob," and "enforcement of law" are, so examination of the annual reports of Adjutants General indicates, actually instances of labor disturbances. Since even in that era strike-breaking was politically dangerous, Adjutants General apparently used what they believed were euphemisms. On the basis of a check on a random sample of the actual events euphemistically described, it seems certain that well over half the instances of active militia service reported to the House committee were strike duty.

That the primary function of the revived National Guard was strike duty

Table 8–3.   Occasions for the use of the militia, 1877–1892

Labor troubles	33	instances
Suppression of riots	14	''
Preservation of order and enforcement of law	12	''
Repression of a mob	11	''
Guarding jails and assistance in making arrests	24	''
Prevention of lynchings	9	''
Natural disasters	4	''
Indian troubles	2	''
Election riots	2	''
Unspecified	1	''
Total	112	instances

Source: House Report No. 754, 52nd Congress, 1st Session, pp. 16–20.

can be clearly inferred from this compilation; and the function is equally evident in the reported conversations of militia officials. In the 1881 convention of the National Guard Association the chief question under discussion was whether or not states ought to maintain cavalry and artillery, both of which, by reason of their equipment, cost much more than infantry. Stated as most of the officers present seemed to think of it, this question was: "Given our function of strike duty, is infantry enough or is cavalry and artillery also necessary?" The Adjutant General of Rhode Island answered: "With our modern breech loading arms, I believe that infantry troops will be found equal to all emergencies in times of riot...." The Adjutant General of Pennsylvania, on the other hand, favored artillery: "...there can be no question of the efficiency of the artillery of the National Guard in putting down riots...a battery loaded with grape and cannister has a most discouraging effect upon a body of rioters..." (*Proceedings, Third Convention*, 1881, pp. 10, 17).

The Adjutant General of Illinois, however, favored both cavalry and artillery:

"We have a battalion of five companies of cavalry, all located in the city of Chicago. It grew out of our riots of 1877, previous to which we had no cavalry in the State. During the riots it was found necessary to have a cavalry among our business men who had seen cavalry serve [i.e., service] during the war. This cavalry was very efficient. As the enemy they were compelled to meet were not armed with long ranged rifles or breech loaders, the cavalry were able to make many successful charges. They also did good service from the rapidity with which they could go from one part of the city to another to quell a disturbance. Our cavalry was not equipped by the State. It belongs, however, to the National Guard, but was equipped and uniformed by the Citizens' Association of the City of Chicago. This association is composed of business men, who look after the best interest of our city. . . .

"We feel that both branches of this service should be encouraged. We all know how effective light artillery may be made upon any unorganized crowd. Canister is very unhealthy indeed for that kind of people, and very effective" (*Proceedings*, pp. 13-14).

Clearly, people who talked about the National Guard in such terms conceived of it as a strikebreaking force. But perhaps the clearest evidence of the primacy of strike duty in the revived militia of the 1880s is the remarkably high correlation between the appropriations for the militia and the number of strikers in each state. In 1891, appropriations for the militia varied widely among the states (See table 8–4). New York appropriated $400,000—as much as the United States Congress; Pennsylvania $300,000. Thirty-seven states appropriated amounts between $3,900 (Delaware) and $244,630 (Massachusetts). Arkansas, Idaho, Mississippi, Missouri, and Wyoming appropriated nothing. It is noteworthy that, by and large, the states with many strikers in 1881-1885 were the ones that appropriated large amounts of money. (For this calculation, the number of strikers was taken from the first part of the decade, while the appropriations were taken from the end of the decade, in order to allow sufficient time for the problem of strikes to impress legislators.) Thus, New York had more strikers than any other state, 283,907; Pennsylvania followed with 198,532. Arkansas, on the other hand, had only 253 in the six years, Idaho and Wyoming had none, and Mississippi 197. Superficially at least, it appears from these examples that there is some close relationship between the number of strikers and appropriations for the militia; and in fact, when these two measures are correlated, the calculation results in the amazingly high figure of $r = +.84$. (A correlation of 1.00 indicates complete interdependence of two variables, while a correlation of $+.00$ indicates complete independence.) This is a spurious correlation, however, in that the states with large appropriations are those with large populations (and hence presumably large tax resources) as well as large numbers of strikers. In order to control the distorting influence of population in this calculation, one can compute a partial correlation, with the influence of population eliminated. Ths results in:

r (appropriations to strikers with population constant) $= +.59$.

This is to say that if the population of each state is assumed to be equal, there is still a correlation of .59 between the appropriations of 1891 and the

Table 8-4.   Militia expenditures, 1891; population, 1890; and number of strikers,
1881-1886

State	Dollars for militia, 1891[a]	Population in 1890[b]	Number of strikers 1881-1886[c]
Alabama	29,300	1,513,401	1,651
Arkansas		1,128,211	253
California	156,573	1,213,298	6,763
Colorado	40,000	413,219	10,720
Connecticut	117,000	746,258	9,236
Delaware	3,900	168,493	1,537
Florida	7,500	391,422	6,178
Georgia	25,000	1,837,353	1,836
Idaho		88,548	
Illinois	132,500	3,826,352	175,837
Indiana	37,000	2,192,404	15,105
Iowa	35,000	1,912,297	15,936
Kansas	22,350	1,428,108	2,291
Kentucky	10,000	1,858,635	3,682
Louisiana	12,000	1,118,588	16,837
Maine	20,000	661,086	2,468
Maryland	40,000	1,042,390	16,347
Massachusetts	244,630	2,238,947	36,695
Michigan	73,286	2,093,890	23,920
Minnesota	40,000	1,310,283	9,792
Mississippi		1,289,600	197
Missouri		2,679,185	4,816
Montana	6,500	142,294	19
Nebraska	12,500	1,062,656	753
Nevada	8,200	47,355	
New Hampshire	30,000	376,530	1,510
New Jersey	148,516	1,444,933	17,082
New York	400,000	6,003,174	283,907
North Carolina	13,000	1,617,949	110
North Dakota	11,000	190,983	1,865
Ohio	87,400	3,672,329	73,286
Oregon	20,000	317,704	585
Pennsylvania	300,000	5,258,113	198,532
Rhode Island	24,000	345,506	2,817
South Carolina	10,000	1,151,149	1,044
South Dakota	4,000	348,600	111
Tennessee	2,900	1,767,518	1,952
Texas	15,000	2,235,527	6,822

Vermont	30,000	332,422	102
Virginia	10,000	1,655,980	6,172
Washington	80,000	357,232	2,171
West Virginia	10,000	762,794	6,851
Wisconsin	69,431	1,693,330	15,217
Wyoming		62,555	576
Total	2,305,186		983,636
	$r_{13.2} = + .588$		

[a] House. Report No. 754, 52nd Congress, 1st session.
[b] Eleventh Census.
[c] *Third Annual Report of the Commissioner of Labor*, 1887 (Washington, D.C.: U.S Government Printing Office), p. 834.

strikers of 1881–1886. Considering all the influences that might lead a state legislature to appropriate money for the militia, considering for example the effect of the Indian menace (still significant in the West), considering, for another example, the effect of the traditionally large appropriations in Massachusetts and Connecticut (which had the highest standards of militia organization throughout the nineteenth century), considering the poverty of the South (which was just beginning to emerge from the miseries of Reconstruction)—considering, then, all these other possible influences on militia appropriations, the figure of .59 is exceptionally high. (Although the correlation pertains to an entire population, it is of some interest to note that, were this a sample of 44 cases out of a larger population, a coefficient as low as +.39 would be significant at the level of 1%. That is, if one were to select figures from the given range for correlation randomly, in only 1% of the correlations would the result be as high as .39.) In short, it is reasonable to infer that the primary motive for the revival of the militia was a felt need for an industrial police.

Notes

1. The report of the Militia Board of 1826 is probably one of the most notable public documents of the nineteenth century and certainly one of the best sources of information for the study of the militia of that era. It is discussed in: John K. Mahon, "A Board of Officers Considers the Condition of the Militia in 1826" *Military Affairs* 15 (1951): 85–94.

2. Versions of the Knox plan were debated, in Congress in the following years: 1797, 1798, 1806, 1808, 1811, 1812, 1813, 1816, 1817, 1823, 1824, and 1831,.

3. In this era few people criticized the election of company officers by militiamen. It took the experience of the Civil War to convince us that elected officers might have more skill in

winning elections than in winning battles. The Militia Board report did, however, suggest—in striking anticipation of the present system—that elected and appointed officers be subject to examination by the War Department. *American State Papers: Military Affairs*, vol. III, p. 444.

4. The estimates, it should be noted, are hardly worthy of credence. One militia general in Kentucky estimated the volunteers as one-fourth of the total for the state, another estimated them as one-twentieth. Only in Virginia and Massachusetts was an accurate count kept, and in these states the volunteers did amount to about one-fourth of the whole. It is highly unlikely that any other state had so high a proportion of volunteers, for in this decade Massachusetts and Virginia had by far the most vigorous militia systems.

5. "Letter from the Secretary of War. . .4 February 1878," Senate Executive Document No. 22, 45th Congress, 2nd Session, Part III, Appendix B, pp. 3–5.

6. The number of men and the expense is based on a calculation from detail given in XIV *Congressional Record* 512-14, 12 January 1893, based on reports of Adjutants General of the states, and on "Report of the Adjutant General," New York Assembly Documents, 1878, vol. 1, no. 6.

7. Frederick T. Wilson, *Federal Aid in Domestic Disturbances*, Senate Document No. 209, 57th Congress, 2nd Session, pp. 192, 198, 201. The Secretary of War boasted that the Army accomplished its mission "without bloodshed" (p. 205).

8. "Report of the Secretary of War, 19 November 1877," House Executive Document 1, part 2, 45th Congress, 2nd Session.

9. Senate Report No. 555. 45th Congress, 3rd Session, pp. 89–101.

9 ADMINISTRATIVE CENTRALIZATION

William H. Riker

Commentary. *This chapter is a summary of the process of centralization of administrative activities in the United States. While it is based entirely on my subjective judgment, most students of American federalism would probably agree with me on most of these judgments. Thus, in the category "external affairs," for example, it seems indisputable that, in 1790, the states controlled the entire military force of the United States, but by 1850 they controlled almost none of it. On the other hand, there may well be dispute about my judgment that only recently has the United States come to share control of civil rights. Subjective as it is, however, I am emboldened to reprint this summary because it coincides extremely well with the data later collected by Alexander (1974) and Pommerehne (1977). Alexander found that in 1962 the federal portion of domestic expenditures was 0.49, and Pommerehne found that in 1965 the federal proportion of all expenditures was 0.55. My judgment for 1964 was similar: that the federal government controlled slightly over half of total administrative activity. (That is, in table 9-1 in this chapter I attribute an average score of 2.8 on centralization, which is slightly on the national side of a scale, where 1.0 is national control and 5.0 is state control.) Similarly, at the earlier end of the time series, I had,*

From *Federalism: Origin, Operation, Significance*, pp. 81–94.

subjectively, assigned the federal government about one-fifth of the administrative control in 1850 and Alexander found that the federal proportion of domestic expenditures was about 0.22.

This chapter contains an examination in 19 categories of action of the degree of centralization (or peripheralization) of federalism in the United States. It is apparent that one theme running through these brief verbal descriptions is that the federal government has acquired more duties, in relation to the states, over the years. Both kinds of governments have grown with the nation, but the federal government seems to have become somewhat more conspicuous than that of the states.

This conclusion is summarized numerically in table 9–1 which indicates, for each of the 17 substantive areas of spending money, the relative position of federal and constituent governments at four time periods. The entries are defined thus

1.   The functions are performed exclusively or almost exclusively by the federal government.
2.   The functions are performed predominantly by the federal government, although the state governments play a significant secondary role.
3.   The functions are performed by federal and state governments in about equal proportions.
4.   The functions are performed predominantly by the state governments, although the federal government plays a significant secondary role.
5.   The functions are performed exclusively or almost exclusively by the state governments.
–   The functions were not recognized to exist at the time.

The choice of a particular entry is, of course, my highly subjective judgment based only on my immersion in the study. Others might disagree with my assignments, but by keeping the discriminations crude, that is, by using only a five-point scale, disagreements are probably minimized. The last row of the table shows the average for each of the time points of all functions then recognized to exist. Since the 17 (or 14, or 15) categories of functions are by no means of equal significance politically or socially, it may well be argued that the average is without meaning. Therefore, I have made the same kind of judgment for possibly equally significant groups of functions (external affairs, internal order, trade, and welfare) and the result is approximately the same.

Table 9–1. The degree of centralization in the United States by substantive functions and at points in time

Functions	ca. 1790	ca. 1850	ca. 1910	ca. 1964
1 External affairs	4	1	1	1
2 Public safety	5	4	4	4
3 Property rights	5	5	4	4
4 Civic rights	5	5	5	3
5 Morality	5	5	5	5
6 Patriotism	3	3	3	3
7 Money and credit	3	4	3	1
8 Transport and communication	4	4	2	2
9 Utilities	5	5	5	4
10 Production and distribution	5	5	4	2
11 Economic development	3	4	3	2
12 Resources	—	—	2	2
13 Education	—	5	5	4
14 Indigency	5	5	5	2
15 Recreation	—	4	4	3
16 Health	—	—	4	3
17 Knowledge	1	1	1	2
Average	4.1	4.0	3.5	2.8

But granted that the federal government has become administratively somewhat more conspicuous than the states, the question remains: Does this table of American experience support the administrative theory of federalism? I think not. Under this theory, administrative centralization is what is supposed to preserve and maintain the central government. But if one looks at the crucial period for the survival of federalism in the United States, that is, from 1790 to 1850, it appears that some functions were centralized and others were decentralized. Military centralization was matched by economic decentralization (cf. rows 1, 7, and 11). We have no easy way of knowing whether or not these reallocations were in areas of comparable importance; but we do know that the reallocations were not all in the same direction—as they have been since the Civil War. And since they are not all in the same direction we cannot affirm that administrative centralization is what preserved the federal bargain in the pre-Civil War era.

On the other hand, the sharing of administration is what is supposed to preserve the guarantees to the states. Yet, according to the table, sharing has declined notably in the last period (i.e., from 1910 to the present) whereas the fundamental guarantees to the states seem as strong as ever. I conclude, therefore, that the administrative theory is totally inadequate to explain the maintenance of federalism. Unfortunately, most American students of the subject have been deeply attracted to the theory; hence it has tended to obscure constitutional realities. I will be content if this essay has no other impact but to disabuse scholars of their faith in the clearly false administrative theory of federalism.

10 PRESIDENTIAL ACTION IN CONGRESSIONAL NOMINATIONS

William H. Riker and William Bast

Commentary. In striking contrast to the progressive centralization of administration, there seems to have been very little centralization of political control. The measurement in chapter 4 (Riker and Schaps) and chapter 5 (Alexander, with Riker) demonstrates, of course, that political relationships between the nation and the states have varied randomly without a trend. But that measurement does not help us explain why the relation is random. Had complete centralization occurred, it would be easy to trace the development of political dominance from the center. Or had the system disintegrated, it would be easy to trace the dissolution of federation. What has happened, however, is something in between, and it is difficult, therefore, to account for something that seems not to change in any specific direction.

In an effort to identify the source of random variation, Bast and I asked: "What kind of institutions or political events would bring about political centralization?" Our answer was that centralization means truly national leadership, that such leadership can exist only through the medium of political parties, that the only agent who might conceivably restructure a

Originally published in Aaron Wildavsky, ed., *The Presidency* (Boston, Little, Brown, 1969), pp. 250–267.

political party for such leadership is the President, and that, therefore, any
institutional arrangement or series of events that induced or prohibited
Presidential leadership of parties would be the marginal forces for or against
centralization. The easiest and perhaps the only way the President might
control his party is to control its nominations for national office, as do, for
example, prime ministers in most parliamentary systems. The place to look
for opportunities for leadership, therefore, is in nominations, which is the
subject of this chapter. That we find twentieth century Presidents, imperial as
they are sometimes said to be, have almost no control of nominations is
convincing evidence that Presidents cannot control their parties and hence
cannot choose congressmen. Instead they must work with congressmen who
are chosen for them. Sometimes, by dint of ideological persuasion,
Presidents may convince their partisans to nominate compatible congress-
men and state officials and then Presidents tend to centralize, as did, for
example, Lincoln and Franklin Roosevelt. But just as easily Presidents may
fail to lead ideologically, in which case the system reverts to its initial state of
balance, perhaps just as the framers intended.

In his recent work, *Presidential Power*, Richard E. Neustadt poses the
question of what a President "can do to make his own will felt within his
own Administration" (Neustadt, 1960, p. vii). This question, so reminiscent of the "prince-books" or "kings' mirrors" of early modern times, is
wholly appropriate again in this century, which has witnessed the
remarkable and world wide revival of popular expectations of effective
executive leaderships. For political scientists with a practical interest in
good government, questions similar to Neustadt's are probably more
appropriate than those questions of constitutional structure and political
behavior with which they have conventionally been concerned. At least for
us it was a conviction of the need for more concentrated executive power
that informed the inquiry reported here into an especially sensitive area of
presidential action.

Presidential Endorsements of Candidates in Congressional Primaries

The constitutional separation of powers, which renders it difficult for
Presidents to influence congressmen, is only partially modified by party
allegiance. As Neustadt properly remarks, the continuing effectiveness of
the forms of this eighteenth century constitutional theory is due to the fact

that the President and his congressional partisans are elected in different ways:

> The White House has too small a share in nominating Congressmen, and Congress has too little weight in nominating Presidents for party to erase their constitutional separation. Party links are stronger than is frequently supposed, but nominating processes assure the separation (Neustadt, 1960, p. 34).

This separation is in sharp contrast to the unification often achieved through party control in parliamentary regimes. In England, for example, the Prime Minister has a great deal to say about who gets nominated for the safe seats of his party and thereby can often exercise a continuing control over both those members of his party who have such seats and those who would like to have them.

While American Presidents cannot easily exercise such control over congressmen, they have often tried to do so. In the sense that they attempt to formulate a popular ideology to which others will adhere simply because it is popular they are in an indirect way also attempting to control the kind of people who are nominated for Congress. But in addition to this general ideological leadership, many of the more capable or ambitious or activist Presidents have tried to influence nominations directly. Ever since Jefferson's time, Presidents have urged their personal or ideological allies to seek nominations and often have helped them to form local coalitions for this purpose. From Jackson's time until the early twentieth century, many Presidents extensively manipulated patronage to affect congressional nominations. But in recent years, especially since the passage of the Seventeenth Amendment and later the Hatch Act, such manipulation has been more difficult. Not only is there relatively less patronage and not only is the civil service somewhat isolated from party politics but also the character of the nominating process has changed. What formerly was done in caucus and convention, where coalitions could be constructed in the privacy of the hotel room, is now done in primary elections. While the President is not debarred from sending agents to help make alliances for his ideological friends whom he hopes to nominate for Congress, often his influence is nonexistent unless he speaks out publicly. And this he is loath to do for reasons that we will examine in detail.

Between 1913 and 1960 there were—so far as we can discover—39 instances in which Presidents have publicly endorsed candidates in congressional primaries of their own parties. Since two of the instances were reendorsements of already endorsed candidates, in fact there were only 37 public interventions in primaries. In each party during this period there were about 12,000 nominations, mostly by primary elections. Thirty-seven is only an infinitesimal fraction of these. Even if one considers only the 31 instances in which Presidents endorsed candidates in Senatorial primaries, this number is less than 5% of the approximately 800 senatorial nominations in each party. Even subtracting from 800 the nominations made in years of presidential elections in which the incumbent was not a candidate, 31 is still less than 5% of the Senatorial nominations. It seems fair to say, therefore, that Presidents have been deeply reluctant to attempt, at least publicly, to control congressional nominations.

Considering that, as Neustadt observes, the curtailment of Presidential power by the separation of branches is maintained as a viable constitutional form owing to the President's lack of control over congressional nominations, considering further that the acquisition of control over nominations would greatly enhance the President's power to influence the whole process of government, and considering finally that Presidents seem to have been exceptionally reluctant to attempt to exercise control over congressional nominations, we are led to ask two questions:

1) Why have Presidents so seldom endorsed candidates in congressional primaries? and

2) Is there any way, given the present state of American politics, that a President might obtain some control over congressional nominations in his own party?

While the first question probably cannot be answered definitively, some of the compelling considerations can be surmised from historial and analytical evidence. As for the second question, which is a matter of practical invention or political engineering, only Presidents themselves can answer it, although the concerned political scientists may make suggestions on the basis of an examination of the outcome of instances of Presidential endorsements.

The basic data for answering both questions are, of course, information about public Presidential activity in congressional primaries. This we have obtained by examining all entries under both Presidential and state politics in the index of the *New York Times* from 1913 to the present. Whenever an entry in the index even hinted at public Presidential endorsement of a candidate in a primary, we examined the news story. If it recorded such an endorsement, we then examined the regional press. A summary of the 39 instances of endorsement that we discovered is set forth in the Appendix. The same material is arranged somewhat differently and even more summarily in table 10–1. Incidentally, we used 1913 as the base year for that was the year the Seventeenth Amendment became operative and thereby took Senatorial nominations out of the privacy of the legislative caucus and into (usually) the public arena of the primary.[1]

Table 10–1. Success and failure of presidentially endorsed candidates in congressional primaries, 1913–1959

Presidential action	Candidate succeeded[a]	Candidate failed
President endorsed incumbent	4 (Tillman, 1918); 8 (Lewis, 1918); 10 (Tillman, 1918); 11 (Frelinghuysen, 1922); 13 (Reese, 1930); 16 (Pepper, 1938); 17 (Thomas, 1938); 19 (Bulkley, 1938); 20 (Thomas, 1938); 21 (Barkley, 1938); 22 (Caraway, 1938); 37 (Kilgore, 1952)	12 (Lenroot, 1926); 23 (McAdoo, 1938); 30 (Wheeler, 1946)
President endorsed incumbent's opponent	5 (Slayden, 1918); 6 (Vardaman, 1918); 9 (Hardwick, 1918); 27 (Fay, 1938); 31 (Slaughter, 1946)	7 (Huddleston, 1918); 18 (Gillette, 1938); 24 (George, 1938); 25 (Lewis, 1938); 26 (Smith, 1938)
President endorsed a candidate when no incumbent was in the primary	1 (Underwood, 1913); 2 (Palmer, 1914); 3 (Ford, 1918); 14 (Burke, 1934); 15 (Fish, 1936); 28 (Johnson, 1941); 29 (Gillette, 1944); 33 (Carrol, 1950); 34 (Loveland, 1950); 35 (Di Salle, 1950); 36 (Granger, 1950); 39 (McKay, 1956)	32 (Hennings, 1950); 38 (Symington, 1952)

[a] Each entry consists of a reference number to an item in the Appendix, plus, parenthetically, the name of the chief congressional figure and the date of the endorsement.

The Reasons for Presidential Reluctance

There undoubtedly exists an old and persuasive tradition in American politics that a congressional nomination is exclusively the business of the state or district the congressman represents. The constitutional provision that each congressman be a resident of the state he represents was undoubtedly intended to prevent that centralized control of nominations that since Tudor days had been a striking feature of the English political system. Similarly, the almost never-violated tradition, which seems to have been in force from 1788 onwards, that Representatives be residents of the districts they represent seems to be an elaborating detail on the constitutional provision about residence.

Presidents have generally felt the force of this tradition. In nearly all the 39 instances we have collected, Presidents in one way or another apologized for intervening in a "local" affair. When Wilson endorsed a candidate in the Georgia senatorial primary of 1918 as part of a general program of eliminating Southern Democrats not sufficiently enthusiastic about the war, he still contrived to make it appear that the impulse for the endorsement originated in Georgia, not in the White House. Thus the endorsement was given in response to an (undoubtedly inspired) request from the editor of the *Atlanta Constitution:*

> Your letter, I observe, is addressed to me by you in your capacity as a member of the National Democratic Committee, and I assume that it is proper for me to answer the question in the interests of the party as a national unit. . . . I have never undertaken and I would not presume to undertake to dictate to the voters of any state the choices they must make, but when my views have been sought by those who seem to have the right to seek them, I have not hesitated to give them. . . . (*New York Times,* August 12, 1918, p. 9. See Appendix, item 9)

Most of the other endorsements Wilson made during that summer had the same form, a local request, followed by a joint explanation and endorsement. Similarly, when Franklin Roosevelt began the purge of 1938, he prefaced his action with a fireside chat that was both a justification and an apology:

> As head of the Democratic party. . .charged with carrying out the definitely liberal declaration of principles set forth in the 1936 Democratic platform, I feel I have every right to speak in those few instances where there may be a clear issue between the candidates for a Democratic nomination involving those principles or involving a clear misuse of my own name (Roosevelt, 1941).

The earlier Roosevelt, who was, if anything, more eager than his younger cousin to acquire power over his congressional partisans, drew back quite sharply when it came to "interfering" in "local" nominations. Much as he disliked Senator Teller (Democrat, Colo.), T. R. would do nothing to help Colorado Republicans agree on a candidate. Perhaps as a result, a few Republican legislators defected to Teller, who was then reelected. Writing to his close friend, Philip B. Stewart of Denver, Roosevelt said, "Of course, now [since his elevation to the presidency over a year previously] I can take no part of any shape or kind in the senatorial contest. The President has no business to interfere" (Morison, 1951–1954, vol. 3, p. 378). Furthermore, although he was a constant behind-the-scenes manipulator of New York politics, although indeed one of his great achievements as President was to wrest control of the New York Republican party from the Platt stalwarts, still in 1906 at the height of his self-assurance and popularity T. R. refused to speak out publicly for Hughes for the New York Republican gubernatorial nomination, even though it was in Roosevelt's own state:

> Most of the people whom I have consulted feel very strongly that such action as you suggest [a public endorsement of Hughes] would be a harm instead of a benefit. . . . They feel that I have gone as far as I can safely go, and that an utterance from us [Roosevelt or his Secretary of War Elihu Root] would have directly the opposite effect of what is anticipated (Morison, 1951–54, vol. 3, p. 466).

This persistent reluctance by Presidents to intervene in congressional primaries is matched by a jealous defense of local autonomy by, of course, those whom the President might oppose. When President Hoover endorsed Representative Reese of Knoxville in 1930 (see Appendix, item 13), Reese's opponent in the primary responded with a blast of rhetoric reminiscent of an earlier era of American politics:

> The time has not yet come in this district when any man, before offering himself for office, must make a pilgrimage to the distant shrine of a great political boss and humbly climb up the golden stairway to the throne and kiss His Majesty's great toe and beg to be annointed with the privilege of asking the voters of his district to support him. . . . I am taking my case to the people of this district. They know me and I trust them (*Knoxville Sunday Journal*, July 27, 1930, p. 4. The orator was Sam W. Price and the district was near Buncombe County, North Carolina.)

A few years later, when the White House endorsed his opponent, Senator Gillette of Iowa's (see Appendix, item 18) most telling argument was that "Tommy Corcoran and his crowd of non-Iowans" were trying to tell the people of Iowa how to vote; and Georgia Senator George described Roosevelt's attempt to purge him by endorsing Lawrence Camp (see Appendix, item 24) as "a second march through Georgia."[2]

Both presidential reluctance and the sense of outrage displayed when Presidents do actually endorse in congressional primaries combine to demonstrate the viability of the tradition that congressional nominations are local affairs into which Presidents ought not to intervene. To demonstrate that the tradition exists does not, of course, explain why it does. We can, however, offer some explanation of its genesis and persistence, without, naturally, having any absolute evidence that our explanation is correct.

The kind of federalism invented in Philadelphia in the summer of 1787 consisted of the creation of a central government endowed with adequate authority to make and carry out national policy along with a bribe to the local politicans who would give up power when the new central government came into existence. This bribe was the guarantee that local politicians would both continue to have offices and continue, despite the transfer of duties and functions to the center, to have a considerable voice in the selection of national officials. The constitutional provisions for the election of the President, for the election of Senators, for the residence of congressmen, and the implied provisions for control of the process of election by state legislatures were part of the content of the bribe. Although these provisions have been greatly modified, especially with respect to the election of Presidents and Senators, the basic content of the bribe still exists today. For example, President Eisenhower was moved to remark after five years in office, "There are no national parties, but forty-eight state parties and they have a right to put in office whom they want" (*New York Times*, October 12, 1957, p. 1). While our kind of federalism allows for repeated centralization of function, it nevertheless maintains a variety of political independence at the periphery. And it is this independence, we believe, that accounts for the Presidential reluctance to engage in nominating congressmen.

Given the political independence of states in our federalism, consider the position of any President who endorses a partisan in a congressional primary. By the very act of endorsement, he transfers the popular decision from one on the candidates to one on himself. Thus, endorsement renders Presidential prestige a subject for electoral decision in a contest in which the President himself has neither a legal nor a traditional role. No prudent man, we believe, would lightly risk prestige in this way, especially considering, as Neustadt points out, that prestige, imprecise as it is, is still one of the main components of presidential power (Neustadt, 1960, ch. 5). If a Presidentially endorsed candidate wins both the primary and general election, the President may perhaps enhance his prestige. But if the candidate loses either one, the President is quite likely to tarnish himself.

Assuming all candidates have an equal chance of winning, the *a priori* probability that a presidentially endorsed candidate will win both elections is at most one-fourth and may be much less. Historically, Presidentially endorsed candidates have won both elections, 17 out of 37 times or about 46%. If the odds that endorsed candidates would win were somewhat better than even, many Presidents might frequently have endorsed. But, probably owing to the structure of our federalism, the odds are not very good; and this fact undoubtedly partly explains the Presidential reluctance.

Complicating all this, moreover, is the structure of our electoral system. A nonincumbent candidate for President can hardly endorse persons in congressional primaries, for the Presidential candidate has not ensured his own candidacy until after most congressional primaries are held. Furthermore an incumbent Presidential candidate for renomination may often and justifiably fear that endorsements in congressional campaigns may hurt his own chances. Hence, regardless of the odds on endorsed candidates, most Presidents have apparently felt that they can endorse only in congressional elections occurring in years without Presidential elections. Thus, 32 of the 37 endorsements we counted occurred during mid-term elections.

Our explanation of Presidential reluctance to endorse is thus twofold. Both the structure of our federalism and the temporal involvement of congressional elections with Presidential ones render Presidents reluctant to enter congressional primaries publicly.

Can a President Influence Congressional Nominations?

From the point of view of states' righters—whether racial or commercial conservatives, both of whom fear national action—and from the point of view of exponents of the separation of powers—who are conservatives of the same two sorts who fear governmental decisions of any kind—the tradition that excludes Presidents from congressional nominations is a morally valuable constitutional restraint. Not surprisingly, therefore, since 1913 the Presidents with conservative ideology have displayed far less interest in manipulating nominations than have those with a more radical orientation. Harding, Coolidge, Hoover, and Eisenhower publicly endorsed candidates in Republican congressional primaries only once each. Wilson, on the other hand, publicly entered 10 Democratic congressional primaries; Franklin Roosevelt entered 16; and Truman entered 9. While complete information on the behavior of earlier Presidents in this century is not available, it appears that this dichotomy holds true for them also. The conservative Taft attempted to manipulate only two nominations

(Riker, 1953, p. 292), while the radical Theodore Roosevelt, so one infers from his letters, maneuvered behind the scenes in perhaps dozens of congressional nominations.

In this essay we reject the moral view of the advocates of states' rights and the separation of powers. We adopt instead the morality implicit in Neustadt's work and in the behavior of Wilson, Truman, and the two Roosevelts. In this latter and activist morality, increases in the President's power to compel congressional decisions are regarded as morally desirable and the constitutional tradition that restricts Presidential participation in primaries is interpreted as an impediment to good constitutional structure. Adopting, as we do, this activist morality, our practical question is: Can a President evade the restrictive tradition that keeps him out of congressional primaries and lessens his ability to influence congressmen?

Manifestly, a President can force himself into any and all congressional nominations simply by announcing a preference among candidates. Such announcements are unlikely to awe congressmen, however, unless they also believe that the President's actions significantly influence the outcome of primaries. Hence, to break the restrictive tradition, a President must not only participate but also participate successfully. "Successfully," means, of course, both that the President's candidate wins and that congressmen infer—whether correctly or incorrectly is irrelevant— that the voters were influenced by the President's announcement. So our question really is: How can a President achieve a reputation for successfully influencing congressional nominations?

Historically, Presidents have tried in two ways, clandestinely and publicly. The clandestine method is to send emissaries, who are often well supplied with the currency of high politics—judgeships, donors of funds, organizers of campaigns, etc.—to participate in local campaigns. The advantage of this method is that if the supported candidate wins, the exaggerations of rumor may gain a President credit for far more than he actually accomplishes, while at the same time, if the candidate loses, the President's prestige is probably not diminished. This method has two disadvantages, however. The currency of high politics is today in limited supply, and the decision in primaries is sufficiently public that the significance of clandestine aid is always disputable. No ambitious and activitist President can ignore clandestine methods. Indeed, all of them in this century have apparently used them to a considerable degree. Nevertheless, the drawbacks of the method are today such that a reputation for influence can probably be acquired only by the public method of endorsement. So we reduce the question further: How can a President gain a reputation for successful endorsements?

To answer this question, we distinguish three kinds of endorsements: 1) endorsements of incumbents; 2) endorsements of opponents of incumbents; and 3) endorsements of candidates in primaries in which incumbents are not running. Further, we point out that in the present state of American politics, the incumbent has a considerable advantage, except perhaps when he is very old or is a first-termer who has not yet acquired leadership in his state or district. Assuming then that incumbents have a great advantage, the effects of endorsements may be analyzed in six cases.

Case 1a: A Presidentially endorsed incumbent wins the primary. Since the presumption is that the incumbent will win anyway, the fact of endorsement will probably be thought to have relatively little significance. Only if it is widely believed that the incumbent is likely to lose his seat can the President be given much credit for the success. This may have occurred in the Kentucky Democratic senatorial primary of 1938, when Senator Barkley, although endorsed, barely beat off the challenge of Governor Chandler (Shannon, 1938). (See Appendix, item 21.)

Case 1b: A Presidentially endorsed incumbent loses the primary. Because of the presumption of success for the incumbent, the fact that he loses may well reflect negatively on the President's prestige. It will be said, for example, that the President was too weak to help a friend or that the voters definitively rejected the President himself. This clearly occurred in 1926 when Coolidge reluctantly and ineffectually endorsed Senator Lenroot of Wisconsin who promptly lost the primary by a wide margin. (See Appendix, item 12). On the other hand, Senator McAdoo's failure in California in 1938 passed largely unnoticed among the more dramatic events of the purge. (See Appendix, item 23.) And Truman's defense of Senator Wheeler in 1946 probably did not detract from the President's prestige when Wheeler lost since Truman then had little prestige to lose. (See Appendix, item 30).

Case 2a: A Presidentially endorsed opponent of an incumbent wins the primary. Since the presumption of success lies with the incumbent, his opponent's victory may well be regarded as quite surprising and thereby will reflect much credit on the President. It may be believed—whether rightly or wrongly is irrelevant—that the President provided the margin of victory. This seems to have occurred for Wilson in the events mentioned it items 6 and 9 of the Appendix. Fay's victory in 1938, however, did not enhance Roosevelt's prestige greatly for it was overshadowed by other events in the purge of that year. (See Appendix, item 27.) Nor did Axtell's victory in 1946 greatly enhance Truman's prestige since the primary was in Truman's own district where he might be expected to have much influence. Furthermore Axtell lost the general election. (See Appendix, item 31.)

Case 2b: A Presidentially endorsed opponent of an incumbent loses the primary. Since the presumption of success lies with the incumbent, his victory does not necessarily reflect great discredit on the President. Wilson was apparently not greatly hurt by Huddleston's victory in Birmingham in 1918. (See Appendix, item 7.) On the other hand, Roosevelt certainly did lose some prestige by the success of incumbents he opposed in 1938. (See Appendix, items 18, 24, 25, and 26.) Yet this loss derives from some of the unique features of the purges rather than from the inherent nature of the events themselves. After much hesitation, Roosevelt undertook the purge with the maximum amount of publicity, aiming, presumably, to unseat a number of partisans. After a brave beginning, the purge rather fizzled out and in the end only the least important of the five endorsed opponents of incumbents won. Quite probably it was the bad batting average after so much publicity that hurt Roosevelt in these instances.

Case 3a: A Presidentially endorsed candidate wins in a primary without an incumbent. In this case there are no guidelines for expectations about the outcome. Since the main unusual feature of such a primary is the President's endorsement, he may well be popularly credited with his candidate's victory. Of course, if there is only one candidate the credit is trivial. (See Appendix, items 2, 15, and 29.)

Case 3b: A Presidentially endorsed candidate loses in a primary without an incumbent. As the exact converse of *Case 3a*, here it may be expected that the President will lose some prestige.

Having distinguished these cases, we are now able to lay down some elementary canons of behavior for a President who desires to win a reputation for successfully influencing primaries.

Our first canon is that a President ought quite frequently to try to influence primaries either clandestinely or publicly. The most striking feature of table 10–1 is, we believe, the paucity of entries, only 39 events in all (really only 37, for two pairs relate to the same primary). Presidents have been too cautiously bound by tradition, unaware that sometimes— even with bad planning—their predecessors have influenced a primary.

Our second canon is that a President ought to avoid *Case 1* endorsements. If his endorsed candidate is successful, the President is given little credit, as indeed happened in 1938. The purge of that year is almost universally interpreted as a failure although five of the six endorsed incumbents were renominated. (See Appendix, items 16, 17, 19, 20, 21, 22, and 23.) On the other hand, if the President's candidate fails, the failure may be credited to the President rather than the candidate, as happened when Coolidge endorsed Lenroot. (See Appendix, item 12.) In short, in *Case 1* endorsements, the President stands to lose very much and gain almost nothing.

It has been the fashion among political scientists to poke fun at the political ineptitude of President Eisenhower. Yet in one instance, at least, he showed a fine sense of political strategy. Despite substantial pressure to endorse Senator Wiley in Wisconsin in 1956 when he was in great danger of losing the nomination to a Representative of the McCarthy wing of the Republican Party, the President refused to endorse his fairly reliable congressional supporter when the state Republican convention endorsed Wiley's opponent. Shortly before this, however, Eisenhower had publicly endorsed Secretary McKay in the Oregon Republican Senatorial primary in which no incumbent was involved. The contrast between the endorsement and the refusal to endorse suggests that Eisenhower believed 1) that, if Wiley won, the President would have exactly the same influence whether or not he endorsed; 2) that, if Wiley lost after Presidential endorsement, the President would have a hostile partisan in Wiley's opponent; 3) that, if McKay was endorsed and won, the President would have a reliable ally; and 4) that, if McKay lost after Presidential endorsement, the winner would not greatly resent the President's endorsement of a cabinet officer. If these were Eisenhower's opinions, then his strategy was very good. It is, indeed, an excellent operative instance of our second canon of Presidential behavior.

Parenthetically, it might be observed that Presidents are under great pressure to make *Case 1* endorsements, especially when the incumbent is a faithful congressional ally who faces a difficult time in the primary. Sometimes the pressure may be so great that the President cannot resist it and indeed there may even be occasions when he may not wish to. If he does decide to endorse an incumbent, however, he should do it long enough in advance and with sufficient material aid to avoid the debacle of the incumbent's defeat. Contrast Wilson's endorsement of Tillman of South Carolina in 1918 or Roosevelt's endorsement of Thomas of Oklahoma in 1938 with Coolidge's endorsement of Lenroot of Wisconsin in 1926. In the former two instances the President acted far enough in advance and with sufficient planning to force the withdrawal of the main opponent from the primary. (See Appendix, items 4, 10, 17, and 20.) In the latter instance Coolidge hesitated and fumbled, watched five of his strongest supporters in the Senate lose in primaries, and then, rather panic-stricken, ineffectually praised Lenroot in a speech that came too late to have any possible influence on the Wisconsin primary.[3] So we add to the second canon this proviso: If the President decides to violate the canon, he ought to do so with planning and care and, above all, he ought not to allow last-minute considerations to move him to an imprudent position.

The third elementary canon we lay down is that in making *Case 2* and *Case 3* endorsements, a President ought to be reasonably sure that his endorsed candidate will win. If he cannot thus assure himself, he should be silent. In both categories of endorsement, the success of the candidate reflects credit on the President, while in most *3b* and *2b* instances the failure detracts from his prestige. Elementary prudence suggests, therefore, that these endorsements be made only when the President has assured himself that his candidates can win.

To justify this canon we will contrast instances of *Cases 2a* and 3a endorsements with instances of *Cases 2b* and *3b*. What makes the difference between them? Since only Wilson, Franklin Roosevelt, and Truman made endorsements in both categories, we will examine only their experience.

In 1918, Wilson undertook to unseat several Southern Democrats who, he believed, were not supporting the war program. In a letter to a significant Democratic official of the district, Wilson denounced Representative Slayden of San Antonio. While he did not endorse a specific candidate, one of Slayden's opponents was Carlos Bee, a brother-in-law of Postmaster-General Burleson. Slayden withdrew and Bee was nominated and elected. Given the Burleson-Bee relationship, there can be hardly any doubt that all this was carefully anticipated in advance by Wilson or his advisors. (See Appendix, item 5.) By letters to prominent Mississippi Democrats, Wilson denounced Senator Vardaman whose only opponent, Pat Harrison, won the seat and held it for many years. This too was a well-prepared action, for Wilson's candidate was also endorsed by the main figures in Mississippi politics including the other Senator. (See Appendix, item 6.) In an obviously inspired and already quoted letter to Clark Howell, Wilson denounced Senator Hardwick and endorsed his opponent William J. Harris, who was nominated and elected. As in the previous case, Wilson was clearly acting in concert with important Georgia politicians. (See Appendix, item 9.) On the other hand, Wilson's one significant failure involved Representative Huddleston of Birmingham, whom Wilson denounced in a letter to a minor party official. (See Appendix, item 7.) Since Huddleston had several opponents, Wilson's inferential blessing was scattered among them in a way that could do no good. Wilson's planning was so ineffectual in this instance that, in response to his letter, the Democrats of Bessemer promptly and with apparent confusion endorsed both Wilson and Huddleston. It thus appears that Wilson's candidate succeeded when the President allied with leading local politicians and concentrated his blessing on one candidate. When the President did neither of these things, his candidate failed.

The same proposition holds for the *Case 3* events in which Wilson was involved. In one instance he arranged for an opponent of Representative

Underwood to withdraw from the Alabama Senatorial primary. Since Underwood, a national figure, was also the leading politician of the state at the time, Wilson was clearly in alliance with the dominant forces of Alabama politics. (See Appendix, item 1). Much the same thing can be said of his other *Case 3* endorsement where, in effect, Wilson acted as a recruiting agent to obtain the strongest possible candidates. (See Appendix, items 2 and 3.) For Wilson the moral is clear. When he acted with significant local forces and concentrated his strength, his candidate won, quite possibly thereby enhancing his strength in Congress.

Much the same generalization can be uttered about Franklin Roosevelt. In those *Case 2* events in which his endorsed candidate lost to an incumbent, Roosevelt opposed a well-entrenched local leader and did not make adequate preparations for his action. (See Appendix, items 18, 24, 25, and 26.) In every one of these instances, the incumbent had lined up a substantial amount of local support *before* Roosevelt endorsed. The most significant episode of this sort was in Georgia, where Roosevelt decided to endorse Camp *after* Senator Russell had already announced his own support of the incumbent, Senator George. Many observers at the time believed that, had Roosevelt acted earlier, he could have obtained Russell's endorsement of Camp or at least his silence. As it was, however, Russell was committed to working for his senior colleague throughout the campaign. The same sort of belatedness characterized Roosevelt's endorsement of Olin Johnson against Senator "Cotton Ed" Smith of South Carolina, of Representative David Lewis against Senator Tydings of Maryland, and of Representative Wearin against Senator Gillette of Iowa. On the other hand, the single instance of *Case 2* in which Roosevelt's endorsed candidate won involved a—probably unanticipated—alliance with a significant local force. While Representative O'Connor was supported by Tammany, his opponent, James Fay, was supported by the Workers' Alliance, a union of WPA workers that had the personnel and the energy to make a full canvass of the district. (See Appendix, item 27.) For these *Case 2* events, the clear conclusion is that Roosevelt's candidate won when he had the support of significant local interests and lost when he did not.

The same is true of Roosevelt's *Case 3* endorsements. In item 15 of the Appendix, Roosevelt's candidate won trivially, for there was no opposition, but in items 14, 28, and 29 his candidates won against significant opponents. In each of these instances Roosevelt sided with dominant local forces. When he endorsed Representative Burke of Nebraska against Governor Bryan in the Nebraska Senatorial primary of 1934, he supported an advocate of national relief against one of its main opponents in the

Democratic Party. When he endorsed Lyndon Johnson in the Texas senatorial primary of 1941, he sided with Speaker Rayburn especially against the notorious party irregular, Martin Dies. When he endorsed ex-Senator Gillette in Iowa in 1944, he made peace with the man who had proved in 1938 that he dominated the Iowa Democracy. Thus, like Wilson's, Roosevelt's candidates won when he allied with local strength and concentrated his blessing.

Finally, the same observation holds true of Truman's endorsed candidates. When in his own district he endorsed Enos Axtell against Representative Slaughter, he was, of course, acting with his own intimate political friends who had long demonstrated their ability to control the local Democratic Party. (See Appendix, item 31 .) When, on the other hand, he endorsed candidates in the Missouri Democratic Senatorial primaries in 1950 and 1952, he was attempting to extend the influence of his friends in the northwestern portion of the state through the state as a whole. (See Appendix, items 32 and 38.) Since there had always been tension between the northwest and the rest of the state in the Democratic party, his candidates' failures may be attributed to the fact that Truman did not ally with the dominant state leaders. Truman's greatest success in endorsements occurred in 1950, when, so he several times hinted in the fall and winter of 1949-1950, he had planned a reenactment of Roosevelt's entry into Democratic primaries. Instead of attacking the South, however, Truman apparently intended to build up the party in the northern Midwest. This was the area he had so triumphantly carried by his whistle-stop tour in 1948. Presumably, he intended in 1950 to use the same means to elect a number of Democratic Senators. He started by picking candidates for the primaries. Thus, he appointed the governor of Colorado to a judgeship, leaving the way clear for Representative Carroll. He encouraged Under-secretary of Argriculture Loveland, to enter the Iowa primary. He endorsed Michael Di Salle in Ohio. And he announced that he hoped that Walter Granger would be unopposed in the Utah primary. (See Appendix, items 33, 34, and 36.) These men all won in the primaries, but lost in the general election, perhaps because Truman never made the anticipated campaign trip. The sudden eruption of the Korean War diverted Truman's energies from domestic politics to international affairs. Had he been able to make the trip, this planned participation in Senatorial nominations and elections might have significantly changed the relation of President and Congress. No permanent consequences flowed from it, however, for the plan was aborted. Nevertheless it is sufficient to point out that Truman's candidates succeeded in the primaries when he carefully planned his strategy and, in Colorado and Utah especially but in the other two states also, allied with the strongest local leadership.

On the basis of these *Case 2* and *3* events we reaffirm our third canon: A President ought endorse only when he has made reasonably sure that his endorsed candidates can win. This means that, unlike Roosevelt in 1938, he must start planning his action many months in advance. It also means that he must have a staff of political secretaries both to inform him about possible endorsements and to help elect his endorsed candidates.

We started with the question of how a President might obtain greater influence over Congress and subsequently we reduced this to the more specific question of how he might obtain a reputation for influencing the outcome of congressional primaries. This latter question we answered with three canons of Presidential behavior: 1) a President ought to try to influence nominations; 2) he ought not endorse an incumbent; and 3) he ought to endorse a candidate only when he has made reasonably sure that the candidate can win. While the latter two canons are quite restrictive, even within the restrictions an activist President has the opportunity to substantially revise the American Constitution. As the nation becomes more centralized, in fact, it may well happen that voters increasingly turn to the President for leadership in congressional nominations. If so, and if several activist Presidents should follow the conservative and cautious canons here set forth for long enough and with enough frequency to destroy the federalistic tradition of noninterference, it might indeed happen that Presidential endorsements would be expected in every congressional primary as a matter of course. Should this occur, the canons we have set forth would be completely superseded, for they are canons of behavior in a transitional situation.

Appendix

List of Instances in Which Presidents Have Endorsed Members of Their Own Parties for Nomination for the House or the Senate[4]

1. Wilson, by letter, asked Representative Henry C. Clayton to withdraw from the special senatorial primary in Alabama, thereby leaving the field clear for Representative Oscar Underwood. In effect, Wilson chose Underwood over Clayton for the senatorship. Clayton withdrew and Underwood was nominated and elected. *Montgomery Advertiser*, October 12, 1913, p. 1.
2. Wilson, by interview, requested Representative A. Mitchell Palmer to withdraw from the Pennsylvania Democratic gubernatorial primary and to enter the Senatorial primary. In effect,

Wilson recruited a candidate where there had been none. Palmer was nominated but lost the election. February 5, 1914.

3. Wilson asked Henry Ford to run for the Democratic as well as the Republican nomination for Senator from Michigan. Ford did so, winning the Democratic, but not the Republican, nomination and losing the general election. *Detroit News*, June 14, 1918, p. 1.

4. Wilson asked Representative Lever to withdraw from the South Carolina Democratic senatorial primary, thus leaving the field open for the reelection of Senator Tillman. Lever withdrew on June 14, 1918. *Charleston News and Courier*, June 14, 1918, pp. 1 and 3.

5. Wilson, by letter, denounced Representative James Slayden of Texas (San Antonio) as an enemy of the administration, but did not endorse either of the other two candidates. Slayden withdrew and Carlos Bee was nominated and subsequently elected. July 26, 1918. *San Antonio Express*, July 25, 1918, p. 1.

6. Wilson, by letter, denounced Senator Vardaman of Mississippi, thereby indirectly endorsing Pat Harrison, the only other candidate in the Democratic Senatorial primary. Harrison won. August 10, 1918. *Natchez Democrat*, August 11, 1918, p. 4.

7. Wilson, by letter, denounced Representative Huddleston of Alabama but did not endorse any of his opponents in the primary. Huddleston was renominated. August 10, 1918. *Birmingham Age-Herald*, August 10, 11, 1918, p. 1.

8. Wilson, by letter, publicly requested (and thereby inferentially endorsed) Senator J. Ham. Lewis of Illinois to seek renomination and reelection. Lewis won the primary but lost the general election. August 12, 1918.

9. Wilson, in a letter to Clark Howell, endorsed William J. Harris for the Georgia Democratic senatorial nomination against Senator Hardwick. Harris won. August 12, 1918. *Atlanta Constitution*, August 12, 1918, p. 1.

10. Wilson, by letter, denounced the claims of Governor Cole Blease, candidate for the South Carolina Democratic senatorial nomination, to be a friend of the administration, thereby inferentially endorsing Senator Tillman, who won. August 17, 1918.

11. Harding in a speech praised the political services of Senator Frelinghuysen of New Jersey, thereby presumably endorsing him for renomination against George L. Record. Frelinghuysen won the primary and general elections. September 4, 1922.

12. Coolidge in a speech at Washington mildly praised Senator

Lenroot of Wisconisn, thereby presumably endorsing him for renomination against Governor Blaine. Blaine won the primary and the general election. September 6, 1926.

13. Hoover, by letter, endorsed Representative B. Carroll Reese of Knoxville, Tennessee, for renomination against Sam Price. Reese won the primary and general elections. July 27, 1930; *Knoxville Sunday Journal*, July 27, 1930, p. 1.

14. Roosevelt, by quoting extensively and with approval in a Green Bay, Wisconsin, speech from the speeches of Representative Edward Burke, a candidate for the Nebraska Democratic Senatorial nomination against Governor Charles Bryan, allowed the press to infer that he (Roosevelt) preferred Burke to Bryan. Burke won the primary and general elections. August 10, 1932.

15. Roosevelt specifically endorsed the unopposed candidate for the Democratic nomination for the House of Representatives in Dutchess County, New York. The Republican incumbent, Hamilton Fish, was reelected. September 25, 1936.

16. James Roosevelt, presumably acting for his father, specifically endorsed Senator Claude Pepper of Florida for renomination against a former governor and representative. Pepper won. February 7, 1938.

17. Roosevelt, by interview, persuaded Representative Disney to withdraw from the Oklahoma Democratic senatorial primary, thus clearing the way for the renomination of Senator Thomas who was reelected. February 13, 1938.

18. Harry Hopkins, presumably acting for the President, endorsed Representative Otha D. Wearin for the Iowa Democratic Senatorial nomination against Senator Guy Gillette, who won the primary but lost the general election. May 27, 1938.

19. After a fireside chat in which he said, "I have every right to speak... where there may be a clear issue between candidates for a Democratic nomination." Roosevelt began a campaign tour, the first step of which was to indirectly endorse Senator Robert Bulkley of Ohio for renomination against a former governor. Bulkley won the primary but lost the general election. July 9, 1938.

20. Roosevelt, in a speech, mildly endorsed Senator Thomas of Oklahoma for renomination against Governor Marland and Representative Gomer Smith. Thomas won the primary and general election. July 10, 1938.

21. Roosevelt, in a speech, strongly endorsed Senator Alben Barkley of Kentucky for renomination against Governor Chandler.

Barkley won the primary and general election. July 9, 1938.

22. Roosevelt, in a speech, mildly endorsed Senator Hattie Caraway for renomination against Representative John McClellan. Mrs. Caraway was renominated and elected. July 10, 1938.

23. Roosevelt, in a speech, strongly endorsed Senator McAdoo of California for renomination against Sheridan Downey. Downey won the primary and the general election. July 17, 1938.

24. Roosevelt, in a speech, strongly endorsed Lawrence Camp for the Georgia Democratic senatorial nomination against Senator Walter George. George won. *Atlantic Constitution*, August 12, 1938, p. 1.

25. Roosevelt strongly endorsed Representative David Lewis for the Maryland Democratic senatorial nomination against Senator Millard Tydings, who won. August 17, 1938.

26. Roosevelt, without mentioning either of the South Carolina Democratic Senatorial candidates by name, discussed them in such a way that his words could easily be interpreted as an endorsement of Olin Johnson again "Cotton Ed" Smith. August 31, 1938.

27. Roosevelt condemned Representative O'Connor of New York City as an enemy of the administration thereby indirectly endorsing James Fay, O'Connor's opponent in the primary. Fay won the primary and general elections. August 17, 1938.

28. Roosevelt praised Representative Lyndon Johnson, running for the Texas Democratic Senatorial nomination in a field of twenty-five candidates. Johnson won. April 3, 1941. *Houston Post*, April 23, 1941, p. 1.

29. Roosevelt indirectly endorsed ex-Senator Guy Gillette for the Iowa Democratic Senatorial nomination. Gillette won both the primary and general election. April 9, 1944.

30. Truman, in a press conference, defended Senator Burton Wheeler from charges made against him by an opponent, Leif Erickson, in the Montana Democratic Senatorial primary. Erickson won the primary and lost the election. July 12. 1946.

31. Truman announced that he opposed the renomination of Representative Roger Slaughter of Missouri, thereby indirectly endorsing Enos Axtell, who won the primary but lost the election. July 19, 1946.

32. Truman announced that he supported Emery Allison for the Missouri Democratic Senatorial nomination. Former Representative Thomas C. Hennings won the nomination and general election. January 6, 1950. *Kansas City Star*, January 7, 1950, p. 3.

33. Truman appointed Governor W. Lee Knous of Colorado to the

federal bench, presumably to withdraw the governor from the Colorado Democratic Senatorial primary and leave the way clear for the nomination of John A. Carroll, who won the primary but lost the general election. March 2, 1950.

34. Truman encouraged, but did not clearly endorse, Albert Loveland for the Iowa Democratic senatorial nomination. Loveland won in a field of five but lost the general election. March 4, 1950. *Des Moines Register*, March 4, 9, 1950.

35. Truman, by announcement, endorsed Michael Di Salle in the Ohio Democratic Senatorial primary where he had only token opposition. Di Salle won the primary but lost the election. February 5, 1952.

36. Truman announced in a press conference that he hoped Representative Walter Granger would be unopposed in the Utah Democratic Senatorial primary. He was, but Granger lost the general election. January 25, 1952.

37. Truman announced he would regard the loss of Senator Harley Kilgore to the Senate as a loss to the country, thereby in effect endorsing Kilgore against Representative Andrew Edmiston. Kilgore won both the primary and the general election. February 13, 1952.

38. Truman endorsed J. E. Taylor for the Missouri Democratic Senatorial nomination, against Stuart Symington and James Slaughter. Symington won the primary and the general election. May 25, 1952.

39. Eisenhower endorsed Douglas McKay for the Oregon Republican Senatorial nomination. McKay won the primary but lost the general election. March 10, 1956.

Notes

1. Several writers have recognized the crucial character of presidential endorsements in congressional primaries, especially in connection with the so-called purge of 1938: Riker, 1953, pp. 285–293; Ranney and Kendall, 1956, pp. 286–289; Key, 1958, pp. 484–487; Shannon, 1938. None of these discussions is completely systematic, however, and none is therefore able to throw much light on our questions, especially since they emphasize the purge of 1938, which is the most dramatic but not the most typical incident in the series. Surprisingly, Neustadt does not discuss the maneuver of Presidential endorsement at all, possibly because it did not occur dramatically during the two administrations he studied in detail.

2. *New York Times*, June 3, 1938, p. 2. In a dramatic story of Roosevelt's attack on George, the *Atlanta Constitution* wailed, "Never before had a President entered Georgia and called for the defeat of one its leading political figures" (August 12, 1938, p. 1).

3. The fallen allies were: Pepper of Pennsylvania, Cummins of Iowa, Stickney of Vermont, Stanfield of Oregon, and McKinley of Illinois. Lenroot was the last—and probably least important—of these. See the *New York Times*, May 23, 1926, p. 3; June 5, 1926, p. 3; July 11, 1926, p. 1; and Appendix, item 12.

4. Dates are those on which the endorsement is reported by the *New York Times*. For those instances in which the regional press gives more detail than the *New York Times*, the names and dates of the appropriate newspapers are added.

11 PARTY ORGANIZATION

William H. Riker

Commentary. This final chapter completes the argument of the last chapter about Presidential inability to control nominations. The President's weakness is a function of party decentralization. It both causes the President's weakness and in turn is itself reinforced by his inability to control.

This brings us to the end of the story: Speaking politically and constitutionally, we have, as these last two selections demonstrate, changed very little. There has been neither political nor constitutional unification because the separation of powers and the framers' kind of federalism have kept political parties local.

That is, we have precisely the system devised in 1787 and embodied in the Constitution. That system is, of course, highly centralized relative to the federation that preceded it, but certainly it is still a federal structure, nothing at all like the unitary governments of western Europe.

The framers' system has permitted a vast amount of administrative centralization, as demonstrated in chapters 4 and 5 on measurement and chapters 8 on the milita and 9 on administration generally. Perhaps indeed

From *Federalism: Origin, Operation, Significance*, pp. 91–101.

the framers intended centralization of functions. But the framers' system has not permitted political centralization, as demonstrated in chapters 10 and 11.

Consequently we have preserved the kind of federalism that the framers invented, so, as argued in the Preface, their centralized federalism has been in fact self-perpetuating. Thus the reinterpretation, promised in the Preface, has been justified.

Party Organization

As nearly all observers have pointed out, political parties are highly decentralized in the United States. They lack unity on a national level with respect to both platforms and leaders. City and county (and, rarely, state) organizations are the bodies that control most nominations for Congress and for state and local offices. Even the nominations to the Presidency are often controlled by confederations of local party and state leaders, rather than by clearly national leaders.

The consequence is, not that states control national decisions—it would take more than local control of nominations to bring about that effect—but that the nation cannot control state decisions. The result is a standoff, which is what, I suppose, is intended in the federal bargain.

The historic localism of our parties is reflected in and probably reinforced by two important constitutional provisions: 1) the requirement that representatives be residents of the state from which elected and 2) the permission to state legislatures to prescribe the manner of elections. The first provision was probably intended to prevent what progressive opinion of the day regarded as an abuse in the English system. Then as now in Britain the Members of Parliament seldom were residents of their constituencies, although then, when many constituencies were rotten boroughs, the lack of residence seemed closely associated with a fundamental distortion of representative government. What the framers therefore required was probably meant as no more than an indirect provision against the abuse of rotten boroughs, but it has operated to require that representation be local and to reinforce the assumption that control of nominations is vested in local party organizations. The second provision, the permission given to state legislatures to govern elections in the absence of national legislation, was intended to reassure the states that they were not being deprived by the Constitution of control of the basic representative process. Hence it was consciously peripheralizing in its intent and doubtless also in its effect.

This localism has been supported by two conditions, one of which is simply tradition and the other the absence of any effective device for unifying party ideologies and organization. About tradition one need say little, except that the force of tradition exists and, given an initial localism, tradition of course perpetuates it. About the absence of any effective device for unification, one needs to say quite a bit to indicate how seriously national leaders have sought for one without, however, conspicuous success.

To examine the absence of a device for unification, consider the operation of the office of the President: first, electorally, the nomination of a candidate for President and then the election of a President, the two electoral processes usually regarded as the most important ones in our political system. At least when the sitting President is not a candidate for renomination in a convention, the process of winning a nomination is a process of forming (over a period of one to two years) a coalition large enough to win. The several prospective candidates naturally have to reward the delegates who enter their several coalitions. Some delegates, especially those who are chosen in primaries, may be rewarded cheaply (i.e., with promises about ideology). But others must be rewarded in more expensive ways, e.g., with promises of high office for their leaders, with promises of specific policy decisions, with promises of help in local elections, etc. In this coalition-building process, the prospective candidates typically devote full time for about two years to bargaining and bargaining and bargaining. If one regards the election campaign as a process of candidates offering bargains to marginal voters, then the bargaining continues right up to the election—and soon after the election is over the bargaining starts again for the next one.

Or consider the President's relationship with Congress: If parties were nationally oriented, then the President would be able to count on substantially complete support from his partisans in Congress. But one of the most well-known facts about our system is that he cannot. Instead, to put any measure through he must bargain, even with his own partisans, whom, in the classic (but false) theory of parties, he has already bought with the cheap currency of ideology.

In short, the life of a President, who is the main national official, is one of constant bargaining—to get the votes to get nominated, to get the votes to get elected, to get the votes to get bills through Congress, to get the votes to get renominated, etc., etc.

This constant bargaining is expensive: Time consumed in making one bargain is consumed forever and cannot be used to make another. And this fact is a significant limitation on what a President can accomplish. Not surprisingly, therefore, most Presidents have tried to invent an ideology which they could persuade their partisans to accept and which, once accepted, would serve as a sufficient reward for votes tendered. Such an ideology would take the place of bargaining and permit its creator to minimize the costs of bargaining itself and thus to accomplish greater numbers of things.

The significant feature of Presidential attempts to substitute ideological commitment for bargaining is that it has usually failed, or at least has not succeeded for very long. Rarely has a President been able to leave it to a successor. Sometimes the effort of creating an ideology takes so much time that its creator is nearly out of office by the time the ideology is beginning to work.

The Presidents who worked hardest and most effectively to create an ideology were: Jefferson, Jackson, Lincoln, Theodore Roosevelt, and Franklin Roosevelt. Let us consider their experience. . . .

The Presidents mentioned are commonly regarded as more effective than most others, and probably the reason they have been more effective is that they have bound voters and congressmen to themselves with an ideological tie that eliminates, to some degree, the high costs of bargaining. But as the survey indicates, no President has been able to create an ideology sufficiently powerful to eliminate bargaining and only Jackson created an ideology that worked as well for his successors as for himself. This relative failure, which I believe is rooted in the decentralized character of the party system, indicates that localism is a powerful agent in maintaining the guarantee to the states in the federal bargain.

What some Presidents have tried to do with ideology, nearly all Presidents have tried by manipulating the organization of their parties. The crucial kind of activity here is the attempt to control the composition of Congress. If a congressman owes his seat to the agency of the President, presumably then he is willing to do what the President asks without much hesitation, thereby also eliminating the President's cost of bargaining. Most Presidents, at least for the last century or so, have campaigned for their partisans for Congress with greater or lesser degrees of enthusiasm. But, given the ideological spread in our parties, given their lack of cohesion in legislative behavior, the election of partisans is not enough.

So most Presidents also have tried to control the composition of their parties by controlling nominations, especially for Congress, but also for state offices such as governorships and party offices such as state chairmanships. Most such attempts are probably made in conversation, often as part of discussions on the allocation of patronage. Hence their frequency and force are difficult for the scholar to assess. It seems likely that in the latter part of the nineteenth century, when the President could dispense large amounts of really valuable patronage, Presidential control of nominations was greater than it now is. But this is a guess for which I know no possible technique of verification. One feature of Presidential attempts to control nominations is necessarily semi-public, however, and hence is something the scholar can assess. This is the attempt to influence the selection of nominees in state party primaries. To influence, the President must ask voters to support a candidate for the nomination and this is necessarily a public act. One way to look at Presidential attempts to control the composition of their parties is, then, to study these semi-public acts. . . .

It is commonly said that the two-party system enforces a kind of ideological conformity on the political system, by forcing parties to present substantially similar candidates. But if, as I have just shown, it allows for organizational decentralization and hence ideological diversity, one wonders how it can simultaneously induce conformity. Actually, however, the two statements are not in conflict. The conformity is induced by the matching of pairs of candidates in elections and exists in each geographic district in which an election is held. (An important special case is the election of the President, in which the district is, effectively if not legally, the whole nation—and it is the operation of the two-party system in this case that usually leads to the assertion that it induces conformity.) But there is nothing in the system to guarantee that all the Democratic members of the electoral pairs will be like each other more than like Republicans. Indeed, so long as the two-party system operates within a decentralized context, the probability is that Republicans and Democrats who face each other in an election will be more alike than either all Democrats or all Republicans. Thus the two-party system induces similarity between parties by districts, but encourages (by perpetuating decentralization) dissimilarity within parties.

So, I conclude, the decentralization of the two-party system is sufficient to prevent national leaders (e.g., Presidents) from controlling their partisans by either organizational or ideological devices. As such, this decentralized party system is the main protector of the integrity of states in our federalism.

BIBLIOGRAPHY

Adams, Henry (1902). *History of the United States During the Second Administration of Thomas Jefferson*. New York: Charles Scribner.

Adams, John Quincy (1928). *Diary*, ed. by Allan Nevins. New York: Longmans, Green.

Adams, John Quincy (1913 ff). *Writings*, ed. by Worthington C. Ford. New York: Macmillan.

Adams, Willi Paul (1980). *The First American Constitutions*. Chapel Hill: University of North Carolina Press.

Alexander, William Paul, Jr. (1973). *Political Centralization in the Federalism of the United States*. Rochester: University of Rochester, xeroxed dissertation.

Ambler, Charles Henry (1913). *Thomas Ritchie: A Study in Virginia Politics*. Richmond: Bell.

Anderson, Dice Robbins (1914). *William Branch Giles*. Menasha, Wisconsin: Banta.

Banzhaf, John F. (1965). "Weighted Voting Doesn't Work." *Rutgers Law Review* 19: 317–343.

Bennett, William H. (1963). *American Theories of Federalism*. Tuscaloosa: University of Alabama Press.

Bradt, R.N., et al. (1955). *Universal Mathematics*. New Orleans: Tulane University Bookstore.

Birch, A.H. (1966). "Approaches to the Study of Federalism." *Political Studies* 14: 15–33.

Boyd, Julian F., ed. (1951 ff). *Papers of Thomas Jefferson*. Princeton: Princeton University Press.

Colegrove, Kenneth (1920). "New England Town Mandates." *Publications of the Colonial Society of Massachusetts* 12: 411–449.

Dawson, R.M. (1948). *Government of Canada*. Toronto: Toronto University Press.

Deegan, John (1979). "Constructing Statistical Models of Social Processes." *Quality and Quantity* 13: 97–119.

DeTocqueville, Alexis de. (1945). *Democracy in America*, ed. by Phillips Bradley. New York: A.A. Knopf.

Deutsch, Karl, et al. (1957). *Political Community in the North Atlantic Area*. Princeton: Princeton University Press.

DeWitt, John (1743). *Political Maxims of the State of Holland*, ed. by John Campbell. London: J. Nourse.

Dikshit, R.D. (1971). "Military Interpretation of Federal Constitutions: A Critique." *Journal of Politics* 33: 180–189.

Dodd, William E. (1902). "The Principle of Instructing United States Senators." *South Atlantic Quarterly* 1: 326–332.

Elazar, Daniel (1962). *The American Partnership*. Chicago: University of Chicago Press.

Eliott, Jonathan (1856). *Debates on the Federal Constitution*. Washington, D.C.: Printed by the editor. 5 vols.

Farrand, Max (1911, 1938, 1964). *The Records of the Federal Convention of 1787*. 4 vols. New Haven: Yale University Press.

Foote, Henry S. (1874). *A Casket of Reminiscences*. Washington, D.C.: Chronicle.

Ford, Worthington C. (1906). *Journals of the Continental Congress 1774–89*. Washington, D.C.: Government Printing Office.

Gastil, Raymond (1978). *Freedom in the World*. Boston: Freedom House.

Grodzins, Morton (1960). "The Federal System." *Goals for Americans*. New York: American Assembly.

Hamilton, J.G. DeRoulhac (1916). "Party Politics in North Carolina, 1835–60." *James Sprunt Historical Publications* 15: 51–70.

Hansen, A.H., and H.S. Perloff (1944). *State and Local Finance in the National Economy*. New York: Norton.

Haynes, George H. (1906). *The Election of Senators*. New York: Holt.

Haynes, George H. (1938). *The Senate of the United States: Its History and Practice*. Boston: Houghton Mifflin.

Haynes, John (1893). "Popular Elections of United States Senators." *John Hopkins Studies in Historical and Political Science* 13: 95–108.

Hoyt, William Henry (1914). *The Papers of Archibald D. Murphey*. Raleigh: North Carolina Historical Society.

Johnson, Claudius O. (1936). *Borah of Idaho*. New York: Longmans. Green.

Key, V.O. (1958). *Politics, Parties and Pressure Groups*, 4th ed. New York: Crowell.

Leach, Richard (1970). *American Federalism*. New York: Norton.

Lemieux, Peter (1978). "A Note on the Detection of Multicollinearity." *American Journal of Political Science* 22: 183–186.

London, Lena (1951). "The Militia Fine, 1830–1860." *Military Affairs* 15: 133-144.

Lothian, William (1780). *History of the United Provinces of the Netherlands.* Dublin: W. and H. Whitestone.

Lynd, Staughton (1967). *Class Conflict, Slavery, and the United States Constitution.* Indianapolis: Bobbs-Merrill.

MacClay, Edgar S. ed. (1927). *The Journal of William MacClay.* New York: Boni.

Mayes, Edward (1896). *Lucius Q. C. Lamar.* Nashville: Publishing House of the Methodist Episcopal Church, South.

McCormac, Eugene (1922). *James K. Polk.* Berkeley: University of California Press.

Miller, J. D. B. (1954). *Australian Government and Politics.* London: Duckworth.

Morison, Etling E. (1951–1954). *Letters of Theodore Roosevelt.* Cambridge: Harvard University Press.

Musgrave, Richard, ed. (1965) *Essays in Fiscal Federalism.* Washington, D. C.: Brookings.

Nagel, Jack (1975). *The Descriptive Analyses of Power.* New Haven: Yale University Press.

Neustadt, Richard E. (1960). *Presidential Power.* New York: John Wiley and Sons.

Nichols, Roy Franklin (1931). *Franklin Pierce.* Philadelphia: University of Pennsylvania Press.

Oates, Wallace (1972). *Fiscal Federalism.* New York: Harcourt Brace Jovanovich.

Pennock, J. Roland (1959). "Federal and Unitary Government-Disharmony and Frustration." *Behavorial Science* 4: 147–157.

Polk, James K. (1910). *Diary*, ed. by Milo M. Quaife. Chicago: McClurg.

Pommerehne, Werner W. (1977). "Quantitative Aspects of American Federalism." In Wallace E. Oates, *The Political Economy of Fiscal Federalism.* Lexington, MA: Lexington Books.

Ranney, Austin, and Willmore Kendall (1956). *Democracy and the American Party System.* New York: Harcourt, Brace.

Riker, William H. (1953, 1964). *Democracy in the United States.* New York: Macmillan.

——————— (1955). "The Senate and American Federalism." *American Political Science Review* 49: 452–469.

——————— (1957). "Dutch and American Federalism." *Journal of the History of Ideas* 18: 495–521.

——————— (1958). *Soldiers of the States.* Washington: Public Affairs Press.

——————— (1958a). "Causes of Events." *Journal of Philosophy* 55: 281–290.

——————— (1964). *Federalism: Origin, Operation, Significance.* Boston: Little, Brown.

——————— (1964a). "Some Ambiguities in the Notion of Power." *American Political Science Review* 57: 341–349.

———— (1975). "Federalism." In Fred Greenstein and Nelson Polsby, *Handbook of Political Science, vol. 5: Governmental Institutions and Process.* Reading, MA: Addison-Wesley.

Riker, William H., and William Bast (1969). "Presidential Action on Congressional Nominations." In Aaron Wildavsky, ed., *The Presidency.* Boston: Little, Brown.

Riker, William H., and Ronald Schaps (1957). "Disharmony in Federal Government." *Behavioral Science* 2: 276–290.

Roosevelt, Franklin D. (1941). *The Public Papers and Addresses of Franklin D. Roosevelt, 1938.* New York: Macmillan.

Royal Commission on the Constitution (1929). *Report.* Canberra: Commonwealth Printing Office.

Rutland, Robert (1975 ff.). *Papers of James Madison.* Chicago: University of Chicago Press.

Sawyer, Edmund (1725). *Memorials of Affairs of State...from The...Papers of...Sir Ralph Winwood.* 3 vols. London: T. Ward.

Schieber, Harry N. (1966). *The Condition of American Federalism: A Historian's View.* Washington, D.C.: Government Printing Office.

Scott, Nancy L. (1856). *Memoir of Hugh Lawson White.* Philadelphia: Lippincott.

Scott, Thomas A. (1877). "The Recent Strikes." *North American Review* 125: 357.

Shannon, Jasper, B. "Presidential Politics in the South." *Journal of Politics* 1: 146–170, 278–300.

Shapley, Lloyd S. (1953). "A Value for N-Person Games." In H.W. Kuhn and A.W. Tucker, eds., *Contributions to the Theory of Games, II.* Princeton: Princeton University Press.

Shapley, Lloyd S., and Martin Shubik (1954). "A Method of Evaluating the Distribution of Power in a Committee System." *American Political Science Review* 48: 787–792.

Sherman, John (1895). *Recollections of Forty Years in the House, Senate, and Cabinet.* Chicago: Werner.

Simeon, Richard (1972). *Federal Provincial Diplomacy.* Toronto: University of Toronto Press.

Smith, O.H. (1858). *Early Indiana Trials and Sketches.* Cincinnati: Moore, Wilstach, Keys.

Smith, Paul Tincher (1919). "Militia of the United States from 1846–1860." *Indiana Magazine of History* 15: 20–47.

Sparks, Edwin Erle (1918). *The Lincoln Douglas Debates of 1858.* Chicago: Hall and McCreary.

Stanhope, Philip, Fourth Earl of Chesterfield (1774). *Letters...to his Son,* ed. by Bonamy Dobrée, 1932. London: Eyre and Spottiswoode.

Straffin, Philip (1977). "Homogeneity, Independence, and Power Indices." *Public Choice* 30: 107–118.

Storey, Moorfield (1900). *Charles Summer.* Boston: Houghton Mifflin.

Sunquist, James (1969). *Making Federalism Work.* Washington, D.C.: Brookings Institution.

Temple, Sir William (1672). *Observations upon the United Provinces of the Netherlands*, ed. by G.N. Clark (1932). Cambridge: Cambridge University Press.

Tyler, Lyon Gardiner (1884, 1896). *The Letters and Times of the Tylers*. Richmond: Whittet and Shepperson.

Upham, Cyril B. (1920). "Historical Survey of the Militia of Iowa." *Iowa Journal of History and Politics* 18: 3–93, 413–440.

Upton, May. Gen'l. Emory (1917). *The Military Policy of the United States*. Washington, D.C.: Government Printing Office.

Wagstaff, H.M. (1910). "Federalism in North Carolina." *James Sprunt Historical Publications* 9: 24.

Wheare, K.D. (1953). *Federal Government*. London: Oxford University Press.

Yellen, Samuel (1936). American Labor Struggles. New York: Harcourt Brace.

INDEX